THE
ART OF
LEADERSHIP
BY SUN TZU

A New-Millennium
Translation of
Sun Tzu's *Art of War*

**Translated and
Annotated, With Cases
by
David H. Li**

THE ART OF LEADERSHIP BY SUN TZU
A New-Millennium Translation of Sun Tzu's *Art of War*

Translated, Annotated, with Cases, by David H. Li
Copyright © 2000 by David H. Li
All rights reserved

Manufactured in the United States of America
Published by Premier Publishing Company
Post Office Box 341267
Bethesda Maryland 20827 USA
Fax: 301-469-6544; Tel: 301-469-7051
Translator's e-mail address: davidli@erols.com

To Charles Liu, business-leader-cum-strategist
Philip Li, executive director of Coro - a non-profit foundation
for training leaders in public service
Volunteers in Year 2000 Presidential Campaign
For your leadership achievements

Library Cataloging Data

Sun Tzu

The Art of Leadership by Sun Tzu - a New-Millennium Translation of Sun Tzu's *Art of War* / translated, annotated, with cases on war, politics, war-simulation, and business, by David H. Li - Bethesda MD: Premier Pub., c2000

272 p.; 23 cm
Includes complete text in Chinese
Includes chronology (p. 212-216), subject index (p. 239-253), index on war cases (p. 254-258), index on politics cases (p 259-264), index on text passages cited in cases (p. 265-266), and bibliography (p. 267-271)
Includes 5 battlefield maps and 6 diagrams

ISBN 0-9637852-9-X (pbk.)

Cover graphics: Invading a citadel, 4th century BCE
from a bronze in the National Museum of Beijing

1. Sun Tzu   2. Art of War   3. Leadership   4. Military history
5. U.S. Politics 2000   5. Bin Fa - English   I. Title

U101 .S95 2000
355.02 20   LC Card No. 00-90336

00 01 02 03 5 4 3 2 1

PREFACE

You pick up this volume and turn to me: "Isn't this Sun Tzu's *The Art of War?*" Indeed it is. "Why are you calling it *The Art of Leadership by Sun Tzu?*" Because *leadership* is what his work — and this book — is about.

Treatise on Leadership

Sun Tzu's work is a treatise *on* leadership — *by* one who aspires to be a leader in war management *for* the eyes of a leader in state governance.

Sun Tzu's work, consisting of thirteen essays, was identified by him, simply, as *Thirteen Essays*. Labeling it as *Sun Tzu's Art of War* was by a well-known annotator, a leader in his own right, some three-quarters of a millennium later — *Sun Tzu* (Tsu = Master), as a tribute to the man: Sun Wu; *Art of War,* in recognition of his contribution: war management.

Sun Wu was a warrior; true. Sun Wu's contribution is on war management; also true. But, while the world reveres at his war-specific contributions, important they assuredly are, Sun Wu has made, in my judgment, an even more important, though much subtler, contribution — his view that war management is a *profession*, that war management is an exercise in *leadership*.

Treatise on War Management as a Profession

In his very first essay, Sun Wu argues that leadership in war management must be separated from leadership in state governance.

This separation, in present-day terms, is *professionalism*. Well understood and well accepted. But, 2,500+ years ago, this was truly a revolutionary idea. Then, heads of state invariably fancied themselves as *both* leaders in state governance *and* commanders-in-chief on the battlefield.

3

Sun Wu's argument is straight forward: if waging war is important, if winning war is important, then entrusting the management of war to a *professional* is equally important. Let the head of a state be the supreme leader and concern himself with state governance. Let a warrior versed in war management be the commander-in-chief to lead in war efforts.

Top-Level Planning

To better appreciate Sun Wu's work as a treatise on leadership, I have grouped his thirteen essays into four parts with appropriate titles.

Leadership must necessarily begin with planning at the top level — the focus of three essays in Part I. Essay 1, Topmost-Level Planning, which Sun Wu envisaged as a summary for his intended head-of-state reader, is on the importance of war and war management, on terms of reference between a head of state, as the leader in governance, and his appointee, as commander-in-chief in war management.

Following that initial essay, the focus shifts to the commander-in-chief's doing *total* planning. Essay 2, Total-Resource Planning, concerns pre-operational planning of human and physical resources; Essay 3, Strategic Planning, is on overall war planning.

Field-Level Planning

In Part II, the focus shifts to the commander-in-chief, as the field marshal, doing *field-level* planning. Essay 4, Formation Planning, is on self-foe assessment. Essay 5, Momentum Planning, discusses the role of momentum in planning to win, while Essay 6, Preparedness Planning, concerns with the need for preparedness in planning to win.

Battlefield Strategies and Battlefield Management

In Part III, the focus shifts to a still lower hierarchical level — to commanders planning *battlefield* strategies. They include: Battlefield Maneuvers (Essay 7); Battlefield Contingencies (Essay 8); and Battlefield Logistics (Essay 9).

Part IV covers special topics in a battlefield setting: Management of Terrain (Essay 10); Deployment of Field Forces (Essay 11); Use of Incendiary (Essay 12); and Use of Intelligence (Essay 13).

Planning to Win My Leadership War

So much for my view that Sun Wu's work is on leadership, on planning and management of war at three hierarchical levels. Let me now turn to *another* leadership planning — to make this volume, upon publication, the leader, the standard of comparison for *all* English translations of Sun Wu's work.

In the marketplace at the moment, there are several dozens of such versions. How to make *this* entry the leader?

One, proficiency in languages. Born in China and earning a baccalaureate degree in Shanghai, Chinese is my mother tongue. Though English is not, I do have an acquaintance with it for some 65 years, and have been in daily contact with it for over 50.

Two, experience in research and writing — I have published 17 single-author book-length work in English while in academia and now in retirement. This book is Number 18. *The Genealogy of Chess* (1998, 383 pages), the result of 18 months' research at the Library of Congress, earned a Book of the Year honor because of its "superb research," and because "It is well written and is compelling reading. One can hardly put it down."

Three, adherence to standards of translation — truthfulness in content, clarity in communication, and elegance in composition. My previous effort at book-length translation, *The Analects of Confucius - a New-Millennium Translation* (1999, 285 pages), is praised for its "valuable feature of line-by-line bilingual text in vernacular English," for its "meticulous annotations."

Case Studies a Distinguishing Feature

But, these are just preconditions. There is a need to differentiate my work from the rest. A feature that clearly distinguishes *this* volume from *all* other English translations of Sun Wu's work is the inclusion of cases.

The value of case studies is well known to academics. As a professor of business administration for over 30 years, I enjoyed using textbooks with cases. Textbooks I wrote *all* have cases.

Sun Wu's work is textbook-quality. I have included twenty-six cases in this volume, two for each essay.

Cases are best added after the text is done; I did exactly that. Cases are most meaningful when they illuminate the accompanying text; I used significance and insightfulness as my criteria.

With these criteria, I did *all* the research, and *all* the writing. To 21 of the 26 cases, I also added references to specific passages in the text. These references are summarized at the top of each case and consolidated into Appendix F. Sun Wu's work is presented as 190 passages in this volume; 71 passages, or 37 percent, are cited in various cases for a total of 115 times.

In keeping with the theme of this volume, the emphasis of all cases is necessarily on leadership, on planning, on leader-leader interaction.

Cases on War Management: 11

Cases included in this volume may be divided into four groups. The first group, 11 in number, is war-related — three on ancient wars and eight on modern wars. Appendix D gives a list of these cases and an index on them.

Let me illustrate how a case is selected. Essay 12, Use of Incendiary, discusses fire. Fire was new technology in Sun Wu's time, equivalent to tanks in World War I or the atomic bomb in World War II. Though leadership and planning played critical roles in both instances, the decision on using tanks was pragmatic while that on using the bomb was philosophical. Opting for concreteness over the abstract, I wrote a case on Cambrai, the site of the world's first tank battle.

Cases on Politics: 11

The second group of cases, also 11 in number, relates to politics. This may come as a surprise, but Sun Wu's leadership concepts and planning emphasis adapt well — perhaps even better — to politics.

Politics is a zero-sum game at its purest. Its rules of engagement are cut-and-dry (vote count), its decision criterion is clear-cut (majority/plurality wins), and its end result is cut-throat (winner takes all).

All 11 cases included in this volume relate to the Year 2000 presidential nomination process — ten on the Republican Party nomination and one on the Democratic Party nomination. Each case has a focus or theme. For example, Essay 12, Use of Incendiary, includes a case related to the South Carolina primary. That primary is known for its "firewall" protective quality; the case is labeled "Momentum versus Firewall."

All cases on politics, except the first one (on the Iowa Straw Poll held on August 19, 1999), were written pari passu with the actual event. "Momentum versus Firewall", for example, was written on February 25, 2000, six days after the South Carolina primary, held on February 19, 2000. Thus, cases as written retain the freshness, the spontaneity, and the excitement while events were still unfolding.

A list of cases related to the Year 2000 presidential nomination process, along with a separate index, is in Appendix E.

Cases on War Simulation: 3

The third group, consisting of three cases, relates to war-simulation games. This may also come as a surprise, but war-simulation games illustrate Sun Wu's concepts simply, clearly, and vividly. Indeed, the world's very first war-simulation game was invented to educate officers and troops in Sun Wu's concepts — leadership, commander's responsibilities, planning as a precondition to winning.

Three species of war-simulation games are included in this volume: (1) Xiangqi, invented in 203 BCE; (2) western chess, a simplified version of Xiangqi; and (3) Kriegspiel, western chess with an element of uncertainty.

Case on Business: 1

The fourth group, on business applications, is represented by a single case. This token representation is intended to suggest that, with business administration being my academic discipline (MBA, University of Pennsylvania's Wharton School; PhD, University of Illinois), I hope to do, some day, a separate volume on the application of Sun Wu's concepts to business.

Other Features

Other features of this volume, taking a leaf from my translation of *The Analects*, include (1) a line-by-line bilingual text, (2) full annotations, (3) the protagonist's year-by-year chronology (Appendix A), and (4) a subject index (Appendix C).

A new feature for this volume is a recapitulation of *all* passages in English (sans the Chinese text and annotations) as Appendix B, intended to make locating specific passages easier.

Dedication

This work is dedicated to two family members and a group. My brother-in-law, Charles Liu, a business-leader-cum-strategist, deserves recognition. He has guided me for decades; it is through his urging that this volume appears so soon — in time to greet the Year 2000 presidential campaign when it is yet to begin in earnest.

Our son, Philip, the second of four Wharton MBAs in our family, also deserves recognition. Philip recently left an excellent position on the Wall Street to be the executive director of a non-profit organization, Coro, whose purpose is to train leaders in the management of non-profit organizations. In applauding his noble pursuit, for each copy of this book sold at list, $1 will be donated to Coro as a gesture of my support.

Year 2000 is memorable in many ways. In the Chinese zodiac, it is the Year of the Dragon — when men/women of magnanimity make their appearance. In the United States, it is a year of exciting presidential nomination contests — thanks to thousands of volunteers. These volunteers are leaders in citizenship now, and leaders in public service later. As the author of a book on leadership, I recognize their contribution in this dedication.

Bethesda, Maryland
March 2000   David H. Li

THE ART OF LEADERSHIP BY SUN TZU
A New-Millennium Translation of Sun Tzu's *Art of War*
Table of Contents

1 计　篇

TOPMOST-LEVEL PLANNING

In ancient China when words were preserved on bamboo strips, writings were terse, and essays rarely had titles. This essay, the first of thirteen, intended by Sun Wu to serve as an overall summary, had no title as originally prepared; the one shown above is supplied by a commentator centuries later. Each of the thirteen essays also begins with "Sun Tzu said," clearly another commentator-supplied addition; these words are *not* included in this translation.

Conversely, for ease in annotation and cross-referencing, essays are segmented into passages, with passage numbers added. The text proper, however, is intact and unchanged. All passages in English, sans footnotes, are recapitulated as Appendix B at the back of this volume.

1.1　　　兵者，国之大事，死生之地，
　　　　　　存亡之道，不可不察也。

War is a major affair of the State[1], a domain deciding life and death, a direction[2] defining existence and extinction. It is not to be left uninvestigated.[3,4,5]

[1] Sun Wu's work is a treatise *on* leadership, *by* one who aspires to be a leader, *for* the eyes of a leader. The phrase *a major affair of the State* in the very first sentence signals Sun Wu's intent: his work is for a leader with the highest rank, a head of state.

Affairs of the State are the domain of heads of state; of these, only two, deemed *major*, expect a head of state's personal involvement: officiating in ceremonies honoring past kings and deciding whether to engage in war. They symbolize a head of state's leadership in peace and in war, respectively.

[2] In *The Analects of Confucius - A New-Millennium Translation* (1999), this translator has rendered *dao* as *direction*, on account of its four attributes: it is abstract, it requires nurturing, it is changeable, and it needs constant vigilance. These four attributes work equally well, perhaps even better, for this work. A head-of-state's role is indeed to define, nurture, adapt, and keep vigilance over direction. Thus, *dao* is rendered as *direction* in this volume. When shown capitalized, as *Direction*, it suggests the *right* direction.

[3] Targeting a head of state as his intended reader, Sun Wu chooses his words with care and expresses them with discreetness — especially in this initial essay. Thus, words such as *must* are absent, so is the imperative mood of expression. Frequently, he uses a double negative to soften the tone. In this volume, Sun Wu's delicate treatment is carefully preserved and occasionally commented upon.

With deliberate wording — "It is not to be left uninvestigated," a double negative — Sun Wu gently reminds his intended royal reader of adverse consequences of neglecting major affairs of the State. Thus, he implies his work's importance and subtly urges his intended royal reader to read on.

[4] One instance of a head of state's neglecting a major affair of the State and its resultant adverse consequences took place in 578 BCE in the state of Lü. That year, 13th Year in Duke Chen's reign, the Duke failed to officiate a state ceremony honoring past kings.

Ignoring an occasion as important as this was probably well known to other heads of state — either through hearing it from envoys or through reading it in *Zuo Zhuan*, an authoritative and almost contemporaneous year-by-year record about heads of state. That specific incident is in *Zuo Zhuan*; the entry is followed by a biting comment: "With Duke Chen being so neglectful, he appears to be giving up life. His end is near."

Indeed, five years later, in 573 BCE, the Duke passed away.

[5] When King Hé Lü, of Wu, read this essay by Sun Wu, in 512 BCE (some 61 years after Duke Chen's passing), he was so impressed that he not only read the first part of the first essay (Sun Wu's realistic expectation), not only the entire first essay (probably Sun Wu's most optimistic expectation), but the entire thirteen essays!

1.2 故经之以五（事），校之以计而索其情：一曰道，二曰天，三曰地，四曰将，五曰法。

For better understanding, it[6] needs to be delineated into five factors and analyzed separately. They are:

One, Direction

Two, *Tian*[7]

Three, Location

Four, Commandership

Five, Support

[6] Sun Wu uses the word *bing* (= war, when used as a noun) only twice in this initial essay (at 1.1 and 1.12). He prefers to refer to it implicitly, as here.

[7] In China, the word *Tian* embodies two entirely different views, a physical (cosmographical) view and a metaphysical (philosophical) view. Not knowing whether his view will be appreciated by his intended royal reader, Sun Wu temporizes.

To play along with Sun Wu, we must also temporize — a rendition of this word into English at this point will tip Sun Wu's hand prematurely; we must defer to Sun Wu until he is ready (at 1.4).

1.3 道者，令上与民同意也。故可与之死，可与之生而不诡也。。

Direction[8] refers to a common goal that molds the subordinates' with the superior's — making them willing to die, to fight, to be unafraid of risks.

[8] Sun Wu places great emphasis on Direction — the molding of a goal common to subordinates and their superior. Indeed, he implies (at 1.9) that it is a precondition before he, Sun Wu, would accept an appointment as a state's commander-in-chief.

1.4 天者，阴阳、寒暑、时制也。

Tian refers to *yin* and *yang*[9], to wintery and summery climates[10], to changes in seasons.

[9] At this point, Sun Wu has to disclose what his view of *Tian* is. Still, he makes every effort to withhold it for as long as he can.

Beginning his disclosure with *yin* and *yang* is artful. These two words, from *I* (*Changes*), the oldest and the most abstruse work in China, can also be viewed physically and metaphysically — thus, Sun Wu still has not tipped his hand even at this point.

[10] By using wintery and summary climates as another representation of *tian*, Sun Wu finally shows his hand: he subscribes to the physical view of *tian*; that is, *tian* = cosmo. For a warrior, where one's day-to-day existence depends on being pragmatic, realistic, and rational, this is not unexpected.

What is difficult for Sun Wu is that, to make sense of his thirteen essays, his intended royal reader has to accept, at least acquiesce to, a physical view of *tian*.

Heads of state invariably hold onto the metaphysical view; that is, *tian* = heaven. Among other reasons, this view allows heads of state to be referred to as *sons of heaven*.

For Sun Wu, another difficulty is that this metaphysical view is held by many important thinkers as well, Confucius among them. (In *The Analects of Confucius - A New-Millennium Translation*, this translator has rendered *tian* as *heaven* throughout the entire volume.)

By presenting his physical view of *tian* simply and unambiguously (only six words in the original), albeit reluctantly, Sun Wu demonstrates his courage.

An exemplary passage by Sun Wu.

1.5   地者，高下、远近、险易、广狭、死生也。

Location refers to land high and low, to land close by and distant[11], treacherous and plain, easily accessible and not easily accessible, deadly and lively.

[11] These two words in Chinese, literally translated as *close by* and *distant* here, have a subtle implication of being *familiar* and *unfamiliar*.

In this translator's assessment, to Sun Wu, physical distance is relatively unimportant — a commander can engage in war while stationed a thousand miles away, as he says at one point (6.11). To

Sun Wu, it seems to this translator, what is critically important is, to coin a term, the *knowledge distance* — how much a commander knows about the land — how *familiar* or *unfamiliar* is a commander with a land on which he is to wage war and risk his men's lives.

1.6 将者，智、信、仁、勇、严也。

Commandership refers to intelligence, trustworthiness, nobleness, courage, and discipline.

1.7 法者，曲制、官道、主用也。

Support refers to military organization, administrative direction, and fiscal appropriation.

1.8 凡此五者，将莫不闻，知之者胜，不知者不胜。

A commander-in-chief is knowledgeable in all these five factors.[12,13] One with such knowledge wins; one without does not win.

[12] This paragraph serves three interrelated purposes. One, it is a convenient point for his intended royal reader to make a self-assessment. In the Spring and Autumn Period (770-476 BCE), a head of state frequently fancied himself as a governor-cum-warrior, and invariably appointed himself as the commander-in-chief in wars. Here, Sun Wu subtly asks: Is your excellency up to it? Isn't winning a war more important than showing off your excellency's bravery?

Two, it is serviceable as a commander-in-chief's job description and the basis for preparing the terms of reference were a head of state persuaded to designate someone as the commander-in-chief.

Three, it serves as a summary of the first part of this initial essay, subtly suggesting that, with the appointment of a commander-in-chief, a head of state's personal involvement in matters of war can rightly come to an end.

The first part of this essay up to this point contains 127 words (not including the first three commentator-added words), which just about fills one scroll of bamboo strips. It is thus convenient for a head of state to carry and read, to reach a decision about war and about appointing someone to be the commander-in-chief.

[13] We may also take a break and offer a summary of the five factors delineated by Sun Wu:

Sun Wu's Factor	Stated as an "Advantage" (in Abstract Terms)	Stated as "in Congruence With" (in Concrete Terms)
Direction	Idea	people
Tian	Timing	nature
Location	Location	geography
Commandership	Leadership	experience, character
Support	Support	resources

1.9   故校之以计，而索其情。曰：主孰有道？将孰有能？天地孰得？法令孰行？兵众孰强？士卒孰练？赏罚孰明？吾以此知胜负矣。

When factors as delineated are analyzed separately, the issues become:

Which head of state has the Direction?

Which commander is more capable?

Which side has natural and geographical advantages?

Which side has better support?

Which army is numerically superior?

Which army is better trained?

Which side's reward-penalty system is more equitable?

With answers to these, I[14] can predict a victory or defeat.[15]

[14] Beginning with this paragraph, the viewpoint shifts — to *I*, to Sun Wu. The word *I* appears for the first time. The tone also change — to the imperative mood.

Thus, Sun Wu, though still writing for the royal eye, now assumes that his royal patron plans to appoint him as the commander-in-chief. He now submits a list of preconditions of winning for his royal patron's consideration.

Two of the preconditions enumerated here are assurances Sun Wu needs from the head of state: (1) the head of state's Direction is, and will continue to be, in congruence with the people's (and Sun Wu's), (2) the head of state will honor his promised infrastructural support.

After the head of state gives assurances to these two issues, Sun Wu claims that the rest is his responsibility and he can take care of them. Thus, he boldly concludes this paragraph with *I*. Unambiguously, Sun Wu declares that he is up to the task — and offers his services.

[15] At the same time, Sun Wu implies that, if these issues (mainly the two involving the head of state) are not to his liking, he may not even wish to be considered as commander-in-chief, since he cannot be assured of victory — and he certainly does not wish to be associated with defeat.

1.10   将听吾计，用之必胜，留之；将不听吾计，用之必败，去之。

For a commander[16] who will follow my plan, using his services results in a sure win — keep him. For a commander who will not follow my plan, using his services results in a sure loss — release him.

[16] This paragraph talks about senior-level staffing, after Sun Wu has assumed the role of the commander-in-chief. The word *commander* here refers to senior officers under Sun Wu's command.

1.11   计利以听，乃为之势，以佐其外。势者，因利而制权也。

A well formulated plan well received builds up momentum; momentum has a significant effect on those in the field. Momentum necessarily changes as conditions change.[17]

[17] Sun Wu has a healthy regard for momentum; Essay 5 is devoted to this issue. Here, Sun Wu talks about the effect of momentum on troop morale, a discourse on organizational behavior.

This is a well crafted passage, full of subtleties. One, it pays tribute to the head of state for appointing him as the commander-in-chief and for accepting his plans. Two, it solicits the head of state's continuing confidence in him on account of the positive effect such confidence has on the entire military operation. Three, it discreetly requests that the head of state's confidence in him remain intact despite day-to-day operational *changes* (here used euphemistically to refer to *reverses*) because, otherwise, momentum could be adversely affected.

1.12 兵者，诡道也。故能而示之不能，用而示之不用，近而示之远，远而示之近。

War involves stratagems.[18] Thus, when competent, feign incompetence; when active, feign inaction; when close in, feign distance; when distant, feign proximity.[19]

[18] In this and two paragraphs following, the overview shifts to enumerating tactics — creating stratagems (four, in this paragraph), designing counter-measures (eight, in 1.13), and initiating attacks (two, in 1.14). Altogether, fourteen tactical measures are cited.

The four stratagems enumerated here are aimed at inducing the enemy to draw wrong inferences and make wrong moves — inviting the enemy to attack on a misconception that we are weak where we are in fact strong, or enticing the enemy to lower their guard on a misreading that we have no plans where we are in fact readying to mount a surprise attack.

As to proximity/distance, they are easier to feign as knowledge distances than as physical distances — that is, when these two terms are interpreted as familiar/unfamiliar (see 1.5n).

1.13 利而诱之，乱而取之，实而备之，强而避之，怒而挠之，卑而骄之，佚而劳之，亲而离之。

With the enemy seeking advantage, bait; in disarray, take; showing strength, prepare; parading power, elude; prone to anger, provoke; displaying caution, agitate; at ease, make work; exhibiting unity, divide.

1.14   攻其无备，出其不意。

Attack when unprepared; advance where unexpected.

1.15   此兵家之胜，不可先传也。

Tactics for winning are as stated; they cannot be predesignated.[19]

[19] This last sentence again emphasizes the need for flexibility and further discourages the head of state from appointing himself as the commander-in-chief.

1.16   夫未战而庙算胜者，得算多也；未战而庙算不胜者，得算少也。多算胜，少算不胜，而况于无算乎！

We can predict a win because we have identified many options through repeated top-level planning. We cannot predict a win because we have identified few options through little top-level planning. With many options, one wins; with few options, one does not win. With no options, how can one win?

1.17   吾以此观之，胜负见矣。

Viewed this way, I can readily predict victory or defeat.[20]

[20] This essay ends with a powerful yet simple message: top-level involvement means top-level planning; proper planning at the topmost level transforms into winning in the field.

Case P-1 Politics. Republican Party Presidential Nomination for 2000 - The Iowa Straw Poll

[Passages referenced: 1.2, 1.8n]

Th e art of leadership is a game, a game aimed at dominance, be it war, business, or politics. Where the aim is *total* dominance, where the winner takes all, it is a zero-sum game. Politics is a zero-sum game. Politics also accords us a good clinical view of the effect of Sun Wu's five factors upon winning a zero-sum game.

The Presidential Nomination Process

In a year divisible by four (such as Year 2000), the United States of America elects a president. Although there are many political parties in the United States, for practical purposes, the election is a contest between the Democratic Party's nominee and the Republican Party's nominee. The winner of this contest becomes the president — the "sum" in this zero-sum game — and occupies the White House beginning on January 20 of the year following election. The loser gets nothing — the "zero."

Although voting for this office takes place in November of such years, preparatory work begins much earlier. Working backward from that November election date, each party's nominee needs to be designated, perhaps by August. Before that, many vie for the honor of being that nominee. Those vying for this honor are known as *candidates*; the vying period is known as the presidential nomination process.

States' Role in the Nominating Process

The United States being a federal form of government, vying begins at the state level. Each state sets its own rules; key provisions include: (1) eligibility requirements for candidates and for voters, (2) time and method of determining winner(s), and (3) the reward to winner(s).

To be recognized as a candidate in a state, a hopeful must first submit x number of signatures representing registered voters in that state (or subdivisions thereof). Gathering these signatures is both time consuming and expensive.

Self-Assessment of Five Factors

From a state's point of view, these rules separate a mere hopeful from a viable — the number of candidates is thus significantly reduced.

From a hopeful's point of view, this is a perfect occasion to do a self-assessment against Sun Wu's five factors (1.2, 1.8n):

Direction - How appealing is my message? Do I have an idea advantage?

Tian - Is my timing right? Do I have a timing advantage?

Location - How does my message appeal to voters of this state? Do I have a location advantage?

Commandership - How am I as a person? Do I have an experience/character advantage?

Support - Are my resources adequate? Do I have a support advantage?

Republican Party's Incentive in 2000

Election-year politics generally creates more interest for the party whose titular head is not the White House occupant. This is so for the Republican Party. But, for Year 2000, this is doubly so. This is because the present White House occupant, having served two four-year terms, is ineligible to succeed himself — the office of the president is now an "open seat." With advantages accruing to an incumbent absent in Year 2000, the Republican Party's gaining control of the office of the president is just as good as the Democratic Party's retaining it.

So, with this attractive scenario, the curtain rises.

Republican Hopefuls

The first state in which candidates vie is Iowa, and the contest is scheduled for January 2000. But, many Republican Party hopefuls, attracted by the "open seat" scenario, have started early, perhaps years early. By August 1999, at least ten prominent members of the Republican Party have expressed an interest in vying for being the nominee. This list is shown in Exhibit 1 (page 22).

The Iowa Straw Poll

A prelude to an actual contest is a "straw poll;" the first one in the nation is also that held in Iowa, in August 1999. For the year 2000 presidential nomination, with the stake high, hopefuls' interest in this straw poll is doubly high, indeed, unprecedentedly high.

A straw poll, as the term suggests, has no substance; it certainly has no official standing. It is invented, several presidential elections ago, by members of the media, for the purpose of creating news to fill voids in coverage.

Case P-1 Exhibit 1
Hopefuls Vying to Be the
Republican Party Nominee for the
Office of the President for Year 2000 Election
As of August 1999
(Listed alphabetically)

Lamar **Alexander** - Secretary of Education in a former Republican administration; former Governor of Tennessee; veteran of 1996 presidential nomination campaign

Gary **Bauer** - former president of a non-profit organization

Patrick Bucannan - press secretary to two former Republican presidents; veteran of 1992 and 1996 presidential nomination campaigns

George W. **Bush** - incumbent Governor of Texas; son of a former President

Elizabeth **Dole** - Secretary of Labor and Secretary of Transportation in a former Republican administration; former president of American Red Cross; spouse of 1996 Republican presidential nominee

Steve **Forbes** - magazine publisher; veteran of 1996 presidential nomination campaign

Warren **Hatch** - senator from Utah

Alan **Keyes** - former ambassador to the United Nations Economic and Social Council; veteran of 1996 presidential nomination campaign

John **McCain** - senator from Arizona

Dan **Quayle** - Vice President in a former Republican administration, former senator from Indiana

An ingenious feature of a straw poll is that each vote cast is to be accompanied by a $25 check — a diabolic twist. Instead of paying *for* votes, illegal in the United States, the straw poll calls for paying *to* vote. Thus, a state party receives some financial reward for mounting such an event.

The straw poll, in spite of its lack of any standing, does serve, in addition to being a cash cow, a very useful purpose — it allows each hopeful to do a comparative assessment early in the process: What is my appeal *in relation to* other hopefuls' appeal?

Results of Iowa Straw Poll

The result of this straw poll, held on Saturday, August 14, 1999, is shown as Exhibit 2.

Case P-1 Exhibit 2
Result of Iowa Straw Poll
August 14, 1999

Bush	7,418	votes	31	percent
Forbes	4,921		21	
Dole	3,410		14	
Bauer	2,114		9	
Buchanan	1,719		7	
Alexander	1,428		6	
Keyes	1,101		5	
Quayle	916		4	
Hatch	558		2	
McCain	83		-	

Alexander Steps Aside

One of Mr. Alexander's keys message is education. Given his experience as Secretary of Education, he is certainly intimately aware of its importance. Indeed, he ran his 1996 campaign with education as his centerpiece, and did well.

But, time has changed. In 1996, he was one of few who stressed education's importance. In 2000, education is at the top of practically every hopeful's list of priorities.

Thus, while his message's appeal remains strong, his *timing* advantage is gone. Unable to differentiate his message from other hopefuls', thus, unable to use education as a leverage to gain *support* advantage, Mr. Alexander wisely announces — on August 16, just two days after the straw poll — his departure as a contestant for the Year 2000 nomination.

Buchanan Leaves the Party

Among the hopefuls, Mr. Buchanan is the only two-time veteran, having campaigned in both 1992 and 1996. Indeed, in 1992, when the White House was occupied by a fellow Republican, President George H. W. Bush (father of Governor George W. Bush, deep in the 2000 race for the Republican presidential nomination), Mr. Buchanan was the only candidate who campaigned against President Bush's reelection bid.

Mr. Buchanan's message is America First, economic self-sufficiency, and non-participation in the North American Free Trade Alliance (NAFTA) and the World Trade Organization (WTO) — a tried-and-true platform that has served him well in the past. Using that same message to oppose President Bush in the New Hampshire primary in 1992, he captured 37 percent of votes cast. He won the 1996 New Hampshire primary with the same message, but his share of the vote was cut to 27 percent.

He now uses the same message in 2000. But, time has changed. Instead of the high unemployment rate in 1992, there is the unprecedented 40-month-long economic growth that is still going strong. Instead of dissatisfaction with the status quo in the past, there is optimism. In short, Mr. Buchanan can offer neither the *idea* advantage nor the *timing* advantage.

In Iowa in 2000, there is also another issue to contend with. By advocating economic self-sufficiency, Mr. Buchanan disdains NAFTA and WTO — and their aim to promote international trade. Iowa being a grain-exporting state, this position is certainly viewed with suspicion. Thus, Mr. Buchanan has no *location* advantage either.

Taking everything into account, Mr. Buchanan also wisely decides to withdraw. On the assumption that his message still has appeal, he leaves the Republican Party shortly thereafter to seek the Reform Party's presidential nomination.

Quayle Bows Out

Mr. Quayle was Vice President during the Bush Administration; before that, he was a senator from Indiana. He is well regarded for his handsomeness, his elegant demeanor, and his family-first advocacy — a gentleman with conservative views.

Though his message has appeal to members of the Republican Party, given a crowded field with many sharing these same views, it is difficult for Mr. Quayle to be in the spotlight long. This is despite his luminous credential of having served as a Vice President.

For 2000, Mr. Quayle is also in a rare dilemma. His vice presidency is in the Bush Administration, and that president's son is in the Year 2000 presidential nomination race.

With the *timing* advantage clearly not on his side, Mr. Quayle also wisely bows out.

Dole Withdraws

Among the initial lineup of ten hopefuls, Mrs. Dole has the unique distinction of being the first woman to contest for the office of the president. In addition to her own distinguished record in public service, her role in helping her husband, the 1996 Republican Party's presidential nominee, is both touching (resigning her Red Cross presidency without regret) and memorable (presiding over many forums with grace).

Mrs. Dole's performance, third with 3,410 votes, is impressive. This is clearly a reflection of the people's high regard for her.

Her message, not surprisingly, emphasizes her unique role as a candidate who knows women's needs best. Thus, her position on family value and her more sympathetic view on abortion — a big issue among Republican Party members — stand out among the hopefuls.

Thus, clearly, Mrs. Dole has the *idea* advantage (more sympathetic to women's causes) and the *timing* advantage (first woman candidate). She can also claim some *location* advantage, as Kansas, her home state, and Iowa are practically neighbors. (Universities in these two states are in the same conference for sporting events.) Her *personality* advantage is certainly second to none.

But, it is the fifth factor, *support* advantage, that gives her pause. Given the excellent showing in her vote-gathering prowess, she has every right to expect strong financial support. But, apparently, it does not come in in sufficient numbers and amount. With a small "war chest" to start with, the lack of healthy replenishments to augment her treasury forces Mrs. Dole, reluctantly, to withdraw from the contest.

And There Are Six

Among the list of hopefuls (see Exhibit 2), only Senator McCain elects not to campaign in Iowa. He is against ethanol alcohol, a corn derivative and an uneconomical gasoline substitute requiring substantial government subsidy — but it is favored by Iowan farmers. Knowing that he lacks location advantage, he wisely refuses to set foot in Iowa.

Thus, before the first actual vote is cast, in Iowa in January 2000, the number of hopefuls is already reduced to six.

Case B-1 Business. Launching a New Product

[Passages referenced: 1.2, 1.16]

The art of leadership in business, as in war and in politics, is also a game — but with a *big* difference. In business, *total* dominance is illegal, at least in the United States of America, unless it is specifically sanctioned by law (such as a utility company or a patent-protected product). Thus, the best a company can — and should — aim for is *pre-eminence*, either for itself, or for one of its products, or both. Regardless, Sun Wu's five factors are eminently applicable.

Applying the Five Factors to Planning a New Product

On Sunday, January 23, 2000, I received a telephone call from my brother-in-law, Charles Liu. He had received a copy of my recently published work, *The Analects of Confucius - A New-Millennium Translation*, thought it was good, and congratulated me. He then asked: "Have you considered translating Sun Tzu's *Art of War*?"

Have I? Doing a book on Sun Tzu's *Art of War* had been at the back of my mind for some ten years, spurred by two influences. One, I am a Xiangqi (Chinese chess) player — from earlier research, I know that Xiangqi was invented specifically to apply principles in Sun Tzu's *Art of War*. I want to improve my game.

Two, during my service as a consultant to the Asian Development Bank, stationing in Shanghai (November 1990 to May 1991), I read in the *China Daily* (an English-language newspaper published in Beijing) that General Norman Schwartzkopf had applied principles in Sun Tzu's *Art of War* in the conduct of Gulf War. I want to learn more.

My brother-in-law's query prompted me to ask again: Is it time for me to do Sun Tzu's *Art of War*?

Let's apply Sun Wu's Five Factors (1.2) and see.

Direction

Direction, when viewed in a business context, is to identify a product's appeal. The idea advantage becomes *What is my product's competitive advantage?* Fashioning to gain an idea advantage becomes *How do I differentiate my product?*

This is top-level planning, using market research information as one of the inputs. Following Sun Wu's "We can predict a win because we have identified many options through repeated top-level planning" (1.16), one perhaps needs to do Sun Wu's five-factor iteration several times before reaching a conclusion.

For market research in the internet age, I first used listings on the Amazon.com website to identify competition — it carries 46 titles on Sun Tzu, many with copious reader comments. I also posted a message on relevant newsgroups: Which translation(s) of Sun Tzu's *Art of War* do you like best?

Armed with this information, I went to the Library of Congress and looked at *all* titles in its vast collection, paying particular attention to those receiving favorable reader comments.

After familiarizing myself with what the field offers, I felt that a book with the following features would maximize my competitive advantage:

· bilingual text - (1) to emphasize my bilingual and bicultural background, (2) to make it parallel to my *Analects* book, and (3) to use it as the second entry for a possible series on Chinese classics with bilingual text

· case studies — in war, in business, and in politics

Tian

Is my timing right? Do I have a timing advantage?

Including case studies from politics has a strong appeal, particularly in the context of Year 2000 presidential election. So, the timing of my work would be good. But, to appeal to readers with interests in politics, to take full advantage of this timing advantage, I need to bring this book out 'way before the Year 2000 presidential election.

Do I have enough time? Can I do the translation this fast? Can I write cases this fast?

Writing cases on the Year 2000 presidential nomination process as it unfolds has a strong appeal to me — information can be gathered contemporaneously with actual events and, thus, with greater detail. These cases will have a freshness, a spontaneity almost like writing reports for a daily newspaper or broadcast.

Given my experience in translating the *Analects*, I am reasonably confident that the text part would pose little problem. I have no assurance with cases on politics: Will they provide enough variety and interest? Since these events are yet to take place, only time will tell. All I can do is to do my best one case at a time.

Location

Do I have a location advantage?

Living in the greater Washington DC area, there is no better place in the United States to feel its political pulse. All the great newspapers are available early in the morning, all major television networks are here. And several all-news radio stations as well.

On top of these, the incomparable Library of Congress is here. I have used its Rare Books collection and produced a book that won a Book of the Year honor. So, if I ever want to write a case on an obscure ancient war, say, I can count on the good old Library of Congress to come up with the needed information.

And, of course, all branches of the Armed Services are headquartered here. Each must have a library open to the public into which I may possibly tap, should a need arise.

Experience and Support

Do I have an experience advantage? Since the translation of my just completed *Analects* has received critical acclaim, I am reasonably confident on this front.

Do I have a support advantage? Being retired and living simply, I have no problem with resource allocation — I have too much free time at my disposal.

All Systems Go

So, the end result of this five-factor iteration is: All systems go.

Endnote

This case is conceived in January 2000, when the decision to do this volume is reached. It is written on Sunday, February 20, 2000, after completing a case on the South Carolina primary, when results of that primary, held on the 19th, are reported in the newspapers.

By mid-February, I have done the text translation for some time, and have written many cases as well. Still, the nomination process is young, and many cases are yet to be identified and prepared.

As you hold this copy, perhaps you can make an assessment: Is the planning for this volume OK? Has the execution deviated much from its plan?

2 作 战 篇

TOTAL-RESOURCE PLANNING

Historians are uncertain whether Sun Wu submitted his thirteen essays to King Hé Lü of Wu all at once or in installments. In this translator's view, the latter was more likely — it would make much better sense for Sun Wu to submit one essay (the initial essay) to a royal reader and then to wait for his reaction, if any. This second essay, which is much more specific and much better focused, suggests that Sun Wu prepared it for King Hé Lü of Wu, perhaps at the latter's specific invitation. Appendix A, Sun Wu's Life, a Chronology, has further details in entries under year 512 BCE.

2.1

凡用兵之法，驰车千驷，革车千乘，带甲十万，千里馈粮，则内外之费，宾客之用，胶漆之材，车甲之奉，日费千金，然后十万之师举矣。

In general, a war campaign requires 1,000 four-horse chariots, 1,000 heavy-armored chariots, 100,000 weapon-carrying soldiers,[1] provisions to last 1,000 miles,[2] expenditures at home and in the field, stipends for advisors and envoys, parts for chariot maintenance, and feed for horses. To marshal a 100,000-member army needs the daily outlay of 1,000 measures of gold[3].

[1] In the Spring and Autumn Period (770-476 BCE), a state's standing may be deduced from its army size, expressed by the number of chariots it maintained. A chariot was drawn by four horses and complemented with 25 weapon-carrying men, mostly foot soldiers and some cavalrymen. A thousand-chariot state, with an army of 25,000 men, would be a second-tier state, behind various Powers, some had as many as 10,000 chariots.

Thus, in this narration, Sun Wu suggests a higher-than-second-tier state, not unlike Wu, readying to channel practically all her resources into a campaign — perhaps against a Power, such as Chü. At that time, King Hé Lü of Wu had intentions to take on Chü to avenge an earlier defeat.

[2] The original gives *li* (= mile); in modern times, it would be given as *Hua li* (= Chinese mile; *Hua* = Chinese), to differentiate it from a British mile. *Li* is a distance measure, equivalent to 500 meters or 0.311 mile. The distance between Wu and Chü (present-day Hubei Province) is about 1,000 *li*, or 500 kilometers, or 311 miles.

Because English text, sans footnotes, will be recapitulated as Appendix B, for convenience, *li* is rendered as *mile* in this volume, recognizing that it is an abbreviated reference to a *Chinese* mile.

[3] The medium of exchange in the Spring and Autumn Period (770-476 BCE) was gold. At that time, a unit measure of gold at the state-treasury level was *yi* (1 *yi* = 24 *liang*; 1 *liang* = 50 grams). Thus, the daily appropriation needed for a 100,000-man campaign is 1,000 *yi* (= 600 kilograms) of gold, or US$6-1/4 million, in Year-2000 dollars converted at the rate of $300 per ounce.

2.2

其用战也，胜久则钝兵挫锐，攻城则力屈，久暴师则国用不足。夫钝兵挫锐，屈力殚货，则诸侯乘其弊而起，虽有智者，不能善其后矣。

故兵闻拙速，未睹巧之久也。夫兵久而国利者，未之有也。

In campaigns, aiming for a protracted win dulls the soldiers and lowers their morale, leaving little to attack the city, but thrusting the army's extended needs upon an inadequate treasury. Dull soldiers, lowered morale, feeble force and depleted treasury allow heads of other states to take advantage and take action. When so, even the intelligent cannot come up with a good solution. Thus, one hears about clumsy but quick wins, but never clever and protracted wins. There is no instance where a state benefits from a protracted war.

故不尽知用兵之害者，则不能尽知用兵之利也。

2.3 善用兵者，役不再籍，粮不三载，取用于国，因粮于敌，故军食可足也。

One who does not fully understand the negative side of war is incapable of fully understanding its positive side. One who knows war knows not to draft men more than once nor to seek provisions more than thrice. Bring in weaponry from the state, but satisfy the army's sustenance needs from the enemy.

2.4 国之贫于师者：远师者远输，远输则百姓贫。近师者贵卖，贵卖则财竭，财竭则急于丘役。屈力中原，内虚于家，百姓之费，十去其七。公家之费，破车罢马，甲胄矢弩，戟楯矛橹，丘牛大车，十去其六。

Long-distance transport of provisions for the troops is the cause of a state's impoverishment. To take care of long-distance transport, people are pushed to poverty. To take care of local troops' demands, prices go up. Paying high prices depletes people's savings and prompts the state to hasten the collection of land taxes. With feeble force and depleted treasury in the field, with reduced abundance at home, people's resources are squandered seven out of ten. With fractured chariots and tired horses, with damaged armor and split arrows, with spent halberds and broken shields, the state's resources are consumed six out of ten.

2.5 故智将务食于敌，食敌一钟，当吾二十钟；萁秆一石，当吾二十石。

Thus, an intelligent commander seeks provisions from the enemy. Consuming one bushel[4] of enemy provisions is the equal of consuming twenty bushels of our own; appropriating one ton[4] of enemy supplies is the equal of appropriating twenty tons of our own.

[4] *Zhong*, a capacity measure, is rendered as *bushel* to accommodate readers when passages sans footnotes are recapitulated in Appendix B. Similarly, *shi*, a weight measure, is rendered as *ton*.

2.6　　　　故杀敌者，怒也；取敌之利者，货也。故车战，得车十乘已上，赏其先得者，而更其旌旗，车杂而乘之，卒善而养之，是谓胜敌而益强。

Hatred destroys enemies; rewards encourage boldness. In combats involving chariots, when ten or more chariots are seized, reward the leader, change their flags, and blend them in deployment. For soldiers captured, treat them well. With wins, we grow stronger.

2.7　　　故兵贵胜，不贵久。
　　　　故知兵之将，民之司命，国家安危之主也。

Thus, in war, quick wins are valued, while protracted ones are not. A commander who knows war [is aware that he] is responsible for people's destiny and the state's security.

Case W-A   Napoleon's Russian Campaign (1812)

[Passages referenced: 1.8, 1.9, 1.16,
2.2, 2.3, 2.4, 2.7, 3.2]

Following the French Revolution (1789-1799), and having become the emperor of France as from 1804, Napoleon Bonaparte (born 1769) was entertaining even grander thoughts. Napoleon was a student of Sun Wu's *Art of War*[1] during his school days — when anything Chinese was fashionable in France. Calling himself *emperor* and thinking in dynastic terms, Napoleon could be excused for trying to emulate olden-day China.

When the work was published, its reviews were most complimentary and its acceptance was immediate. Anyone who was, or planned to serve, in France's army — whether as a commander or an officer — was expected to read the work and master it.

The Direction

By 1810, France had been in a state of war for some 20 years — for the people of France there was fatigue, disenchantment, and, above all, resentment toward new tax levies and renewed military service.

Though Napoleon's plan to become Emperor of the entire Europe was aimed at French people's sense of patriotism, they nevertheless realized that it was more for personal glory than for national security. France had proved herself; the need for further proof was not apparent.

Napoleon Looking Eastward

For Napoleon, his grand design was but a few minor pieces short of completion. Taking stock and looking westward, only Britain and Spain needed to be taken care of; looking eastward, Russia's Tsar Alexander appeared restless.

---

[1] Napoleon read a French translation of this work, by J. J. M. Amiot, a native of Toulon, France, and a Jesuit missionary in China. While in China, at the request of Monsieur Bertin, Minister of State under King Louis XV, Amiot translated Sun Wu's work as *Art Militaire des Chinois ou Recueil d'anciens sur la Guerre* (Paris: Didot l'aîné, 1772).

Napoleon had defeated Russia twice, in 1805 and 1807. On both instances Tsar Alexander (born 1777) was Russia's commander-in-chief, who quickly gave up — more a result of intimidation than of military action.

Sun Wu foresaw potentially disastrous consequences when a head-of-state, lacking expertise, assumes the commander-in-chief role. "A commander-in-chief is to know all these five factors [Direction, timing, location, commandership, support]. One with such knowledge wins; one without does not win." (1.8)

Napoleon Sought Quick Resolution

In the light of these past experiences, Napoleon may be excused if he considered Russia, despite her size, an easy prey.

Now, in 1810, Napoleon looked forward to another quick campaign and to Tsar Alexander's quick surrender. Napoleon fully appreciated quick wins, valued by Sun Wu: "quick wins are valued, while protracted ones are not." (2.7)

Napoleon's self-confidence, with respect to Russia, was undoubtedly justified. This self-confidence allowed Napoleon to gloss over a step on which he always did, well and thorough — planning. Somehow, Napoleon had forgotten what Sun Wu had said on another occasion: "Winning a war is best accomplished by planning." (3.2)

Russia Made Four Plans

Napoleon's sable rattling put Tsar Alexander on guard. In 1810, Tsar Alexander, now in his early 30s, and no longer an apprentice in leadership, decreed his staff to submit plans in anticipation of Napoleon's probable attack.

Four plans were submitted. The first one, submitted in late 1810, was by Count Ludwig von Wolzogen, adjunct to the tsar. Mainly on policy issues, Wolzogen advocated a protracted war — exploiting France's weakness in depleted treasury and Napoleon's for quick resolution. Sun Wu said as much: "In campaigns, aiming for a protracted win dulls the soldiers and lowers their morale, leaving little to attack the city, but thrusting the army's extended needs upon an inadequate treasury." (2.2)

In January 1811, Count d'Allonville, a French expatriate, submitted his. In addition to concurring with Wolzogen's protracted war, his also sought Prussia's assistance. Sun Wu anticipated this third-party risk well: "Dull soldiers, lowered morale, feeble force and depleted treasury allow heads of other states to take advantage and take action." (2.2)

Both Wolzogen and d'Allonville also foresaw Napoleon's aiming at Moscow, and suggested (1) non-confrontational retreat until Moscow — forcing Napoleon's troops to lengthen their logistical support line, and (2) scorched-earth policy — denying Napoleon's troops to stock provisions en route. The former suggestion clearly took Sun Wu's caution to heart: "Long-distance transport of provisions for the troops is the cause of a state's impoverishment," (2.4) while the latter was a countermeasure to Sun Wu's strategy: "satisfy the army's sustenance needs from the enemy." (2.3)

Plans Three and Four

A third plan was submitted by Tsar Alexander's tutor and military adviser, General Ernst von Phull. A brilliant theoretician, Phull's plan was more tactical; his was also subjected to many changes along the way. A 1812 pre-operational version was based on the assumption that Napoleon would split his forces and use different routes in reaching Russia's western expanse. He thus advocated stationing 120,000 Russian troops at one strategic location and 80,000 at another, aiming at ambush should Napoleon's troops indeed pass through.

The fourth plan was submitted by General Barclay de Tolly, Minister of War — and the only line person in the quartet. His was confrontational, aiming at meeting Napoleon's troops earlier, around an area known as Pripet Marshes, a north-south divide near one of Russia's border states.

Tsar Adopts Plan

Of the four plans, the first two addressed long-term policy issues with no immediate applicability. Still, it was good to have them, as Sun Wu said: "We can predict a win because we have identified many options through repeated top-level planning." (1.16)

For immediate resolution, the choice was between Plan Three and Plan Four. Given Tsar Alexander's past experiences with Napoleon, he was understandably uncomfortable with Barclay's plan, which was decidedly more confrontational. He elected Plan Three, by Phull.

Plan in Turmoil

The Phull plan, requiring a split up of the Russian forces and seeking a wait-and-see posture, was not well received by officers in the field. They felt that the Russian troops were ready. They wanted a more aggressive posture. They wanted action. They sided with Barclay — the only line person with field experience.

Barclay was also dismayed by his plan's rejection. He was reluctant to give up his plan. There were rumblings of his wanting to act on his own initiative, if the situation called for.

Tsar Assumed Commandership

There were also schemes to bring Phull down. There were, thus, confusion at the headquarters. Further, a field commander was yet to be appointed.

One of two leading candidates for field commandership was General Mikhail Iillarionovich Golenishchev-Kutuzov, whom Napoleon had defeated earlier. General Kutuzov's personal view was that the Russian army could not stand up to Napoleon's. His defeatist attitude incurred the tsar's ire; he was relieved of his command of the Danube Army despite his success in fighting the Turks.

The other leading candidate for field commandership was General Levin August Benningsen, a German, who was quite unpopular. One reason was his implication in the murder of Tsar Paul, Tsar Alexander's father.

In the end, Tsar Alexander assumed the commandership — again. Against Napoleon, it was for the third time — and the score was 0:2 in Napoleon's favor.

Napoleon Marched In

For this campaign, Napoleon amassed a force 500,000 strong. Since he was assuming field commandership himself, Napoleon thought he could do planning on an *ad hoc* basis — after all, it would be but another short campaign requiring few decisions.

With supreme confidence, Napoleon and his troops arrived at Koenigsberg on June 12, knocking at Russia's door.

The sheer size of Napoleon's army personally led by him was a stun — the Phull plan did not anticipate either and, thus, addressed neither contingency in planning. Suddenly, many options became few options; much planning became little planning. "We cannot predict a win because we have identified few options through little top-level planning." (1.16)

Faced with this unanticipated reality and unsure of himself, Tsar Alexander decided to leave field commandership to generals.

Thus, finally and officially, General Barclay took over.

Planning Ended and Action Began

With these steps, the planning phase of this great campaign ended. Action began.

Before we leave the rest to military historians, let us evaluate the situation by means of the following questions raised by Sun Wu (1.9):

> "Which head of state has the Direction?
>
> "Which commander is more capable?
>
> "Which side has natural and geographical advantages?
>
> "Which side has better support?
>
> "Which army is numerically superior?
>
> "Which army is better trained?
>
> "Which side's reward-penalty system is more equitable?"

Can we predict a victory or defeat for Napoleon?

Reference:

Richard K. Riehn, *1812: Napoleon's Russian Campaign* (New York: McGraw-Hill, 1990)

R. Ernest Dupuy (ed), *The Harper Encyclopedia of Military History* (New York: HarperCollins, 1993), entry under "The Napoleonic Wars, 1800-1815," pp. 827-830

David Eggenberger (ed), *An Encyclopedia of Battles* (New York: Dover, 1967, 1985), entry under "Napoleonic Empire Wars," pp. 295-296

George Bruce (ed), *Harbottle's Dictionary of Battles* (London: Hart-Davis, 1971), entry under "Borodino - *Napoleonic Wars*," p. 46

Case P-2 Politics. Republican Party Presidential Nomination for 2000 - The Iowa Caucus - The Forbes Candidacy

[Passages referenced: 2.2, 2.7]

By Year 2000, the Republican Party has been out of the White House for eight years — the last White House occupant hailed from the Republican Party being President George H. W. Bush. Thus, it is anxious to regain that office in 2000. Indeed, assuming that its majority in both the Senate and the House of Representatives is retained, the Republican Party can score a clean sweep and control both the executive and legislative branches of the Federal government.

Against this background, influential members of the Republican Party, those holding offices in the Congress (senators and representatives) or in state capitols (governors, senior-level cabinet members, and state legislators), start early and work hard — their object is to identify a person, deemed most electable, as the Party's nominee for Year 2000.

The "Establishment" Candidate

Influential members in power, collectively, are reverentially known as "the Establishment." For the office of the president for Year 2000, the Establishment has accorded Governor George W. Bush the honor of being the most electable. Soon, the media anoint Governor Bush "the 'Establishment' candidate."

Young (born 1948), energetic and capable, Governor Bush is certainly a worthy designee. Although still in his early fifties, he is already in his second term as the governor of the state of Texas — and he won his re-election by a landslide. Being the son of a highly respected former president (with one of his accomplishments the winning of the Gulf War), Governor Bush has a high "name recognition" advantage as well.

Looking ahead to the November general election, the fact that Governor Bush is the chief executive of the second most populous state (after California) in the nation is another plus. Capturing a large block of electoral votes certainly counts a great deal toward capturing the White House.

Mr. Forbes Plans Another Run

Mr. Steve Forbes is the publisher of a highly respected magazine on investments bearing his family name. Early on, Mr. Forbes came upon "flat tax" as a means of simplifying income-tax administration. It generated a lot of favorable attention, since it is at once straight forward (one rate) and attractive (lower tax burdens).

Mr. Forbes used flat tax as his theme in seeking the Republican Party's nomination in 1996. He did well at the beginning, capturing the Delaware and Arizona primaries, but bowed out later.

With the stake even higher for Year 2000, Mr. Forbes readies to make another run at the nomination.

Concentrated Effort and Quick Decision

Mr. Forbes realizes that he is pitted against a formidable challenge — an Establishment candidate has an overwhelming support advantage that is hard to overcome. He must find ways to blunt it — instead of a 50-state all-front confrontation, do a few states; instead of a protracted contest, demonstrate prowess and force a head-to-head decision quickly.

This is very much what Sun Wu has suggested: "In war, quick wins are valued" (2.7); "aiming for a protracted win dulls the soldiers." (2.2)

Results of the Iowa Caucus

The result of this very first state-wide contest, the Iowa caucus, held on Monday, January 24, 2000, is shown as Exhibit 1.

Case P-2 Exhibit 1
Result of Iowa Caucus
(With 94% Reporting)
January 24, 2000

	Votes	Percent	Delegates
Bush	34,618	41	10
Forbes	25,542	30	8
Keyes	12,030	14	4
Bauer	7,171	9	2
McCain	3,964	5	1
Hatch	868	1	-

Intrinsic Assessment of Forbes's Performance

Comparing his 2000 performance with that in 1996, Mr. Forbes has reasons to be pleased. In 1996, Mr. Forbes had only 10 percent of the total votes; in 2000, he triples that figure. In 1996, he lagged behind as an also-ran; in 2000, he is a solid second.

Comparative Assessment of Forbes's Performance

But, has Mr. Forbes accomplished what he sets out to accomplish? Mr. Forbes presents himself as a conservative and portrays Governor Bush as a moderate. What Mr. Forbes wants is an early one-on-one showdown with Governor Bush — with Mr. Forbes representing the conservative wing and Governor Bush the moderate wing.

This, of course, is good thinking — slightly opportunistic, but good. However, to bring this about, Mr. Forbes must first show a commanding vote-gathering prowess among conservatives in the race. Has he done that?

Performance of the Conservative Wing

Messrs. Keyes and Bauer are self-designated conservative. Their view on abortion is well known; indeed, this is their claim to fame, and is at least as strict as Mr. Forbes's. So, Mr. Forbes cannot claim any idea advantage over them.

In terms of support advantage, Mr. Forbes clearly has it. He has spent $31 million in 1999 — $25 million of his own, and $6 million from donations — while Messrs. Keyes and Bauer operate on tight budgets.

But, this huge spending disparity is not matched by Mr. Forbes's vote superiority — barely 20 percent higher than the two combined. This vote differential is certainly not overwhelming enough to blow Messrs. Keyes and Bauer away.

Thus, while Mr. Forbes's 2000 performance is much better than that in 1996, it still falls short of his quick-knockout-and-early-decision strategy.

Alaska Results Are Heartening

The following day, Senator Hatch expresses his desire to withdraw. That is good news — one conservative less in the race.

In the meantime, straw poll results from the state of Alaska are coming in. These are shown in Exhibit 2 on page 41.

Case P-2 Exhibit 2
Result of Alaska Straw Poll
January 25, 2000

Bush	1,537	votes	36 percent
Forbes	1,532		36
McCain	412		10
Keyes	411		10
Bauer	207		5
Hatch	163		4

Here, Mr. Forbes is only five votes shy of that gathered by Governor Bush. This is indeed good news.

On to New Hampshire

With such favorable results — tripling the 1996 performance in Iowa, barely five votes behind the front-runner in Alaska — the picture is rosy. As to the quick-knockout-and-early-decision strategy, perhaps results from the New Hampshire primary will shed additional light. That primary is but one week away.

On to New Hampshire. And now there are five.

3 谋 攻 篇

STRATEGIC PLANNING

3.1

凡用兵之法，全国为上，破国次之；全军为上，破军次之；全旅为上，破旅次之；全卒为上，破卒次之；全伍为上，破伍次之。

In war, taking the enemy's state whole is superior to taking it disintegrated, taking the enemy's army whole is superior to taking it splintered, taking the enemy's battalion[1] whole is superior to taking it shattered, taking the enemy's squadron whole is superior to taking it smashed, taking the enemy's company whole is superior to taking it crushed, taking the enemy's unit whole is superior to taking it demolished.

[1] In olden China, an army was composed of three battalions. A battalion consisted of 12,500 men; a squadron, 500; a company, 100; a unit, 5.

3.2 是故百战百胜，非善之善者也；不战而屈人之兵，善之善者也。
故上兵伐谋，其次伐交，其次伐兵，其下攻城。

Thus, engaging in 100 wars and winning 100 is not the best of the best; winning the enemy's army without engaging in war is. Winning a war is best accomplished by planning; the next best, by diplomacy; the next best, by combat in open field; the worst, by invading the citadel.

3.3 攻城之法，为不得已。修橹轒辒，具器械，三月而后成；距闉，又三月而后已。
将不胜其忿而蚁附之，杀士三分之一，而城不拔者，此攻城之灾也。

Invade the citadel only when there is no alternative. Repairing weaponry, readying chariots, and preparing equipment take three months. Deploying them with proper support takes another three months. Impatient and restless, the commander orders the troop to climb walls and invade the citadel. The result is the deaths of one third of his men, yet the citadel is still not taken. These are the perils of invading the citadel.

3.4　　　故善用兵者，屈人之兵而非战也，拔人之城而非攻也，毁人之国而非久也，必以全争于天下，故兵不顿而利可全，此谋攻之法也。

Thus, one who knows war takes the enemy's army without engaging in combat, takes the enemy's citadel without invading it, and takes the enemy's state without sieging it. He takes them whole and readies to contest for leadership in the world. These are the results of strategic planning — the troops are not fatigued and resources are intact.

3.5　　　故用兵之法，十则围之，五则攻之，倍则战之，敌则能分之，少则能守之，不若则能避之．

故小敌之坚，大敌之擒也。

Deploy troops thus: when we are superior by tenfold, siege; superior by fivefold, attack; superior by twofold, divide; even, fight; inferior, withdraw; much inferior, elude. An inferior force, regardless of how strenuously they fight, become but prisoners of the superior force.

3.6　　　夫将者，国之辅也。辅周则国必强，辅隙则国必弱。

The commander assists the state. Proper assistance strengthens the state; inadequate assistance weakens it.

3.7   故君之所以患于军者三：不知军之不可以进
而谓之进，不知军之不可以退而谓之退，是谓縻军；不知
三军之事，而同三军之政，则军士惑矣；不知三军之权，
而同三军之任，则军士疑矣。三军既惑且疑，则诸侯之难
至矣。是谓乱军引胜。

A head of state harms his troops three ways. Ordering the troops to advance not knowing that they should not, or ordering them to retreat not knowing that they should not — the troops are misengaged. Involving in troops administration not knowing military affairs — the troops are perplexed. Participating in troops command not knowing military hierarchy — the troops are suspicious. Perplexed and suspicious troops cause disasters, as they invite heads of other states to invade. A disorganized army allows the enemy to win.

3.8   故知胜有五：知可以战与不可以战者胜，识
众寡之用者胜，上下同欲者胜，以虞待不虞者胜，将能而
君不御者胜。此五者，知胜之道也。

On win indicators, there are five. Knowing when to fight and when not to fight wins. Knowing how to handle numerical superiority and inferiority wins. Molding superiors and subordinates to the same goal wins. Waiting for tired troops while rested and at ready wins. Being capably commanded without constraint from the head of state wins. These are the five **ways** to winning.

3.9   故曰：知彼知己，百战不殆；不知彼而知己，
一胜一负；不知彼不知己，每战必殆。

Therefore, with knowledge of our enemy and knowledge of ourselves, we will not be in a precarious position — not even once in 100 battles. Knowing not our enemy but only ourselves, we are as likely to win a battle as to lose one. Knowing neither our enemy nor ourselves, we will lose every battle.

Case W-B   World War II - Battle for Normandy (1944)

After United States became a participant in the World War II by declaring war against Germany, Marshal Joseph Stalin of Russia, needing to relieve Germany's pressure on Russia, demanded that the Allies open a second front by invading France.

Operation Overlord

At a meeting in Tehran in December 1943, President Franklin Roosevelt of the United States, to quell Stalin's insistence, assured him that Operation Overlord, as this operation was dubbed, would be on for Spring 1944. Asked as to who would be in command, Roosevelt could not give an answer. He promised a selection within a few days after that meeting.

With Roosevelt at that meeting was General George Marshall, his Chief of Staff. Roosevelt was in a dilemma. On one hand, he wanted to give the command to Marshall — a deserved recognition for a distinguished career. On the other hand, Marshall was too valuable — Roosevelt simply could not spare him.

Eisenhower Appointed

Roosevelt asked Marshall for his preference. Marshall was also in a dilemma. Given his age (born 1880), before his career came to an end, he probably had at most one more opportunity to serve as a field marshal; this one could be it. On the other hand, Marshall appreciated his value to the president and his duty to the country. He wanted the president to decide.

Thereupon, the president dictated the following to Stalin:

From the President to Marshal Stalin:

The immediate appointment of General Eisenhower to command of Overlord operations has been decided upon.[1]

Eisenhower Encountered Overlord

In December 1943, after being designated the Supreme Allied Commander, Eisenhower was briefed on the Overlord operation — still a planning paper of the Chief of Staff to the Supreme Allied Commander (COSSAC).

[1] Stephen E. Ambrose, *The Victors - Eisenhower and His Boys: The Men of World War II* (New York: Simon & Schuster, 1998), pp. 51-52.

The COSSAC plan called for a three-division attack. Eisenhower commented that, were this operation his (at the time, Eisenhower did not know that Operation Overlord would be his), he would broaden it to a five-division attack, plus two divisions in floating reserve.[2]

Eisenhower then had a meeting with General Bernard Montgomery of Britain. Montgomery was unfamiliar with the proposed invasion plan; he was scheduled to be briefed in London later. Eisenhower wanted Montgomery to urge COSSAC planners to add strength, for which Eisenhower would accept a one-month delay.[3]

Object of Operation Overlord

Montgomery, by working closely with the COSSAC staff, was credited as the principal architect for a revised plan. On April 7, 1944, in briefing Winston Churchill, Britain's Prime Minister, and Eisenhower, who became the Supreme Allied Commander on January 15, 1944, Montgomery said:

> The object of Overlord is to secure a lodgement on the continent from which further offensive operations can be developed. ...
> For the initial operations I am General Eisenhower's ground force commander.[4]

Plan of Operation

The plan, as revised by Montgomery with Eisenhower's concurrence, included the following:

[2] Carlo D'Este, *Decision in Normandy* (New York: Dutton, 1983), pp. 24, 55.

[3] This was what Eisenhower said he said, as quoted in Alfred D. Chandler (ed), *The Papers of Dwight David Eisenhower* (Baltimore 1970), Volume V, p. 134. Montgomery, in his *Memoirs* (London, 1958), p. 210, noted that "He [Eisenhower] had only a sketchy idea of the plan and [said] that it did not look too good." D'Este, *Decision in Normandy*, p. 56.

The relationship between the two was, apparently, strained. Montgomery said of Eisenhower: "When it comes to war, Ike doesn't know the difference between Christmas and Easter." Eisenhower said of Montgomery: "Monty is a good man to serve under, a difficult man to serve with, and an impossible man to serve over." D'Este, *Decision in Normandy*, pp. 50n, 51n, 55-56.

[4] D'Este, *Decision in Normandy*, p. 75.

Strength:
> five divisions, on five divisional fronts, plus one airborne division

Strategies:
> · early capture of a port to avoid total dependence on artificial harbors [code-named Mulberry, specially developed for this invasion]
> · control over main centers of road- communications
> · clearance of minefields by engineers
> · heavy air and naval gunfire support
> · deep thrust by armored formations to control Caen and Bayeux

Assignment:
> · British [and Canadian] army: from Bayeux east to the Orne River [the Sword, Gold, and Juno beaches]
> · American army: from Bayeux westward [the Utah and Omaha beaches], also Cherbourg

Concerns:
> · adequacy of landing crafts
> · capture of airfields

Time table:
> · D-Day: June 5, 1944

Germany's Defense

For Germany, the defense line was the Atlantic Wall — 3,000 miles of coastline. Nicknamed Hitler's Fortress Europe, it was continuous and designed not to be outflanked. Germany's other advantages included numerical superiority in manpower — some 50 to 60 divisions[5] — and familiar lines of communication.

Also, she had panzer divisions. In addition to tanks, which were in abundance, these divisions also had a large number of self-propelled vehicles, equipped with guns and rocket launchers. A very intimidating assemblage of modern technology.

---

[5] Nigel Bagnall, "Omaha Beach (1944)" in Jon E. Lewis (ed), *The Mammoth Book of Battles* (New York: Carroll & Graf, 1995), pp. 341-358, at p. 343.

Montgomery's counterpart on the ground was General Erwin Rommel, commander of German [Seventh] Army in Normandy and Brittany. The commander-in-chief was Herr Adolf Hitler himself; his personal approval was needed for all major actions.

Case W-B Exhibit 1
World War II - Battle for Normandy
June 6, 1944

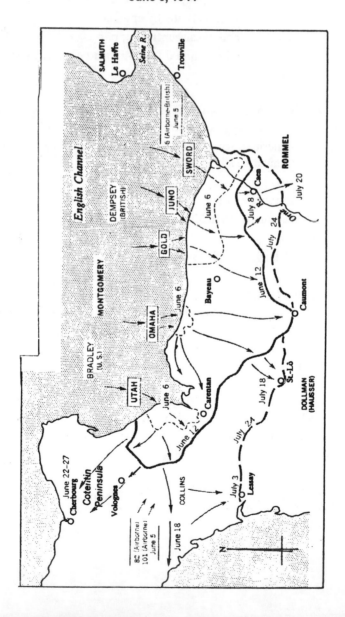

Anticipated Reactions

Montgomery foresaw a potential conflict in Germany's deployment of panzer divisions. These divisions, under the commandership of General Geyr von Schweppenburg, were positioned near Paris to move toward Normandy or the Pas de Calais — intended for large-scale counterattacks. Rommel's strategy in the deployment of panzer divisions was defensive — to defeat Allies' invasion on the beaches.

Lack of cooperation from von Schweppenburg prompted Rommel to appeal to Hitler directly for control of panzer divisions. Hitler, after agreeing, then reversing, finally compromised by moving three panzer divisions from von Schweppenburg's control to Rommel's control, as mobile reserves.[6]

Weather in D-Day Planning

The D-Day was set at June 5, 1944. A number of factors governed that selection,[7] among which were (1) long period of daylight, to maximize Allied's air power; and (2) nearly full moon, to expose beach obstacles at low water and to aid the airborne troops.

The H-Hour was also set, by taking tidal condition into account — rising tide to facilitate landing crafts to ground, unload, and withdraw. The H-Hour was to be staggered, varying by one hour from the easternmost (assigned to British and Canadian forces) to the westernmost (American). H-Hours for the next two days, June 6 or June 7, were also calculated.

Weather Forecast on June 3 and at Early Hours of June 4

The evening of June 3 (Saturday), Group Captain J. M. Stagg, senior meteorologist, reported to Eisenhower and his commanders that:[8]

- a high-pressure system was moving out and a low was coming in
- the weather on June 5 would be overcast and stormy
- cloud base was at 500 feet
- wind velocity was at Force 5
- conditions were deteriorating

[6] E'Este, *Decision in Normandy*, pp. 115-116

[7] Bagnall in *The Mammoth Book of Battles*, pp. 342-343.

[8] D'Este, *Decision in Normandy*, p. 70.

Conditions were not favorable, but final decision need not be made — except, perhaps, for American navy carrying General Omar Bradley's troops for Omaha and Utah beaches; they were ready to sail out from American ports. Eisenhower decided to let them start the voyage.

At 4:30 a.m. on June 4 (Sunday), Stagg reported that sea conditions were slightly better than anticipated but overcast would remain.

The operation was predicated on Allied's having air superiority. Without it, the Allied would have no advantage, and the landing would be too risky. Eisenhower, with no dissenting opinion from the commanders, declared a 24-hour postponement.

Weather Forecast Late June 4

At 9:30 p.m. on June 4, Stagg reported that the bad weather, which earlier forced a 24-hour postponement, was improving:[9]

- a rain front over the planned assault area was expected to move in two or three hours
- the clearing would last until Tuesday morning, June 6
- high wind would moderate
- cloud condition would be favorable to bombing
- heavy sea would still be running
- cloud base might not be high enough to permit spotting for naval gunfire

Eisenhower to Decide

Eisenhower was then faced with a critical decision. These weather conditions were barely tolerable for the operation being planned. Were this postponed again, the next date with the right conditions of moon, tide, and daylight would be June 19.

What to do? In the meantime, Eisenhower was reminded by Admiral Bertram Ramsay, of Britain, the commander-in-chief of Allied Naval Forces, that a decision had to be made within the next 30 minutes.

Eisenhower turned to Montgomery and asked: "Do you see any reason for not going on Tuesday?" "I would say 'Go'," replied Montgomery.

At 9:45 p.m., Eisenhower announced his decision: "Let's go." Thus, Operation Overlord was on.

[9] Bagnall in *The Mammoth Book of Battles*, p. 341-342.

D-Day of Operation Overlord

On D-Day, June 6, the Allies, under Montgomery, had seven infantry divisions, three airborne divisions, two commando brigades and three armored brigades. They were opposed by three infantry divisions and one Panzer division, under General Paul Hausser, the German 7th army of Rommel's Army Group B.

Up to the last minute, Calais was the pretended invasion place, luring much of German armors there. Later, due to French sabotage of telephone links and Hitler's refusal to launch Panzers in reserve, German reactions were slow and ineffective.

Accomplishments and Casualties of Operation Overlord

Accomplishments on D-Day were as follows:[10]

- Allied's airborne troops and parachutists landed on, and secured both flanks of, beaches
- Utah beach - US 101st infantry, 82nd airborne, and 4th seaborne divisions - achieved most of their objectives; by midnight, secured an area 4 miles wide by 9 deep inland
- Omaha beach - US 1st and 29th divisions - landed at wrong places and suffered 3,000 casualties; by midnight, moved inland by slightly over 1 mile
- Gold beach - British 50th division - took Bayeux against heavy German opposition
- Sword beach - British 3rd division - advanced inland but unable to take Caen due to strong Panzer 21st division
- Juno beach - Canadian - advanced seven miles to within sight of the main Caen road

Casualties for Allied are as follows:

- 2,500 killed, mostly at Omaha
- 8,500 wounded or missing

By June 12, the Allied had linked up to form a bridgehead 80 miles long by 10 deep.

[10] George Bruce (ed), *Harbottle's Dictionary of Battles* (London: Hart-Davis, 1971), entry under "D-Day - *Operation Overlord - World War II*," p. 76.

Case P-3 Republican Party Presidential Nomination for 2000 - The New Hampshire Primary - The McCain Candidacy

[Passages referenced: 1.2, 3.8]

The event in Iowa, concluded on January 24, 2000, is a caucus, where voters identify their allegiance openly. The alternative is the primary, where voting is by secret balloting. In many presidential nominating cycles in the past, the first state in the nation to use primary is New Hampshire. Year 2000 is no exception.

McCain Takes a Leaf from Sun Wu

Of the ten the Republican Party hopefuls in the initial lineup — now reduced to five — only John McCain, senator from Arizona, elects to forgo Iowa, choosing New Hampshire as the arena to do his first battle. This is Sun Wu pure and simple. Two of "the five ways to winning" Sun Wu identified are: "Knowing when to fight and when not to fight," and "Waiting for tired troops while being ready and rested." (3.8)

Of course, while in New Hampshire, Senator McCain is not idle. He is busy holding "town hall meetings," delivering his message to the voters face-to-face, and, in the process, refining it to be more in tune with them — another Sun Wu's winning ways: "Molding to the same goal." (3.8) The fact Senator McCain can refine his message without interference from others is still another of Sun Wu's win indicators: "Being capably commanded without constraint from the head of state." (3.8)

Indeed, Senator McCain recognizes his underdog role and acts accordingly, another of Sun Wu's winning ways: "Knowing how to handle numerical superiority and inferiority." (3.8)

Well, well, well. Senator McCain has applied *all* of Sun Wu's five winning ways!

Bush's Strategy

Buoyed by the commanding results from the Iowa caucus, Governor Bush exudes exuberance and self-confidence. His responsibilities as governor of Texas clearly heavy, he makes only infrequent visits to New Hampshire, leaving mundane campaign matters to his capable staff. Indeed, Governor Bush has twice declined invitations to appear in debates with rivals in New Hampshire.

The widely held view of Governor Bush is his "inevitability," that is, his being the Republican Party's nominee is inevitable. Working under this premise, Governor Bush's message is comforting and all-embracing, focusing on his being a "compassionate conservative," and a "uniter and not a divider." He advocates tax cuts without much specifics as to who might benefit therefrom.

But, with pre-primary New Hampshire opinion poll showing Senator McCain leading (by 3 to 6 points), his campaign staff has increased Governor Bush's exposure in the state. On the weekend before the primary, January 29, former president Bush and Mrs. Bush join their son, Governor Bush, in campaign appearances.

These appearances generate a great deal of good will — "like father, like son," "a great family," "image of trustworthy leader," are praises often heard. Other, however, feel that they would prefer hearing specifics on issues than seeing the governor flipping pancakes.

Manchester Union Leader Endorses Forbes

Just before the primary, the *Manchester Union Leader*, the largest daily in New Hampshire, weighs in. It gives its endorsement to Mr. Forbes.

Results of the New Hampshire Primary

The results of the New Hampshire primary, held on Tuesday, February 1, 2000, are shown as Exhibit 1.

Case P-3 Exhibit 1
Result of New Hampshire Primary
February 1, 2000

	Votes	*Percent*	*Delegates*	
			Added	*To Date*
McCain	115,545	49	10	11
Bush	71,120	30	5	15
Forbes	29,615	13	2	10
Keyes	15,170	6	-	4
Bauer	1,671	1	-	2

Mr. Forbes Reevaluates

Among the five, only Mr. Forbes is a repeat. In the 1996 primary, he received 12 percent of votes cast. Now, in this 2000 primary, he receives 13 percent of votes cast, and a distant third-place finish. The improvement is marginal.

Mr. Forbes recognizes that he is dealt another setback. The probability of implementing his original game plan — presenting himself as a more-conservative alternative to Governor Bush in a one-on-one showdown — seems to be further reduced.

Before the primary, a staff member in Governor Bush's campaign comments: "If you base your strategy on one or two states, and you can't win those one or two states, you are pretty well boxed in." Though the comment is directed at Senator McCain's strategy of bypassing Iowa, it applies equally well to Mr. Forbes's campaign.

But, with the Delaware primary a few days away, where Mr. Forbes won in 1996, he decides to press on.

Governor Bush Reevaluates

Results of the New Hampshire primary certainly give Governor Bush pause. Using Sun Wu's five factors to make a one-on-one Bush-McCain comparison (1.2), Governor Bush has an overwhelming support advantage, factor 5 — financially, organizationally, and politically.

On personality/experience, factor 4, Senator McCain's highly touted war record can, to a large extent, be countered by Governor Bush's excellent administrative record as the governor of Texas — probably even, at best a slight advantage to Senator McCain.

On timing and location, factors 2 and 3, neither candidate has any advantage.

On the idea/message front, factor 1, it is clear that Senator McCain's "reform" is captivating, and "fixing social security" resonates well. In addition, Senator McCain's message-delivery system seems ingenious. Instead of advertising, which costs money, Senator McCain substitutes with "Straight Talk Express," giving media, hungry for stories, unlimited personal access — and sympathetic write-ups or close-ups afterward.

Instead of Governor Bush's making his presence scarce, Senator McCain uses the "town hall meeting" for face-to-face give-and-take — unthreatening, intimate, receptive — and appreciative recall comes primary time.

That is it: the idea advantage. It is idea, both its content and its delivery, that gives Senator McCain an advantage — and that is No. 1 on Sun Wu's list.

Senator McCain Reevaluates

Clearly, Senator McCain has reason to be pleased — his margin of win over Governor Bush is greater than that in the pre-primary poll. The message is clearly on target — the idea advantage is with Senator McCain — reform, saving social security are issues of interest to a large number of voters.

Is there a timing advantage as well? An interesting essay in the Winter issue of *National Interest* suggests that, when time is ripe, a "hero" will come forward to instill honor, self-reliance, equality, individualism, and courage in America's heart. Is this the time? Can Senator McCain be that "hero"?

Personality advantage? Clearly demonstrated — with flying colors.

Support advantage? Clearly lagging. That is the factor requiring Senator McCain's attention the most.

On to South Carolina

Looking ahead, the next battleground is South Carolina. Primary on February 19. Eighteen days away.

4 形 篇

FORMATION PLANNING

4.1

昔之善战者，先为不可胜，以待敌之可胜。不可胜在己，可胜在敌。故善战者，能为不可胜，不能使敌必可胜。

In the past, those who knew war first made sure that no one could win over them, then sought opportunities to win over the enemy. Ensuring that no one wins over us depends upon ourselves, seeking to win over the enemy depends upon the enemy. Thus, he who knows war can be sure that no one wins over him, but cannot be sure of a win over the enemy.

4.2

故曰：胜可知，而不可为。

不可胜者，守也；可胜者，攻也。守则有余，攻则不足。

Thus, winning may be predicted but cannot be forced. Unable to win, defend. Capable of winning, attack. Defend because we are inferior. Attack because we are superior.

4.3 善守者，藏于九地之下；善攻者，动于九天之上，故能自保而全胜也。

He who knows how to defend conceals as if hiding in nine levels below. He who knows how to attack bursts as if descending from nine levels above. Thus, he protects himself while winning totally.

4.4 见胜不过众人之所知，非善之善者也；战胜
而天下曰善，非善之善者也。故举秋毫不为多力，见日月
不为明目，闻雷霆不为聪耳。

A not-unexpected win that is foreseen by the populace is not the best of the best; a hard-fought win that is praised by the world is not the best of the best. One who can lift a feather is not acknowledged as a man of great strength; one who can see the sun and moon, not a man of clear vision; one who can hear thunder and storm, not a man of sharp hearing.

4.5 古之所谓善战者，胜于易胜者也。故善战者
之胜也，无奇胜，无智名，无勇功。故其战胜不忒；不忒
者，其所措必胜，胜已败者也。故善战者，立于不败之地，
而不失敌之败也。是故，胜兵先胜而后求战，败兵先战而
后求胜。

I n the past, those who knew war won with ease. Thus, their wins were not regarded as unusual, their intelligence was not praised, and their bravery was not recognized. They won without flaw. Their measures were winning measures, applied to an enemy who had already lost. Thus, he who knows war takes a position that cannot be defeated, and takes on an enemy that is already defeated. A winning army takes a winning position and then takes action, a losing army takes action and then expects to win.

4.6 善用兵者，修道而保法，故能为胜败正。

O ne who knows war is vigilant on Direction and protective of support. Direction and support govern win or loss.

Support is gauged in five steps: first, gauge length; second, gauge volume; third, gauge quantity; fourth, gauge weight; fifth, gauge winning. Land yields length; length yields volume; volume yields quantity; quantity yields weight; weight yields win.[1,2]

[1] In this passage, Sun Wu presents his assessment figuratively. Land, measured by length, denotes a state's size. This *length* measure (land) establishes a state's total *volume* (productive capacity), total *quantity* (aggregate output), total *weight* (value of aggregate output expressed in gold), and winning prospects. Land also determines a state's population, hence, the size of a state's army.

[2] The sequence of presentation suggests that, in Sun Wu's view, a win is predicated on the size of a state's human and material resources.

4.8   故胜兵若以镒称铢，败兵若以铢称镒。

In war, [support received by] a winning army is like a kilogram to [the enemy's] gram;[3] [support received by] a losing army is like a gram to [the enemy's] kilogram.

[3] Footnote 2 in Essay 2 gives the following relationship: 1 *yi* = 24 *liang*. A *zhu* is 1/24 of a *liang*. Thus, with 1 *yi* = 24 *liang* = 576 *zhu*, Sun Wu suggests a ratio of 576:1, a loop-sided comparison between a winning army and a losing army. Because of our need to recapitulate in Appendix B, for convenience, measures more familiar to western readers are used here — *zhu* is rendered as gram, and *yi* as kilogram — resulting in a slight exaggeration.

4.9 称胜者之战民也，若决积水于千仞之谿者，形也。

In war, the winning army may be likened to water rushing down from a mile-and-half-high[4] mountain to the stream. This is formation.

[4] The original gives "a thousand-*ren*-high mountain," where a *ren*, a height or distance measure, equals 2.5 meters or 8.2 feet. A thousand-*ren*-high mountain is thus about 1.5 miles high.

Case W-2   Korean War - Truman and MacArthur   (1951)

[Passages referenced: 1.3, 1.12, 1.13, 1.14, 3.8, 3.9, 4.1, 4.6]

After United States decided to intervene, on behalf of the United Nations, in Korea, President Harry S. Truman installed General Douglas MacArthur, Commanding General, U.S. Army, Far East, as the Supreme Commander, Allied Powers, and Commander in Chief, United Nations Command. General MacArthur's charge was to follow the United Nations mandate.

Decisions in Writing

President Truman had a standing practice of requiring all decisions in writing to avoid misunderstanding and misconstruction. But, once a decision was reached, President Truman would leave it to whomever entrusted for implementation without interference — exactly what Sun Wu would want a leader to do. "Being capably commanded without constraint from the head of state wins." (3.8)

The United Nations mandate was clear. And General MacArthur understood this perfectly, when he pledged his "complete personal loyalty to you" — a classical example of a common goal molding the subordinates' with the superior's (1.3)

Presidential Memorandum to General MacArthur

On December 5, 1950, a presidential memorandum was sent to General MacArthur. It directed that "no speech, press release or other public statements concerning foreign or military policy should be released until cleared by the State Department or the Department of Defense" and that "advance copies of speeches or press releases be submitted to the White House."

Korean War

The Korean War, sometimes waxing and other times waning, produced frustrations to people in Washington as well as to men on the field. When waning, the United Nations command, with General MacArthur as its Commander in Chief, had to make plans to evacuate its troops from Korea altogether. When waxing, General MacArthur had hoped to receive authority to confront China in her home territory. But, General MacArthur's charge, the United Nations mandate, was to maintain status quo — to keep United Nations command's presence in Korea south of the 38th parallel.

General MacArthur Making Public Statements

A World War II hero instrumental in securing Japan's unconditional surrender, General MacArthur found this limited aim confining. In February 1951, in direct contravention of a presidential memorandum dated December 5, 1950 (quoted above), General MacArthur made an open appeal to extend the war — while President Truman, on behalf of the United Nations, was negotiating a cease fire.

In March, General MacArthur repeated his threat to extend the war — again without prior clearance from Washington, in open defiance of the presidential order. His statement appeared in the *New York Times* of March 24, 1951.

Here, Sun Wu's caution is, perhaps, worthy of quoting: "One who knows war is vigilant on Direction and protective of support. Direction and support govern win or loss." (4.6) Sun Wu also said the following: "In the past, those who knew war first made sure that no one could win over them, then sought opportunities to win over the enemy. Ensuring that no one wins over us depends upon ourselves, seeking to win over the enemy depends upon the enemy. Thus, he who knows war can be sure that no one wins over him, but cannot be sure of winning over the enemy." (4.1)

General MacArthur in Correspondence With Minority Leader

In between these two statements by General MacArthur, the Republican Party leader in the House of Representatives (the minority leader), Joe Martin, a persistent critic of the president's war policy, chimed in to support General MacArthur's position to extend the war. Later, he read a letter from General MacArthur, expressing his concurrence with Mr. Martin's view.

This was April 5. Writing to and concurring with the opposition party leader on war policy — without prior clearance — was another violation unbecoming of a field general.

General MacArthur as Hero

Were this transgression committed by a field general with lesser stature, that general would be relieved of his command immediately. But, this field general was General MacArthur. And General MacArthur was a hero. And General MacArthur was popular in the States.

After several days' consultation with General Marshall, Secretary Acheson, Mr. Harriman, and General Bradley,[1] at 1 a.m. on April 11,

1951, President Truman issued a statement to the public and an order to General MacArthur.

President's Statement on April 11, 1951

With deep regret I have concluded that General of the Army Douglas MacArthur is unable to give his wholehearted support to the policies of the United States Government and of the United Nations in matters pertaining to his official duties. In view of the specific responsibilities imposed upon me by the Constitution of the United States and the added responsibility which has been entrusted to me by the United Nations, I have decided that I must make a change of command in the Far East. I have, therefore, relieved General MacArthur of his commands and have designated Lt. Gen. Matthew B. Ridgeway as his successor.

Full and rigorous debate on matters of national policy is a vital element in the constitutional system of our free democracy. It is fundamental, however, that military commanders must be governed by the policies and directives issued to them in the manner provided by our laws and Constitution. In time of crisis, this consideration is particularly compelling.

General MacArthur's place in history as one of our greatest commanders is fully established. The Nation owes him a debt of gratitude for the distinguished and exceptional service which he has rendered his country in posts of great responsibility. For that reason I repeat my regret at the necessity for the action I feel compelled to take in his case.

Order by the President to General MacArthur, April 11, 1951

I deeply regret that it becomes my duty as President and Commander in Chief of the United States military forces to replace you as Supreme Commander, Allied Powers; Commander in Chief, United Nations Command; Commander in Chief, Far East; and Commanding General, U.S. Army, Far East.

[1] Though accorded an unwarranted reputation as one fond of giving "snap judgments," President Truman, in matters relating to national security and war, relied on the collective recommendations of a team consisting of General George C. Marshall, Secretary of Defense; Dean Acheson, Secretary of State; W. Averell Harriman, Special Assistant to the President on foreign policy; General Omar N. Bradley, a fellow Missourian, who served informally as Chief of Staff to the President.

President's Radio Report to the American People, April 11, 1951

That same evening, at 10:30, President Truman delivered a radio report to the American people. The beginning and concluding paragraphs are as follows:

My fellow Americans:

I want to talk to you plainly tonight about what we are doing in Korea and about our policy in the Far East.

In the simplest terms, what we are doing in Korea is this: We are trying to prevent a third world war. ...

We do not want to widen the conflict. We will use every effort to prevent that disaster. And in so doing, we know that we are following the great principle of peace, freedom, and justice.

References

Public Papers of the Presidents of the United States: Harry S. Truman (Washington: General Public Administration)

Lloyd C. Gardner, *The Korean War* (New York: Quadrange Books,1972)

Francis Howard Heller, *The Truman White House* (Lawrence: Regents Press of Kansas, 1980)

R. Ernest Dupuy, *The Harper Encyclopedia of Military History (New York: HarperCollins, 1993),* entry under "The Korean War," pp. 1360-1363

George Bruce (ed), *Harbottle's Dictionary of Battles (London: Hart-Davis, 1971),* entry under "Thirty-Eighth Parallel - *Korean War,*" pp. 251-252.

Endnote

An excellent account of the Korean War and General MacArthur's role is in Eliot A. Cohen and John Gooch, *Military Misfortunes: The Anatomy of Failure in War* (New York: Free Press, 1990), Chapter 7, "Aggregate Failure: The Defeat of the American Eighth Army in Korea, November - December 1950," at pp. 165-195. At the time of this volume's publication, Cohen is Bradley Senior Research Associate at Harvard University's Olin Institute for Strategic Studies, while Gooch is Professor of History at the University of Lancaster, England.

Concerning General MacArthur, Cohen and Cooch first quoted Clay Blair, *The Forgotten War: America in Korea, 1950-1953* (New York: Times Books, 1988, at p. 464): "reckless egotistical strategy after Inchon ... an arrogant, blind march to disaster." (p. 169)

Cohen and Cooch later cited the following passages in Sun Wu's *Art of War* in support of their analysis (pp. 177-178, Sun Wu's passages are represented by renditions in this volume, with passage number added):

The Chinese PLA [People's Liberation Army] did not fight this [North Korea People's Army's] way. ... They followed thereby the maxims of Sun Tzu, from whom Mao Zedong had derived much of the PLA's doctrine:

- War involves stratagems. [1.12]
- Thus, when competent, feign incompetence; when active, feign inaction; when close in, feign distance; when distant, feign proximity. [1.12]
- With the enemy seeking advantage, bait; in disarray, take; showing strength, prepare; parading power, elude; ... ; exhibiting unity, divide. [1.13]
- Attack when unprepared; advance where unexpected. [1.14]

Cohen and Cooch also said the following, quoting Alexander George, *The Chinese Communist Army in Action: The Korean War and its Aftermath* (New York: Columbia University Press, 1967), pp. 7ff, on understanding the enemy:

American intelligence treated prison-of-war information with reserve, failing to believe that Chinese enlisted men would possibly have as much knowledge of their organizations and overall strategy as they claimed. In this they failed again to understand the peculiar nature of their opponents, who stressed the importance of explaining their mission in great detail to their men. (p. 180)

Cohen and Cooch ended their analysis with an observation:

... the proclivity of large and successful military organizations to see all wars as pretty much the same. They are not ... (p. 195)

a quotation from S. L. A. Marshall, *Sinai Victory* (New York: Morrow, 1958), p. 6:

[understanding] the mind and nature of the probable enemy, compared to which a technical competence in the handling of weapons and engines of destruction is of minor importance. Failing in the first, one will most likely fail in everything. (p. 195)

an assertion by General Matthew Ridgeway, the commander of the Eighth Army in Korea in 1950:

We are not adapting our tactics to the enemy and to the type of terrain encountered. (p. 281)

and their own conclusion:

... military organizations must seek out the most difficult kind of intelligence — knowledge of themselves. (p. 195)

On Cohen and Cooch's conclusion, perhaps we may add a passage from Sun Wu:

Therefore, with knowledge of our enemy and knowledge of ourselves, we will not be in a precarious position — not even once in 100 battles. Knowing not our enemy but only ourselves, we are as likely to win a battle as to lose one. Knowing neither our enemy nor ourselves, we will lose every battle. (3.9)

Case P-4 Republican Party Presidential Nomination for 2000 - The Delaware Primary -The Media

[Passages referenced: 1.16, 4.4, 4.9]

The South Carolina primary is scheduled for February 19, 2000. After New Hampshire, it is 18 days away. A lot of time — time to think, time to do more planning, time to identify new options. After all, this is Sun Wu: "We can predict a win because we have identified many options through repeated top-level planning." (1.16)

Governor Bush's New Message

Back in the governor's mansion in Austin, Governor Bush and his policy group go back to do another round of top-level planning.

First, there is the message content. Clearly, Senator McCain's, "reform," resonates. Clearly, voters are interested in their pocket books, either now (tax cut) or later (social security). Conversely, "compassionate conservative," though good as an overall theme for the campaign, suffers in its lack of specificity — it has to be shelved for a while.

How about the governor's record in Texas in attracting women and minorities into his administration? How about his landslide win in his governorship reelection campaign? — old hats, people know these already. But, can these be repackaged? These are solid achievements that need be brought up in every gathering.

And there is the message delivery. The governor needs to be in the public more, to interact with voters more, to talk about his messages more.

Senator McCain's Momentum

The win in New Hampshire puts Senator McCain in new-high grounds. Not only the win, which is a surprise in itself, but the *margin* of the win, which is the surprise of surprises. It is probably beyond the fondest dreams of even Senator McCain himself.

Well, Sun Wu knows that all along. "A not-unexpected win that is foreseen by the populace is not the best of the best" (4.4) proves the reverse: an unexpected win that is *not* foreseen by the populace is the best of the best.

The "not foreseen by the populace" clearly includes the media. To cover their embarrassment, they reward Senator McCain's win with superlatives — "smashing win," "McCain Trounces," and such. They also honor him with his photograph on newsmagazines' covers — not one, not two, but all three. *Time. Newsweek. U.S. News and World Report.* The works. The red-carpet treatment. The media darling.

This is certainly a moment to be treasured. Sun Wu has "been there, done that," and appreciates the momentum a win can generate. "In war, the winning army may be likened to water rushing down from a mile-and-half-high mountain to the stream." (4.9)

Delaware Primary: a Testing Ground

The next major battleground is certainly South Carolina, where both Governor Bush and Senator McCain will appear. But that is a fortnight away.

From the Bush camp, seeing Senator McCain in the limelight for that long a period is clearly unbearable. It needs to be blunted. Besides, the new message needs to have a test market.

Where? Delaware. A small state, but The First State nevertheless — the first state to rectify the Constitution, a historically significant moment that is preserved on the state's license plates.

And There Are Four

The timing is just right. One week after the New Hampshire primary. The location is right also. On the way to South Carolina.

Governor Bush spends three days in Delaware. A huge investment considering that Delaware can deliver only 12 delegates. But the aim is not to claim these delegates, valuable they certainly are, but to test the new message, to test the delivery of the new message.

Too bad that Senator McCain has chosen not to compete in Delaware. These decisions are made 'way ahead; with a low-budget campaign, such as Senator McCain's, he has to bypass Delaware in favor of South Carolina.

On February 4, just four days before the Delaware primary, Mr. Bauer announces his withdrawal from the race. Though Mr. Bauer's presence has not been an important factor in the race so far, from a planning standpoint, his departure simplifies matters.

And now, there are four.

Results of the Delaware Primary

Results of the Delaware primary, held on Tuesday, February 8, 2000, are shown as Exhibit 1.

Case P-4 Exhibit 1
Result of Delaware Primary
(100% of Precincts Reporting)
February 8, 2000

	Votes	Percent	Delegates
Bush	15,102	51	12
McCain	7,547	25	-
Forbes	5,857	20	-
Keyes	1,138	4	-

Governor Bush Reevaluates

The Bush win is fully expected, but his receiving a clear majority is not anticipated, given Mr. Forbes's participation. It must be rated as an excellent performance.

Against Senator McCain on a one-on-one basis, the margin is more than two-to-one, also highly satisfying. The fact that Senator McCain has never set foot in Delaware is a demerit, but that is beyond Governor Bush's control.

In any event, the main purpose for Governor Bush in Delaware is not to win, important though it is, but to test the new message. The new message: "a reformer with results" is certainly effective — catchy, modest, with a hint of experience in administration that Senator McCain lacks. Well done.

Forbes Withdraws

Mr. Forbes won the Delaware primary in 1996, and counts on Delaware to deliver the same to boost his candidacy. The third-place finish is clearly disappointing, particularly since he lags behind Senator McCain, a candidate in absentia.

Having spent $66 million of his own fortune in this Year 2000 run, garnering but 61,860 votes — compared to $37.4 million he spent in 1996, and receiving 1,424,898 votes — the handwriting is on the wall. Satisfied that his main message, flat tax, is well understood, though not well received against an unprecedented 40-month economic growth, Mr. Forbes feels that it is time to call it quits.

On February 9, 2000, one day after the Delaware primary, Mr. Forbes officially withdraws from the race.

On to South Carolina. And now, there are but three.

5 势　篇

MOMENTUM PLANNING

5.1　　　　　　　凡治众如治寡，分数是也；斗众如斗寡，形名是也。三军之众，可使毕受敌而无败者，奇正是也；兵之所加，如以碫投卵者，虚实是也。

M anaging a large army is no different from managing a small army; the key is divisional organization. Giving directives to a large army is no different from giving directives to a small army; the key is command hierarchy. A three-battalion army[1] surrounded by the enemy may suffer no loss; the key is orthodox and unorthodox formations. A superior army overpowers, as if throwing stones at eggs; the key is a firm formation against a façade formation.

> [1] In the Spring and Autumn Period (770-476 BCE), a large army was divided into three complementing battalions, known as the upper battalion, the center battalion, and the lower battalion.

5.2　　　　　　　凡战者，以正合，以奇胜。故善出奇者，无穷如天地，不竭如江河。终而复始，日月是也；死而复生，四时是也。

I n war, use orthodox formations to engage the enemy, but use unorthodox formations to win. One who is adept can produce unorthodox formations as infinitely as sky and earth and as inexhaustibly as oceans and rivers — repeating as day and night, regenerating as the four seasons.

5.3　　　声不过五，五声之变不可胜听也；色不过五，五色之变不可胜观也；味不过五，五味之变不可胜尝也。

In tone there are but five; still, the variation of these five tones can produce melodies beyond anyone's ability to assimilate. In color there are but five; still, the combination of these five colors can produce paintings beyond anyone's ability to appreciate. In taste there are but five; still, the combination of these five tastes can produce cuisines beyond anyone's ability to associate.

5.4　　　战势不过奇正，奇正之变不可胜穷也。奇正相生，如环之无端，孰能穷之？

In formations, there are but two, orthodox and unorthodox; still, their variations are endless. Orthodox and unorthodox formations evolve in infinite cycles. Who can exhaust them?

5.5　　　激水之疾，至于漂石者，势也；鸷鸟之击，至于毁折者，节也。

Water rushing down can move stones; this is momentum.[2] Falcons charging in can crush their preys; this is swiftness.[3]

[2] This sentence echoes the very last sentence in the preceding essay, where winning a war is likened to rushing water's *formation*. Here, Sun Wu adds another dimension to the power of rushing water — momentum.

[3] This sentence, together with the preceding one, demonstrates the advantage of momentum and timing. In the preceding one, a contrast between soft and hard — with momentum, the soft wins over the hard. This sentence, a contrast between large-clumsy and small-lithe — with timing, the clumsy wins over the lithe.

5.6   是故善战者，其势险，其节短。势如扩
弩，节如发机。

Thus, one who knows war builds momentum as if spontaneous, readies for swiftness as if instantaneous.[4] Spontaneous momentum is like a bow completely extended; instantaneous swiftness is like weaponry fully ready.[5]

[4] *As if* are key words in this sentence. Momentum gives the appearance of spontaneity, but, in fact, it is the result of careful building; swiftness gives the appearance of instantaneousness, but, in fact, it is the result of patient waiting. In both instances, the underlying action, unseen, is preparation — and, from that, generalizing, the underlying unseen action is planning.

[5] This sentence elaborates on the unseen action underlying the appearance — an arrow readying for projection is the result of the archer's extending the bow; a stone ball readying for release is the result of the crew's placing the ball into the catapult.

5.7   纷纷纭纭，斗乱而不可乱也；浑浑沌沌，形
圆而不可败也。乱生于治，怯生于勇，弱生于强。治乱，
数也；勇怯，势也；强弱，形也。

In the midst of turmoil and tumult, fight chaos but avoid being chaotic. In the midst of confusion and commotion, form into circles to avoid loss. [The enemy's] Chaos is the result of [our] discipline; [the enemy's] cowardice, the result of our courage; [the enemy's] weakness, the result of [our] strength. The difference between discipline and chaos is organization; between courage and cowardice, formation; between strength and weakness, momentum.[6]

[6] This passage neatly summarizes the role of organization, momentum, and formation in war.

5.8　　　故善动敌者，形之，敌必从之；予之，敌必取之。以此动之，以卒待之。

Thus, one who can outmaneuver the enemy creates [illusory] formations for the enemy to follow; creates [empty] opportunities for the enemy to take. Thus outmaneuvered, our men are ready.

5.9　　　故善战者，求之于势，不责于人，故能择人而任势。任势者，其战人也，如转木石；木石之性：安则静，危则动，方则止，圆则行。故善战人之势，如转圆石于千仞之山者，势也。

Thus, one who knows war makes use of momentum but does ont blame his men; he deploys men in the light of momentum. Momentum, in relation to deploying men, may be likened to propelling wood and stones. Wood and stone remain stationary on a plane, but move about on a slope; remain still as squares, but become mobile when round. Thus, one who knows how to deploy men deploys them as propelling round stones from a mile-and-half-high mountain. This is momentum.[9]

[9] The final sentence neatly summarizes the theme of this essay — momentum, as the final sentence in the preceding one summarizes the theme of that essay — formation. Beautiful writing at its very best.

Case W-D Vietnam War - Kennedy Speech (1954)

[Passages referenced: 1.9, 2.1, 2.2,
2.3, 2.4, 4.6, 5.7, 5.8]

Senator John F. Kennedy (D-Massachusetts, later President of the United States, 1961-63), delivered the following speech on the Senate floor on April 6, 1954.

The time has come for the American people to be told the blunt truth about Indochina.

Two Alternatives

Inasmuch as Secretary Dulles has rejected, with finality, any suggestion of bargaining on Indochina in exchange for recognition of Red China, those discussions in Geneva which concern that war may center around two basic alternatives:

The first is a negotiated peace, based either upon partition of the area between the forces of the Viet Minh and the French Union, possibly along the 16th parallel; or based upon a coalition government in which Ho Chi Minh is represented. Despite any wishful thinking to the contrary, it should be apparent that the popularity and prevalence of Ho Chi Minh and his following throughout Indochina would cause either partition or a coalition government to result in eventual domination by the Communists.

The second alternative is for the United States to persuade the French to continue their valiant and costly struggle; an alternative which, considering the current state of opinion in France, will be adopted only if the United States pledges increasing support. Secretary Dulles' statement that the "imposition in southeast Asia of the political system of Communist Russia and its Chinese Communist ally ... should be met by united action" indicates that it is our policy to give such support; that we will, as observed by the *New York Times* last Wednesday, "fight if necessary to keep southeast Asia out of their hands"; and that we hope to win support of the free countries of Asia for united action against communism in Indochina, in spite of the fact that such nations have pursued since the war's inception of a policy of cold neutrality. ...

Commitment and Prospect

Certainly I, for one, favor a policy of a "united action" by many nations whenever necessary to achieve a military and political victory for the free world in that area, realizing full well that it may eventually require some commitment of our manpower. ...

But to pour money, material, and men into the jungles of Indochina without at least a remote prospect of victory would be dangerously futile and self-destructive. ...

In February of this year, Defense Secretary Charles Wilson said that a French victory was "both possible and probable" and that the war was going "fully as well as we expected it to at this stage. I see no reason to think Indochina would be another Korea." Also in February of this year, Undersecretary of State Smith stated that "The military situation in Indochina is favorable. ..."

Less than two weeks ago, Admiral Radford, Chairman of the Joint Chiefs of Staff, stated that "the French are going to win." And finally, ... Secretary of State Dulles stated that he did not "expect that there is going to be a Communist victory in Indochina"; that "in terms of Communist domination of Indochina, I do not accept that as a probability." ...

Victory Appears Remote

Despite this series of optimistic reports about eventual victory, every Member of the Senate knows that such victory today appears to be desperately remote, to say the least, despite tremendous amounts of economic and material aid from the United States and despite a deplorable loss of French Union manpower. The call for either negotiations or additional participation by other nations underscores the remoteness of such a final victory today, regardless of the outcome at Dien Bien Phu. It is, of course, for these reasons that many French are reluctant to continue the struggle without greater assistance; for to record the sapping effect which time and the enemy have had on their will and strength in that area is not to disparage their valor. ...

Enemy Everywhere and Nowhere

I am frankly of the belief that no amount of American military assistance in Indochina can conquer an enemy which is everywhere and at the same time nowhere, "an enemy of the people" which has the sympathy and covert support of the people. As succinctly stated by the report of the Judd Subcommittee of the House Foreign Affairs Committee in January of this year:

Until political independence has been achieved, an effective fighting force from the associated states cannot be expected ... The apathy of the local population to the menace of Viet Minh communism disguised as the nationalism is the most discouraging aspect of the situation. That can only be overcome through the grant of complete independence to each of the associated states. Only for such a cause as their own freedom will people make the most heroic effort necessary to win this kind of struggle.

War of Colonialism

This is an analysis which is shared, if in some instances grudgingly, by most American observers. Moreover, without political independence for the associated states, the other Asiatic nations have made it clear that they regard this as a war of colonialism; and the "united action" which is said to be so desperately needed for victory in that area is likely to end up as unilateral action by our own country. Such intervention, without participation by the armed forces of the other nations of Asia, without the support of the great masses of the people of the associated states, with increasing reluctance and discouragement on the part of the French — and, I might add, with hordes of Chinese Communist troops poised just across the border in anticipation of our unilateral entry into their kind of battleground — such intervention, Mr. President, would be virtually impossible in the type of military situation which prevails in Indochina.

References

David L. Bender (ed), *The Vietnam War: Opposing Viewpoints* (St. Paul: Greenhaven Press, 1984); Kennedy's speech is excerpted at pp. 22-25

W. Scott Thompson and Donald D. E. Frizzell (ed), *The Lessons of Vietnam* (New York: Crane, Russak, 1977); one four-star general in the United States Army is quoted as saying: "The French haven't won a war since Napoleon. What can we learn from them?" (p. 22)

George Bruce (ed), *Harbottle's Dictionary of Battles* (London: Hart-Davis, 1971), entries under "Dien Bien Phu - *French-Vietnamese War*," p. 80; and "Vietnam War," pp.265-268

Endnote: On Sun Wu

Though Mr. Kennedy is unlikely to be aware of Sun Wu's work, his speech underscores many points made by Sun Wu 2,500 years earlier:

· Which head of state has the Direction (1.9)

· To marshal a 100,000-member army needs the daily outlay of 1,000 measures of gold (2.1)

· There are no instances where states are benefitted by protracted wars. (2.2)

· One who does not fully understand the negative side of warfare is incapable of fully understanding its positive side. (2.3)

· Long-distance transport of provisions for the troops is the cause of a state's impoverishment. (2.4)

· Direction and support govern win or loss. (4.6)

Endnote: On Dien Bien Phu

An interesting account of the French-Vietnamese War, circa 1953, is "Dien Bien Phu (1953)" by Charles Mey, in Jon E. Lewis (ed), *The Mammoth Book of Battles* (New York: Carroll & Graf, 1995), at pp. 433-443. One excerpt (pp. 437-438):

The besieged French have six batteries (24 guns) of 105 mm, one battery of four 155 mm howitzers and thirty-two 120 mm heavy mortars. Colonel Piroth, who commands the base artillery, considers they can stop any enemy infantry attack, and are good enough for effective counter-battery work. He said: "No Viet Minh gun will fire three rounds without being destroyed." The French have underestimated the enemy's artillery strength, the supply of ammunition, the skill of his gunners and the effectiveness of his camouflage. ...

The Viet Minh 105s, in fact, are undetectable and practically invulnerable, because they are well dug-in, though this is at the expense of wide fields of fire and large handling crews. Dummy guns are used by the Viet Minh to deceive the French spotters in the base.

The last paragraph is reminiscent of Sun Wu: "Thus, one who can outmaneuver the enemy creates [illusory] formations for the enemy to follow; creates [empty] opportunities for the enemy to take. Thus outmaneuvered, our men are ready." (5.8)

After stating that Colonel Piroth could not face the defeat of his artillery and took his own life, Mey observed that

> Its [Dien Bien Phu's] ultimate destruction was due to the inability of the French to sustain an adequate supply of men, ammunition and provisions for the besieged garrison. To this must be added the brilliance of General Giap's powers of leadership and the unexpectedly high quality of his battalions. (p. 443)

A relevant passage from Sun Wu might be the following:

> [The enemy's] Chaos is the result of [our] discipline; [the enemy's] cowardice, the result of our courage; [the enemy's] weakness, the result of [our] strength. (5.7)

Case P-5 Republican Party Presidential Nomination for 2000 - The South Carolina Primary - The Bush Candidacy

[Passages referenced: 1.13, 5.8]

The Delaware primary, although an interlude, serves three very useful purposes. It shows that Senator McCain has momentum — drawing 25 percent of votes without even showing up. It also shows that Governor Bush's new message is working — receiving a majority of votes cast. It further shows that Mr. Forbes's message has lost its attractiveness in the context of a prosperous Year 2000.

Mr. Forbes's withdrawal a day after the Delaware primary allows, for practical purposes, a head-to-head confrontation between Governor Bush and Senator McCain. The stakes are high — and getting higher.

South Carolina as Home Territory

The first arena for a head-to-head confrontation after Delaware is South Carolina. A conservative state. A state where Governor Bush has the endorsement of the former governor and the establishment. A state where Governor Bush can rightly claim as his. In South Carolina, Governor Bush has a clear location advantage.

Relaxed and poised, Governor Bush's new message, "reformer with results", also resonates. A new message. A new ball game. Playing at home.

Reformer vs. Astronaut

The "reformer with results" message is devilishly clever. Voters are clearly thirsty for "reform" — campaign finance reform, to be specific — and that is Senator McCain's message. With some $70 million in his war chest, largest ever and mainly from special interests, Governor Bush cannot talk about campaign finance reform. But he can certainly talk about Texas's educational reform and such. It is not campaign finance reform, but it is certainly reform.

The "reformer with results" message seems to bother Senator McCain. He counters with "If Governor Bush is a reformer, I am an astronaut." It is a "sound bite" alright, but it really does not have any punch.

Maneuver and Outmaneuver

Just clipping Senator McCain's wings in his campaign message is not enough, the Bush camp needs to outmaneuver the senator in other ways as well. This, of course, is Sun Wu: "one who can outmaneuver the enemy creates [illusionary] formations for the enemy to follow; creates [empty] opportunities for the enemy to take. Thus outmaneuvered, our men are ready." (5.8)

How?

Well, Sun Wu has an excellent recipe: "With the enemy seeking advantage, bait; showing strength, prepare; prone to anger, provoke." (1.13)

Senator McCain Slips

There is a little fund-raising event for Senator McCain in Washington, with lobbyists in evidence. About $250,000 are raised. May this be used to claim that Senator McCain is no better? Probably not. Indeed, influential newspapers are coming to Senator McCain's defense.

There is a televised debate, where the three remaining candidates participate. Some pundits say that it is well done; others say that it lacks the drama of a head-to-head debate — the third candidate is a drag, preventing the heat level from going up further.

But, it is bad enough — at least for Senator McCain. In one heated exchange, Senator McCain somehow compares Governor Bush to President Clinton in terms of trustworthiness.

Bingo! This is it.

Negative Advertising Proliferates

Comparing a Republican candidate's trustworthiness to President Clinton's is probably the last thing a Republican voter wants to hear. The Bush camp quickly airs an ad, chiding Senator McCain of this indiscretion: "Disagree with me, fine. But never compare me to Clinton on trustworthiness."

In the meantime, to counter Senator McCain's ingenious plan to score a breakthrough in South Carolina[1], many influential people, sometimes known as *religious right*, make telephone calls to their fellow faithfuls, seeking their support and asking them to come out and vote in the forthcoming primary.

New Voters and Turnout

It is said that, in politics, a week is like a year — meaning that a lot may happen in a few days. There are 18 days between the New Hampshire primary and the South Carolina primary. Clearly, a lot more may happen.

The McCain camp hopes to have a large turnout. In New Hampshire, a lot of young people turned out — and mostly they voted for Senator McCain, giving him the win. Senator McCain seeks a repeat performance.

What is the critical number? According to the McCain camp, with turnout below 350,000, Governor Bush wins. Above that, Senator McCain becomes competitive. Over 450,000, Senator McCain has an advantage.

These are indeed big numbers, considering that, in 1996, only 275,000 turned out to vote.

Big Turnout and Big Results

As it turns out, the turnout is indeed heavy. Huge. Twice the 1996 turnout.

Exit polls suggest that those who turn out to vote are regular Republicans — and they vote for Governor Bush, not for Senator McCain. Thus, pundits predict a big win for Governor Bush — some say "of blown away proportions."

---

[1] Senator McCain's ingenious plan to score a breakthrough in South Carolina is presented as Case P-6. That case, because of its theme, is included as a case study under Essay 12, though prepared immediately after this one. Case P-6 may thus be read immediately following this one as well.

The telephone bank operated by religious right is certainly awesome. It delivers. The Establishment candidate wins.

Results of the South Carolina Primary

The results of the South Carolina primary, held on Saturday, February 19, 2000, are shown as Exhibit 1.

Case P-5 Exhibit 1
Result of South Carolina Primary
(99% of precincts reporting)
February 19, 2000

	Votes	Percent	Delegates Added	To Date
Bush	301,050	53	34	61
McCain	237,888	42	3	14
Keyes	25,510	4	-	4

On to Michigan

Finally, on a head-to-head basis, Governor Bush has scored a win over Senator McCain. Is this win big enough?

By the same token, Senator McCain has suffered his first head-to-head defeat. Is this bad enough? Is negative advertising the culprit? Is the slip-of-tongue remark on Governor Bush's trustworthiness that important? Is this reparable?

Well, pundits have weighted in. They are saying that Michigan, three days away, might be Senator McCain's last hurrah.

There is not enough time to deliberate. On to Michigan.

6 虚 实 篇

PREPAREDNESS PLANNING

6.1　　　孙子曰：凡先处战地而待敌者佚，后处战地而趋战者劳。故善战者，致人而不致于人。

One who arrives at the battlefield to await for the enemy's arrival is at ready. One who arrives at the battlefield to meet the enemy is not at ready. One who knows war outmaneuvers the enemy but is not outmaneuvered by him.

6.2　　　能使敌人自至者，利之也；能使敌人不得至者，害之也。故敌佚能劳之、饱能饥之、安能动之者，出其所必趋也。

Maneuvering the enemy so that he comes to where we want him is the result of our bait. Maneuvering the enemy so that he cannot go to where he wants is the result of our blockade. We make him occupied instead of at ease, make him hungry instead of well fed, make him move about instead of at ready. We attack where he must come out to defend.

6.3 行千里而不劳者，行于无人之地也；攻而必取者，攻其所不守也；守而必固者，守其所必攻也。

Marching a thousand miles and not feeling tired, it is because the march is through unpopulated land; attacking a position and producing a sure win, it is because the attack is on the undefended; defending a position and ensuring a secure hold, it is because the defense is against an expected attack.

6.4   故善攻者，敌不知其所守；善守者，敌不知其所攻。微乎微乎，至于无形；神乎神乎，至于无声，故能为敌之司命。

Thus, against one who is adept at offense, the enemy knows not how to defend; against one who is adept at defense, the enemy knows not how to attack. Being minuscule and approaching infinitesimal, we are almost invisible. Being elusive and approaching imaginary, we are almost inaudible. We are thus in control of the enemy's destiny.

6.5 进而不可御者，冲其虚也；退而不可追者，速而不可及也。

Advancing as to be beyond defense, it is because we smash the façade. Retreating as to be beyond pursuit, it is because we move with swiftness.

6.6 故我欲战，敌虽高垒深沟，不得不与我战者，攻其所必救也；我不欲战，画地而守之，敌不得与我战者，乖其所之也。

Thus, if we are determined to fight, the enemy will have to come out and fight, even though they are stationed on high grounds or behind deep channels; this is because we attack a position he must rescue. If we are determined not to fight, the enemy will not engage us in a fight, even though our defense is but a line on the ground; this is because we compel him to deploy his forces elsewhere.

6.7   故形人而我无形，则我专而敌分；我专为一，敌分为十，是以十攻其一也。则我寡而敌众，能以众击寡者，则吾之所与战者约矣。

Thus, with the enemy visible and us invisible, we are consolidated but the enemy is scattered. With us consolidated and the enemy scattered in ten different positions, our attacking force is ten times that of the defending force. Even when our total man-count is inferior to the enemy's, our attacking force is numerically superior to the enemy's; this is because the enemy's force at any position must necessarily be limited.

6.8   吾所与战之地不可知，不可知，则敌所备者多，敌所备者多，则吾所与战者寡矣。

Where we plan to fight is not to be known to the enemy. Without this knowledge, the enemy has to guard many positions. With the enemy guarding many positions, wherever we attack, the defending force will be numerically inferior to ours.

6.9   故备前则后寡，备后则前寡；备左则右寡，备右则左寡；无所不备，则无所不寡。

Thus, [the enemy's] guarding his front exposes his back, guarding his back exposes his front, guarding his left exposes his right, guarding his right exposes his left. Guarding his every position exposes his every position.

6.10   寡者，备人者也；众者，使人备己者也。

Being exposed is the result of guarding many positions. Being numerically superior is the result of forcing the enemy to guard many positions.

6.11   故知战之地，知战之日，则可千里而战；不知战地，不知战日，则左不能救右，右不能救左，前不能救后，后不能救前，而况远者数十里，近者数里乎！

Knowing where and when to fight, the battle line may be as long as a thousand miles. Not knowing where and when to fight, even though the battle line is but a few score miles, or perhaps but a few miles, the left cannot rescue the right, the right cannot rescue the left, the front cannot rescue the rear, the rear cannot rescue the front.[1]

> [1] This paragraph reemphasizes the importance of planning and, with it, of taking initiative. The miserable scenario in the second sentence describes vividly the helplessness of an army that is at his enemy's mercy.

6.12   以吾度之，越人之兵虽多，亦奚益于胜哉？
故曰：胜可为也。敌虽众，可使无斗。

In my estimation, while the army of Yuè[2] has an advantage in number, that is not necessarily an advantage in winning a war. Winning is the result of planning. Although the enemy is more numerous, it can be rendered non-combative.

> [2] Yuè, south of Wu, is situated in present-day Zhejiang Province. Yuè was a long-time foe of Wu, against which King Hé Lü vowed to revenge. See also Item 2 under 512 BCE in Appendix A.
>
> This is the first time Sun Wu mentions a specific state as a potential enemy, suggesting that, by this time, Sun Wu was writing specifically for the eyes of King Hé Lü of Wu.

6.13   故策之而知得失之计，作之而知动静之理，形
之而知死生之地，角之而知有余不足之处。

With planning, we identify strategies for winning and losing. With provocation, we deduce the enemy's movement and deployment. With formation, we explore terrains the enemy thrives and disdains. With skirmishes, we assess our preparedness and deficiencies.

6.14 故形兵之极，至于无形；无形，则深间不能窥，智者
不能谋。

The ultimate of formation is formless. Being formless, it is beyond the cleverest intelligence[3] were they in our innermost, and beyond the most intelligent planners were they in the enemy's employ.

[3] Sun Wu has a healthy regard for the role of intelligence. Essay 13 deals specifically with this issue.

6.15   因形而措胜于众，众不能知；人皆知我所胜之形，而莫知吾所以制胜之形。故其战胜不复，而应形于无穷。

The masses do not understand why a particular formation wins. All they know is that a specific formation wins, but do not know what causes that formation to win. Formations are specific to a specific enemy; they do not recur. They adapt endlessly.

6.16 夫兵形象水，水之行，避高而趋下；兵之形，避实而击虚。水因地而制形，兵因敌而制胜。故兵无成势，无恒形。

Formations may be likened to water. Water formation avoids the high ground but seeks the low plain; military formations bypass the firm but attack the façade. To flow, water accommodates the terrain; to win, formations accommodate the enemy. In war, momentum is not set, formation is not constant.

6.17   能因敌变化而取胜者，谓之神。故五行无常胜，四时无常位；日有短长，月有死生。

One who is all-winning over an enemy in all kinds of maneuvers is a wizard. This is because, among the five elements, none is always predominant; of the four seasons, none is ever-present; of days, some are long and others short; the moon waxes and wanes.[4]

[4] The implication is that an all-winning commander is a rarity. Even in the natural world, constancy is hard to come by.

   Chinese thinking in Sun Wu's time, mainly from *I (The Book of Changes)*, is that nature holds five elements — metal, wood, water, fire, and earth — in a closed cycle. Moving in the right-to-left direction cited here (anticlockwise), one element is the cause of another element's existence (e.g., with water, tree grows); moving in the left-to-right direction (clockwise), one element is the cause of another element's demise (e.g., with a metal saw, trees fell). Thus, "among the five elements, none is always dominant."

Case W-E   Gulf War - Desert Storm (1991)

To honor Sun Tzu, the National Defense University, Ft. McNair, Washington DC, held a "Sun Tzu Art of War in Information Warfare" research competition. Award-winning essays are collected in Robert E. Neilson (ed), *Sun Tzu and Information Warfare* (Washington: National Defense University Press, 1997).

One of the award-winning essays is by Colonel Adolph Carlson, United States Army. Though entitled "Information Management and the Challenge of Battle Command," his essay, in this case writer's view, deals with leadership, with leadership style, with leader-to-leader communication.

Carlson's essay covers two case studies — one is excerpted below, the other one appears later in this volume as Case W-H. For ease in reading, references to the other case are replaced by []; plural-to-singular correspondence is introduced as needed. Passages omitted are noted by ellipses (...).

This paper will examine [] case studies to show that decision making under the pressure of ongoing operations involves a fundamentally different mental process than planning in advance of operations. Moreover, because decisions during the conduct of operations must be made in the shortest time and under the most demanding conditions, the opportunities for consultation among various command echelons are minimized, resulting in the possibility of conceptual divergence between senior and subordinate commanders. ...

Desert Storm, February 1991

The four days of Desert Storm's ground operations in February 1991 seemed to most Americans to be a remarkable military achievement and a satisfactory ending to what could have been a long and bloody war. Army Chief of Staff General Carl Vuono captured the public's mood when he said:

> For as long as Americans honor their history, these 100 hours of Operation Desert Storm will be remembered as one of the most powerful applications of military might and one of the most flawlessly executed campaigns in the annals of warfare.[1]

[1] Quoted in AUSA Institute for Land Warfare, *The U.S. Army in Operation Desert Storm* (Arlington, AUSA, June 1991), p. 24.

Desert Storm, Dissension and Frustration

It came as something of a shock, then, when one year after the event *Army Times* writer Tom Donnelly revealed that the theater command structure was "riven by disputes"[2] over how the ground battle should be waged. Donnelly related that the theater commander and chief, General H. Norman Schwarzkopf, was often at odds with his subordinate land force commanders, Lieutenant Generals John Yeosock, Commander 3d Army; Gary Luck, Commander XVIII Airborne Corps' and Frederick Franks, Commander VII Corps. The principal target of Schwarzkopf's frustration, Donnelly reported, was Franks, who was "not aggressive enough in attacking Iraq's Republican Guard."

Schwarzkopf later added to the controversy in his October 1992 autobiography. Schwarzkopf described Franks' plan as "plodding and overly cautious."[3] Schwarzkopf told of his frustration in finding that, on the morning after the beginning of the ground attack [G+1], VII Corps had not advanced at a rate commensurate with other units in the attack, most notably the 24th Infantry Division in the adjacent XVIII Airborne Corps. In the end, Schwarzkopf toned down his criticism, saying that he had been "too hard" on VII Corps' "slow progress during the battle" and conceding that Franks had been "faced with the challenge of accomplishing [the] mission while sparing the lives of as many of his troops as possible." ...

Building a Case Against Franks

The fact that Schwarzkopf stopped short of indicting Franks did not deter others from building a case against him. In June 1993, retired Air Force Colonel James G. Burton, a fourteen-year veteran of the Pentagon and noted critic of Army testing and acquisition, published an article in which [] he claimed to have had a premonitory insight into Franks' failings.

Burton charged that Franks's unhurried maneuver was the result of rigid adherence to a doctrine not suited to the demands of modern maneuver warfare.[4] He argued that Franks could not keep pace with the demands of the ground war because of his overriding concern that

[2] Tom Donnelly, "The Generals' War," *Army Times*, 2 March 1992, pp. 8, 16-18.

[3] H. Norman Schwarzkopf, *It Doesn't Take a Hero* (New York: Bantam Books, October 1992), p. 433. Other pages referenced are pp. 381, 452-456, and 482.

the formations under his command remain synchronized." The result was a linear, ponderous maneuver which permitted the Iraqi Republican Guard, Franks' objective, to escape. Burton declared that the events of the ground war proceeded at a rate "much quicker than Franks could handle," suggesting that "dinosaur blood runs freely through his veins."

War Fighting Cultures and Leadership Styles

In a June 1994 article, retired Marine Corps Lieutenant General Bernard E. Trainor described Franks as "respected in the Army," but "known to be slow and deliberate in all that he did ... not what Schwarzkopf was looking for as leader of the main attack against the Iraqis."[5] Trainor concluded that Franks "could have been more aggressive," but traced the root of the problem to "a complex combination" of factors, including "different war fighting cultures" and "leadership styles." ...

Problem of Perception

A comprehensive survey of the details of the [] Franks case illustrates that an organization's warfighting culture will shape a subordinate commander's evaluation of information and interpretation of direction. Moreover, when a unit is detached from one organization and placed under the operational control of another, it will carry with it the warfighting culture of its parent command. This phenomenon affects mission analysis, appraisal of enemy capabilities, appreciation for ambient conditions, and promulgation of subsequent guidance.

Mission Analysis

The mission of Central Command included geographic and enemy-oriented objectives. [] Central Command's mission required it to "eject Iraqi Armed Forces from Kuwait" and "destroy the Republican Guard."[6] Strictly speaking, in neither mission was one component more important than the other, but [] Schwarzkopf chose to concentrate on the enemy-oriented aspects of their missions. [] Schwarzkopf told his subordinates "we need to destroy not attack, not damage, not

[4] James G. Burton, "Pushing Them Out the Back Door," *Proceedings*, June 1993, pp. 37-42.

[5] Bernard E. Trainor, "Schwarzkopf and His Generals," *Proceedings,* June 1994, pp. 46-47.

[6] United States Department of Defense, *Final Report to Congress* [Title V Report], April 1992, pp. 73.

surround — I want you to *destroy* [emphasis in the original] the Republican Guard."

Appraisal of Enemy Capabilities

In the [] Frank case, the corps-level appraisal of enemy capabilities was inconsistent with the theater commander's. []

Schwarzkopf viewed the enemy's collapse on G-Day as prelude to a general rout. Schwarzkopf was contemptuous of the enemy facing VII Corps. He said: "The enemy is not worth [expletive deleted]. Go after them with audacity, shock action, and surprise."

To Franks, however, the indicators that suggested to Schwarzkopf that Iraqi forces were in flight painted a different picture, that they were concentrating, possibly for offensive action. Franks expected to fight five heavy Republican Guard Forces Command [RGFC] divisions, four of which were estimated to be 75-100% effective on the eve of the ground attack, the fifth 50-75% effective.[7]

Intelligence had warned that "[t]he RGFC is the best equipped and best trained force in the Iraqi ground forces ... untainted by years of defensive warfare ... a highly motivated and trained offensive force. ..."[8] During the Iran-Iraq war, the RGFC "assumed a tactically offensive role: the counterattack." []

Schwarzkopf based his judgments on data provided by remote sources: intercepted messages and technical surveillance. In contrast, Franks made decisions based on battlefield data, which he believed to portray the situation with greater fidelity. Non-contextual electronic data tracking vehicular movement presented no coherent, persuasive grounds to expect that the anticipated meeting engagement would be anything less than originally anticipated.

Supervision of Operations

[] Schwarzkopf's direction was more direct, but may have been too metaphoric. In his 14 November 1990 commander's briefing, he directed: "I want the VII Corps to *slam* [emphasis in the original] into

[7] United States Department of Defense, *Final Report to Congress* [Title V Report], p. 256. In addition, four regular Iraqi armored divisions [the 10th, 52nd, and 12th, rated at 50-75% effective, and the 17th, rated at 75-100% effective] were identified either in or in reinforcing distance of the VII Corps' zone of action.

[8] National Training Center Handbook No. 100-91, *The Iraqi Army - Organization and Tactics* (National Training Center: S2, 177th Armored Brigade, January 1991), p. 26.

the Republican Guard." Schwarzkopf's memoir implies that he intended the attack to be swift and agile, but the language invokes an image of irresistible mass.

Once operations were in motion, [] Schwarzkopf conveyed direction [not] in person, but [] by electronic means. For Franks, the additional guidance did not clarify.

On 25 February, Schwarzkopf called the VII Corps command post and talked to Colonel Stan Cherrie, corps G-3 [Franks was forward with the 3d Armored Division]. Schwarzkopf reportedly told Cherrie to keep pressuring the enemy: "I want you to keep the Bobby Knight press[9] on them."[10]

This was another example of metaphoric language intended to be emphatic, but which was too imprecise to convey intent. Not until 26 February was the more specific direction passed to VII Corps, to change the operation from "deliberate operations to a pursuit."[11]

Appreciation of Ambient Conditions

[] the deficiencies alleged against Franks were the difficulties of night operations. In Franks's case, Schwarzkopf's anger at what he perceived to be VII Corps' failure to "make good progress during the night" of G-Day suggests that [] he could not visualize his subordinate's predicament.

Because of his wide span of control over U.S. and coalition forces, Schwarzkopf's staff relied on computer graphic displays of information, which were necessarily abridged. These displays precluded from absorbing the details of any specific component of the operation, even in the area of main attack.

Since his map showed only movement, he was inclined to think that a lack of movement equated to a lack progress. In his own words, "They seem to be sitting around." He could not appreciate the difficulties of the 1st Infantry Division's consolidating a beachhead,

[9] A "press" in basketball is a term used to describe a defense which takes the initiative away from an offensive team by coordinated action all across the court. Bobby Knight, Indiana University basketball coach, was famous for employing this tactic.

[10] Rick Atkinson, *Crusade* (New York: Houghton Mifflin, 1993), p. 421.

[11] Richard M. Sqain, *Lucky Way* (Ft. Leavenworth KS: U.S.Army Command and General Staff College Press, 1994), p. 252.

the passage of 7000 vehicles of the British 1st armored Division, and then the 1st Division's redeployment to join 1st and 3d Armored Divisions.[12] []

Phenomenon of Conceptual Divergence

[This case illustrates] a common problem: diverging concepts of ongoing operations leading to dysfunction misunderstanding at different levels in the chain of command. This divergence is a natural consequence of on-the-spot decision making when conditions preclude consultation and coordination. ...

Critical Relevance of Context

The transmission of data without the associated context further diminishes the clarity of a message, especially when the receiver is in a different contextual environment than the sender. The more impersonal the means of transmission, the greater the lack of context will produce misinterpretation. Any alternative to face-to-face consultation reduces the ability of senior and subordinate commanders to communicate clearly. The use of non-specific or metaphoric language carries with it the greater risk that the image the sender intends to communicate will not match with the image invoked in the mind of the receiver. ...

Role of Intermediate Commanders

Significantly, [] there was a level of intermediate command between the corps and theater commanders. []

In Franks' case, the intermediate commander was Yeosock, Commander of the 3d Army. ... Yeosock occupied a post which required either that he advocate his subordinates' views to the superior or that he compel his subordinates to alter operations in accordance with the superior's guidance. ...

He chose to be distant from and incommunicative with his subordinates. For [] Franks, this remote style of command may have been the most difficult aspect of his new environment because it represented a major cultural change. ...

If the span of Schwarzkopf's military and political responsibilities tied him down to the war room at Riyadh, Yeosock's immobility is more difficult to justify. ... Had he been closer to the action, he could either have argued credibly that Franks' judgments were sound, or

[12] Peter S. Kindsvatter, VII Corps in the Gulf War: Ground Offensive," *Military Review*, February 1992, pp. 24, 28.

alternatively pressed Franks to execute in a manner more in line with Schwarzkopf's concept. ...

Morale Factor

Another factor that Schwarzkopf might have considered before publishing his memoirs is the impact of his criticism on the morale of the rest of the officer corps. ...

The practice of blaming failure on subordinates was [] much more unseemly in the wake of victory, regardless of how far short that victory fell of the commander's claims. Although the Gulf War ended before the decline of morale [] could become a factor, the question nonetheless remains: what will be the impact of Schwarzkopf's criticism of Franks on the officer corps as a whole?

Conclusion

[] Franks was never indicted, so his reproof takes the form of faint praise in Schwarzkopf's memoir and pettifoggery from the likes of Burton. [] We will never know whether more rash maneuver on the part of VII Corps would have resulted in an American unit falling into a carefully laid Iraqi ambush. ...

Case P-7 Republican Party Presidential Nomination for 2000 - The Michigan Primary and the Arizona Primary

[Passages referenced: 1.16, 6.1, 6.2,
6.3, 6.5, 6.6, 6.12, 6.13]

The South Carolina primary gives Governor Bush the win he desperately needs — the first win over Senator McCain on a head-to-head basis. Now, each has won a primary — the score is tied. But, for Governor Bush, the more important point is that, with this win, he has gained the momentum while arresting Senator McCain's.

Governor Bush Gains Momentum But Loses Financial Advantage

Over the weekend, pundits are now rooting for Governor Bush. One says that, now, the burden is on Senator McCain. If he cannot win Michigan and Arizona, Senator McCain's home state, it would mean four straight for Governor Bush (counting his win in Delaware) — enough to knock Senator McCain out of the race.

Governor Bush's South Carolina win, however, comes at a high price. To ensure a must-win, the Bush camp has spared no expenses, dipping into the war chest freely, and dropping its balance — and its financial-support advantage over Senator McCain — to an uncomfortable low. Indeed, in January 2000, Senator McCain raises, for the first time, more funds than Governor Bush, $6.5 million to $2.5 million.

Maneuver and Outmaneuver

Each camp now readies for the crucial third round — each tries to maneuver the other without being outmaneuvered. As Sun Wu so aptly says: "One who knows war outmaneuvers the enemy but is not outmaneuvered by him." (6.1)

Senator McCain realizes that negative advertising hurts him more than Governor Bush. "With skirmishes, we assess our preparedness and deficiencies." (6.13) He seeks truce on negative advertising with Governor Bush. Governor Bush declines. "Maneuvering the enemy so that he cannot go to where he wants is the result of our blockade." (6.2)

Senator McCain Continues His New Strategy

In South Carolina, an "open" primary state, Senator McCain made a valiant effort to woo both independents and Democrats to counter Governor Bush's establishment-endorsed candidacy — and lost. Michigan has the same scenario — open primary, Establishment candidate — but Senator McCain elects to continue with his strategy.

Why? Senator McCain sees a big difference in the two states. In South Carolina, religious right dominates; this is not so in Michigan. In Michigan, only the establishment. South Carolina's religious right is not only big and strong, it also has no opposition. Michigan's establishment may well be just as big and just as strong — but there is opposition, from two fronts.

First, the political front — from Democrats. Many Democrats openly say that they plan to vote for Senator McCain just to spite the governor — of Michigan. DOGG — Democrats Out to Get Even with the Governor — is such an institution.

Second, the religious front — from Catholics. The religious right in South Carolina has uncomplimentary comments on the Pope and on Catholicism. Senator McCain's efforts to rally Catholics in South Carolina are helpful in cutting down the margin of loss, but not decisive — the counter-rally of the religious-right faithfuls is simply too much. With the religious right absent in Michigan, a void, rallying the Catholics in Michigan is a different story — "attacking a position and producing a sure win, it is because the attack is on the undefended." (6.3)

Planning, Not Number, Wins

This repeated planning by Senator McCain is clearly useful. "We can predict a win because we have identified many options through repeated top-level planning." (1.16) "With planning, we identify strategies for winning and losing." (6.13)

Sun Wu's comment that number alone is not controlling is also reassuring to Senator McCain: "while [our rival] has an advantage in number, that is not necessarily an advantage in winning a war. Winning is the result of planning. Although the enemy is more numerous, it can be rendered non-combative." (6.12)

Senator McCain Seizes Middle Ground

Governor Bush's coy relationship with the religious right also gives Senator McCain an opening — seizing the middle ground. This forces

Governor Bush to defend from the right, a somewhat constrained position. "if we are determined to fight, the enemy will have to come out and fight, even though they are stationed on high grounds or behind deep channels; this is because we attack a position he must rescue." (6.6)

Thus, with repeated planning, with self-confidence, the battleground is reset.

Results of the Michigan Primary

Results of the Michigan primary, held on Tuesday, February 22, 2000, are shown as Exhibit 1.

Case P-7 Exhibit 1
Result of Michigan Primary
(100% of Precincts Reporting)
February 22, 2000

McCain	626,244 votes	50 percent
Bush	535,840	43
Keyes	65,028	5

Bush Plans a One-Two Knockout Punch

On the same day as the Michigan primary, Arizona also has a primary. Arizona is Senator McCain's home state; he can certainly look forward to a more hospitable reception. Still, his relationship with the governor, also a Republican, is cordial at best, not close.

Early on, the governor of Arizona has endorsed Governor Bush — when Senator McCain's candidacy was at best a "favorite son" variety, lacking evidence of viability.

Regardless, the Bush campaign, taking advantage of momentum generated by the South Carolina win, now makes big plans for the two primaries on February 22. A one-two knockout punch, no less.

One, a staggering blow to Senator McCain by winning the Michigan primary. With expert guidance from Michigan's governor and the establishment, this can be anticipated without question.

Two, a knockout punch by aggressive action in Senator McCain's home territory. "Advancing as to be beyond defense, it is because we smash the façade." (6.5) This is accomplished by investing in a $2 million ad campaign in Arizona.

Senator McCain Shows Weariness

On the eve of the Arizona primary, Senator McCain returns from campaigning in Michigan. He shows weariness. The results of primaries in Michigan and Arizona may well determine his future. The next day, he casts his vote in Phoenix — and waits for the results to come in.

Results of the Arizona Primary

Results of the Arizona primary, held on Tuesday, February 22, 2000, are shown as Exhibit 2.

Case P-7 Exhibit 2
Result of Arizona Primary
(99% of Precincts Reporting)
February 22, 2000

McCain	179,610 votes	60 percent
Bush	106,626	36
Keyes	10,626	4

Senator McCain Leads in Delegate Count

With the double win in Michigan and Arizona, Senator McCain may be excused if he is pleasantly surprised. Another surprise is that he now leads in delegate count, his 96 to Governor Bush's 67 and Mr. Keyes's 4.

Of course, with 1,034 needed to secure a nomination, it is just the beginning.

Bring on Virginia. Bring on Washington. Bring on South Dakota. These are the next battlegrounds. On February 29, only one week away.

7 军争篇

BATTLEFIELD MANEUVERS

7.1　凡用兵之法，将受命于君，合军聚
众，交和而舍，莫难于军争。
军争之难者，以迂为直，以患为利。

Among the processes of war — the commander's receiving his
commission from the head of state, the commander's gathering
men to form the army, the armies' engaging in combat — none is
more demanding than maneuvering. Maneuvering is demanding
because one must regard the circuitous as straight-forward, the
disadvantageous as advantageous.

7.2　　　　　　　　故迂其途而诱之以利，后人发，
先人至，此知迂直之计者也。

[The enemy] must be persuaded to take a circuitous route by
tempting him with advantages. Thus, even though we begin later
than the enemy, we arrive at the battlefield ahead of him.[1] This is
using straight-forwardness and circuitousness in planning.

> [1] This sentence echoes the very first sentence in the preceding
> essay: "One who arrives at the battlefield to await the enemy's
> arrival is at ready."

7.3　　　　故军争为利，军争为危。举军而争利则不及，
委军而争利则辎重捐。是故卷甲而趋，日夜不处，倍道兼
行，百里而争利，则擒三将军；劲者先，罢（疲）者后，
其法十一而至。五十里而争利，则蹶上将军，其法半至。
三十里而争利，则三分之二至。

Maneuvering is to seek advantage — and maneuvering is hazardous. Seeking advantage by moving an entire army results in falling behind in arrival; seeking advantage by moving only men results in leaving behind weaponry.

Seeking advantage 100 miles away by taking weaponry and by advancing day and night without rest, the commanders of all three battalions are likely to be captured; among men, one in ten might arrive, robust ones first, and tired ones lagging behind.

Seeking advantage 50 miles away, the commander of the front battalion is likely to be captured; among men, one in two might arrive. Seeking advantage 30 miles away, two men in three might arrive.

7.4　是故军无辎重则亡，无粮食则亡，无委积则亡。

An army without weaponry is lost. An army without provisions is lost. An army without supplies is lost.

7.5　　　　故不知诸侯之谋者，不能豫交；不知山林、险阻、沮泽之形者，不能行军；不用乡导者，不能得地利。

Thus, without knowing other heads of state's plans, we cannot seek alliance. Without knowing contours of mountains and forest, of hazards and blockades, of channels and rivers, we cannot move troops. Without local guides, we cannot take advantage of the terrain.

7.6　故兵以诈立，以利动，以分合为变者也。故其疾如风，其徐如林；侵掠如火，不动如山；难知如阴，动如雷震。掠乡分众，廓地分利，悬权而动。

Thus, war is built on stratagems, acts on advantages, adapts with formations. Moving swiftly, the thrust is like gust; moving deliberately, the pace is like forest. In attack, the energy is like fire; in defense, the sturdiness is like mountain; unknowable as the moon; unstoppable as thunder. In exploiting the countryside, split men; in expropriating land, control advantageous points. Weigh alternatives before redeploying.

7.7   先知迂直之道者胜，此军争之法也。

One who knows the straight-forward from the circuitous wins. This is battlefield maneuvering.

7.8   《军政》曰："言不相闻，故为金鼓；视不相见，故为旌旗。"故夜战多金鼓，昼战多旌旗。夫金鼓旌旗者，所以一民之耳目也；民既专一，则勇者不得独进，怯者不得独退。此用众之法也。

According to *Military Practices*:[2] "When words cannot be heard, use gongs and drums; when positions cannot be seen, display banners and flags."

Use gongs and drums for night-time battles, use banners and flags for day-time battles. Gongs, drums, banners, and flags set the pace for the men.

With men moving in unison, the brave cannot advance by himself, and the timid cannot retreat by himself. These are ways to manage men.

[2] *Military Practices* appears to be a work on military affairs that is no longer extant.

7.9   故三军可夺气，将军可夺心。
是故朝气锐，昼气惰，暮气归。故善用兵者，避其锐气，击其惰归，此治气者也。

Destroy the morale of enemy's three battalions; demolish their commanders' resolve. During the day, the morale is high; in the evening, low. Thus, to one who knows war, avoid when the enemy's morale is high and attack when his morale is low. These are ways to manage morale.

7.10

以治待乱，以静待哗，此治心者也。

Be at ready and await for the disorganized; be quiet to await for the boisterous. These are ways to manage resolve.

7.11

以近待远，以佚待劳，以饱待饥，此治力者也。

Be close by and await for the distant. Be at ease to await for the exhausted. Be fed to await for the hungry. These are ways to manage strength.

7.12

无邀正正之旗，勿击堂堂之陈，此治变者也。

Cross not well-displayed flags; attack not well-deployed formation. These are the ways to manage contingencies.

7.13

故用兵之法：高陵勿向，背丘勿逆，佯北勿从，锐卒勿攻，饵兵勿食，归师勿遏，围师必阙，穷寇勿迫，此用兵之法也。

Thus, in maneuvers, with the enemy situated on high grounds, do not advance uphill; with the enemy coming down from high grounds, do not intercede frontally; with the enemy's feigning defeat, do not pursue; with the enemy's best troops, do not attack; with the enemy's bait, do not accept; with the enemy's retreating, do not block; with the enemy's being surrounded, do leave an opening; with the enemy's fleeing, do not press. These are ways to manage maneuvers.

Case P-8 Republican Party Presidential Nomination for 2000 - Governor Bush at Bob Jones University - Idea, Personality, Support

[Passages referenced: 1.2, 1.3, 1.8n, 1.16, 6.6, 7.1, 8.2, 10.11, 10.14]

South Carolina is Governor Bush's home territory. Surrounded by old friends, with a former governor of South Carolina leading a statewide endorsement of his candidacy, Governor Bush can be at ease. He is in good hands. At the same time, coming out of the New Hampshire primary, where Governor Bush suffered his first loss — unexpected and unexpectedly large — he needs to regain his footing, his aura of inevitability.

New Options and New Plan

Governor Bush and his policy group need to do some thinking, to come up with new options, new strategy, new plan. "We can predict a win because we have identified many options through repeated top-level planning." (1.16)

Engage Senator McCain in debates is one. Force Senator McCain to leave his high ground to fight is another. "If we are determined to fight, the enemy will have to come out and fight, even though they are stationed on high grounds or behind deep channels." (6.6)

But these are measures to arrest Senator McCain's momentum. We need more.

How about a new label? "Reformer with results." Short and sweet. Positive. Marvelous alliteration. Excellent. But we still need more.

How about a talk at the Bob Jones University? someone suggests.

Bob Jones University

The Bob Jones University is famous — famous not in the academic-excellence sense, famous not in the athletic-prowess sense, but famous for its social-value sense. It accepts black students only because the alternative is a loss of funding. It disallows interracial dating; it views Catholicism as "satanic counterfeit."

Governor Bush at Bob Jones University

But, Bob Jones University is also a regular campaign stop for Republican Party dignitaries — including presidential nominees, *especially* presidential nominees. Ronald Reagan, while the

Republican Party nominee, did (President, 1981-89); George H. W. Bush, while the Republican nominee, did (President, 1989-1993); and Bob Dole did (nominee, 1996 — with Senator McCain giving the nominating speech at the Republican convention).

So, to Governor Bush, it is but a campaign stop. The fact that this is the primary season and not the general election time never crosses his mind. The important thing is that all Republican dignitaries did — including Governor Bush's father.

So, Governor Bush, for practical purposes, makes a courtesy call at Bob Jones University. Interracial dating is banned at the university, regrettable and offensive, but it is not for Governor Bush to criticize — Governor Bush is but a guest, and a guest behaves with all the civility at a guest's command.

Indeed, Governor Bush's family record is unambiguous on this front. His younger brother, Governor Jeb Bush of Florida, and the First Lady of Florida, are an interracial couple. Governor Bush's reelection, by a hugh margin, is mainly attributed to the support of women and minorities.

That Bob Jones University has anti-Catholic views only shows that university's religious intolerance, not anybody else's. Here, Governor Bush can cite from his family record and from his governorship record. His younger brother, Governor Jeb Bush of Florida, is Catholic. His reelection as governor of Texas in a landslide is a reflection of the hugh support Governor Bush enjoys in the Mexican-American community, whose religion is overwhelmingly Catholicism.

After Governor Bush's Bob Jones University Visit

So, innocently — perhaps, hastily (immediately after a difficult New Hampshire loss) as well as unthinkingly (arranged by old friends with good intentions) — Governor Bush gives a talk at Bob Jones University. It is well received. It is also well publicized.

First, there are accusations from the McCain camp. Then the religious right comes to Governor Bush's defense. One thing leads to another. Ugly becomes uglier. A little courtesy call has become cause célèbre.

Well, Sun Wu has warned the difficulties of maneuvering. "Among the processes of war ... none is more demanding than maneuvering. Maneuvering is demanding because one must regard the circuitous as straight-forward, the disadvantageous as advantageous." (7.1)

Questions By Pundits

After South Carolina, the twin wins by Senator McCain in Michigan and Arizona causes everyone to question the propriety of Governor Bush's visiting Bob Jones University. Pundits, with a lot of air time or news space to fill between these primaries (held on February 22) and the next series (in Virginia, Washington, and South Dakota, on February 29), begin to ask: Why did Governor Bush do it?

Sun Wu Answers

Why did Governor Bush do it? To Sun Wu, this is a classic example of why the study of leadership "needs to be delineated into five factors and analyzed separately." (1.2)

In the context of Governor Bush's Bob Jones University visit, the factors particularly relevant are: Direction (message), Commandership (messenger), and Support. (1.2, 1.8n)

Direction

For Governor Bush's Year 2000 campaign, the Direction — "a common goal molding the subordinates' with the superior's" (1.3) — is presumed to be one agreed upon between Governor Bush and his policy group *before* the campaign begins.

Since Governor Bush is the establishment candidate, "the policy group" may be presumed to represent, and speak for, the leadership in the establishment ("the superior" in Sun Wu's quote), while Governor Bush is their appointed or designated representative ("the subordinate") in this scenario. The message ("the Direction") is a molding of the superior's and the subordinate's goals.

The critical point, as Sun Wu sees it, is that, (1) the subordinate does *not* have to accept the appointment as the commander, and (2) he accepts it *only when* he finds the Direction acceptable, resulting in "the commander's receiving his commission from the head of state". (7.1)

After the commander accepts the commission, the leadership ("the head of state" in Sun Wu's phraseology) *must* step aside. The show is now the commander's; the leadership has *no* business changing the Direction. Sun Wu is emphatic on this point: "[In the midst of a campaign,] orders from the head of state are not accepted." (8.2)

Commandership

Once Governor Bush finds the Direction as set by the policy group ("the establishment") acceptable and accepts the appointment as the commander ("the establishment candidate"), the policy *group*'s role as a surrogate of the establishment should end. As needed, the commander may establish a policy *staff*, working strictly for the candidate, and *not* for the establishment.

Support

Sun Wu's view on support is equally clear — *before* appointment, the head of state commits to the support he is to provide; *after* appointment, the head of state's role is to honor this commitment *unconditionally* — and nothing else.

Sun Wu's Answer in Summary

So, to the question: "Why did Governor Bush appear at Bob Jones University?", Sun Wu might answer it this way: It is an example of a breakdown in the agreed upon division of responsibilities.

• Governor Bush is a moderate Republican - he accepts the role as the establishment candidate only because its Direction, as set, is moderate

• Once Governor Bush accepts as the appointment as the establishment candidate, the establishment should not dictate any changes in Direction

• By the same token, the establishment should not provide any "support" unless specifically directed by the candidate — "When adjunct commanders are enraged and disobedient, when they vent their indignation by engaging the enemy in combat without authorization, when their whereabouts are not reported to the commander, the result is collapse." (10.11)

Governor Bush Apologizes

On Sunday, February 27, 2000, Governor Bush sends a letter to Cardinal John O'Connor of New York and other Catholic officials in other states, apologizing for not "disassociating myself from the anti-Catholic sentiments and racial prejudice" when he visited Bob Jones University.

In the meantime, a major player in the religious right group whose organization made any number of anti-Catholic calls in South Carolina has left for Mexico — in one report, at the direction of the establishment. Is this a manifestation that "leads to defeat," as Sun Wu warns? (10.14) Only time will tell.

On to Virginia, Washington, and South Dakota, whose primaries and caucus are only two days away.

Case WS-1   Xiangqi - World's First War-Simulation Game
(203 BCE)

[Passages referenced: 1.2, 3.8, 4.7, 5.3,
10.12, 10.17, 11.8, 11.30]

Many board games have a dual purpose. In addition to being entertainment vehicles, they also have an educational component — encouraging players to think, to deduce real-life principles the game being played simulates.

Weiqi: The World's Oldest Simulation Game

The world's oldest board game still in play is *Weiqi* (*wei*, as a verb = circumscribe or surround; *qi* = board game), sometimes known as *go* in the west. The object of the game is to circumscribe the opponent — or, failing that, to control more territory than the opponent.

Invented by Emperor Shun (reign 2255-2206 BCE), Weiqi is played on a 19x19 square board by two players using undifferentiated "stones" except as to color (black and white). The real purpose of Weiqi was to impress upon the citizenry the importance of flood control, a natural hazard untamed in Emperor Shun's time (and, perhaps, even now).

As a simulation game, black represents nature. Playing first and placing a stone on any one of 361 possible points, the move suggests that flood may strike anywhere, anytime. White, representing the human race, defends to keep flood in check. Each then plays in turn.

The message in Weiqi as a simulation game is simple: flood control requires constant vigilance. One slip, one oversight, water gains the upper hand — controlling it requires a lot more effort. If still paid little attention, black's (water's) thrust may be so overwhelming as to be beyond arresting, and white (the human race) loses unceremoniously.

Hán Xin Sought a Diversion for His Troops

During a reciprocal surveillance between the armies of Hàn (under the command of Hán Xin, its commander-in-chief) and Chao (an ally of Chü), stationed on opposite banks of the Mian-Màn River to await the spring's arrival for a decisive battle, Hán Xin felt that his troops needed a diversion that would be both entertaining as well as educational.

Antecedents to Xiangqi

At that time, two board games were popular, Weiqi and Liubo. The value of Weiqi as a simulation game was not lost on Hán Xin, but the game took too long to play. Further, its theme, flood control, was not germane to the setting at hand — waiting for an opportune time to wage a decisive battle.

Liubo was a much simpler game to play — six playing pieces on each side, with moves chance-dictated. Hán Xin disdained the chance element in Liubo, but liked the idea of differentiated playing pieces.[1]

Xiangqi - The World's First War-Simulation Game

Since Hán Xin's aim was to impart Sun Wu's teachings through game playing, with neither Weiqi nor Liubo serviceable, in the end, Hán Xin invented one himself.[2]

Foot Soldiers First

Hán Xin's invention focused on foot soldiers. He was one once; his new game, invented in their honor, was to suggest that he cared for them. As Sun Wu said: "When a soldier is treated as a loving son, he will be willing to die with the commander." (10.17)

Hán Xin's invention has five playing pieces as foot soldiers — each symbolizing an army's five weapon-carrying battalions — spear, halberd, dagger, sword, or crossbow.[3]

---

[1] Detailed discussion of both Weiqi and Liubo as antecedents to Xiangqi may be found in this case writer's *The Genealogy of Chess* (Bethesda: Premier, 1998, 383 pages), Chapter 7, Antecedents to Chess in the Chinese Environment, pp. 117-131.

[2] Hán Xin's process in inventing Xiangqi is detailed in this case writer's The Genealogy of Chess, particularly Chapters 8-13, pp. 132-235.

[3] Hán Xin was also aware of the number Five's special significance in Chinese classics. *I (Book of Changes)* talks about Nine-Five as being the ultimate. Sun Wu refers to the number repeatedly: "it [war] needs to be delineated into five factors ..." (1.2); "On win indicators, there are five." (3.8); "Support is gauged in five steps: ... step 5, gauge winning." (4.7); "In tone there are but five; .... In color there are but five .... In taste there are but five ...." (5.3)"

Chariots and Other Playing Pieces Added

Hán Xin's invention places two chariots on each wing, and two horses (cavalry, officers on horses) to the interior side of each chariot — Chariot-Horse on the left wing and Horse-Chariot on the right wing. These again reflects the real-life army formation in Hán Xin's time.

In the middle of all these, Hán Xin added a commander, on rank 2, affording an unobstructed view and line of communication with all other playing pieces — "when officer-soldier communication is haphazard, ... the result is ruin." (10.12)

A commander's aide-de-camp is represented by an adjutant, placed immediately behind the commander.

With 11 playing pieces on each side, the world's first war-simulation game was set. The initial array is shown as Exhibit 1.

Case WS-1 Exhibit 1
Initial Array of Xiangqi as
Invented by Hán Xin (203 BCE)
With 11 Playing Pieces on Each Side

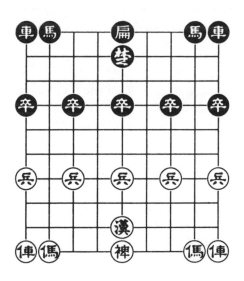

State Color

Hán Xin decided that the two sides are to bear state colors of Chü (black) and Hàn (red). This color representation of the two sides' playing pieces remains to this day.

Movement of Playing Pieces: Forward and Lateral

The main thrust of this new game is forward movement: "Readying for combat, induce our men to move ahead .... Advancing deep into enemy territory, encourage our men to move forward ...." (11.30)

With foot soldiers, Hán Xin also allowed lateral movement — but only after reaching enemy territory. "Attacking inside the enemy territory, move deep and in unison to overpower the enemy." (11.8)

With chariots and horses, recognizing that the commander, aided only by the adjutant, is no match to an onslaught of the enemy's chariots, horses, and foot soldiers converging and charging down in unison, Hán Xin allowed them to move backward to assist in defense.

Take the Enemy's Commander a Thousand Miles Away

Hán Xin was fond of Sun Wu's saying that "The conduct of war is to carefully evaluate the enemy's intentions, concentrate our forces, and take the enemy's commander a thousand miles away. This is the intelligent approach to conducting war." (11.30)

This winning-a-thousand-miles-away feature is the *telepotency* attribute[4] — when a commander has control of a file (with no other playing pieces intervening), the opposing commander cannot move into that file.

Immediate Success and Subsequent Modifications

When Hán Xin introduced his invention, known as The Game to Capture Xiang Qi, to his officers and troops in 203 BCE, it was an immediate success. One fortuitous reason was that there was a big reward for Xiang Qi's (Prince of Chü's) head. There was incentive to play the new invention — to learn secrets to capture the Prince of Chü in real life.

With the heroic death of Prince of Chü (he took his own life by the riverside instead of fleeing on a boat at his disposal), thus ending the Chü-Hàn Conflict (206-202 BCE), the game went into dormancy.

[4] This attribute is dubbed telepotency by this case writer in his *First Syllabus on Xiangqi* (Bethesda: Premier, 1996, 160 pages), at p. 17.

The game was revived, along with several successful modifications, some eight centuries later, during the Tang dynasty (618-907). After adding two cannons in year 818 to honor the invention of gunpowder, the total number of playing pieces on each side became 16. This number remains unchanged to this day.

Initial Array of Xiangqi

The initial array of these 16 playing pieces and their approximate representation in western chess figurines is shown as Exhibit 2 below.

Case WS-1 Exhibit 2
Initial Array of Xiangqi and
Their Approximate Representation
in Western Chess Figurines

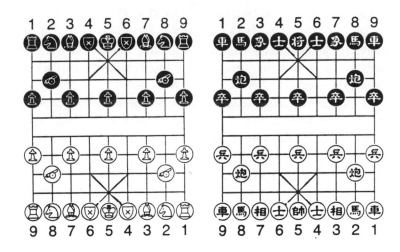

Influence on Other Board Games

In addition to successful modifications incorporated into the game, there were also many unsuccessful attempts. Though these attempts failed to gain a foothold into Xiangqi, they did influence board games in other land.[5]

The second emperor of the Tang dynasty (Tai-zong, reign 626-649) experimented with playing pieces with symbols (instead of with ideograms), with three dimensional playing pieces, and with abridged 8x8 playing board (down from 9x10). These experiments were forerunners of 8x8 western chess.[6]

Another wave of experimentation came during the North Sung dynasty (1079-1126). The 10x11 and 11x11 board sizes influenced the design of Shatranj ul Kebír (the Great Chess, 10x11+2) in Persia, and Wa Shogi/Xiangxi (11x11) in Japan.

A well-known historian at the time, Sima Guang (1019-1086), designed a heptagonal Xiangqi to simulate the Seven Powers during the Warring State Period (475-221 BCE). Another anonymous developer designed (in 1151) a triangular Xiangqi to simulate the Three Kingdom Period (220-280). Neither attempt had any lasting influence, either in China or abroad.

---

[5] The cross-border westward dissemination of Xiangqi, first via Persian merchants in Chang-an, capital of China in Hán Xin's time, to Persia, and later to India, is given in this writer's *The Genealogy of Chess*, in Chapter 16, Chess After Invention: Westward Dissemination, at pp. 275-303. Xiangqi's eastward dissemination is in the book's Chapter 17, Chess After Invention: Eastward Dissemination, at pp. 304-330.

[6] In this case writer's *The Genealogy of Chess*, at p. 258 as on back cover, there is a photograph showing a piece of silk brocade from the Tang dynasty (618-907), with an 8x8 playing board with alternate squares shaded — identical to the playing board currently in use for modern western chess.

8　九　变　篇

BATTLEFIELD CONTINGENCIES

8.1　凡用兵之法：将受命于君，合军聚众，圮地无舍，衢地合交，绝地无留，围地则谋，死地则战。

Guidelines of war are: the commander is to receive his commission from the head of state; the commander is to gather men to form the army;[1] the army is not to encamp in hazardous land, is to rendezvous with allied forces at cross-roads, is not to linger in isolated land, is to negotiate its way out of circumscribed land, and to fight its way out of deadly land.[2]

[1] In the original, though the first 14 words of this sentence are identical to those in the preceding essay, they serve different purposes. Here, they lead off as two basic guidelines in a series of many other; in the preceding essay, as two initial steps in the processes of war. Thus, this sentence is rendered as a declarative here, and as a narrative in the preceding essay.

[2] Maneuvering out of these and other situations, from an operational standpoint, is fully discussed in Essays 10 and 11. Here, a representative sample of these situations and their handling are introduced — as guidelines in troop movement en route to the front.

8.2　途有所不由，军有所不击，城有所不攻，地有所不争，君命有所不受。

[In the midst of a campaign,] Some roads are deliberately averted, some armies are purposely ignored, some citadels are voluntarily bypassed, some lands are intentionally not fought, the head of state's decrees are not accepted.[3]

[3] In this long sentence, only the last point is critically important —
and *very* difficult for a head of state to accept. Here, Sun Wu wants
King Hé Lü, who is reading it, to accept it, at least to acquiesce to
it. Thus, Sun Wu writes most discreetly; indeed, he camouflages
this point as a series of battlefield guidelines — dubbed as five
advantages — on the pretense of gaining time and conserving
resources en route to the front.

8.3
故将通于九变之利者，知用兵矣。
将不通于九变之利者，虽知地形，不能得地之利矣。
治兵不知九变之术，虽知五利，不能得人之用矣。

A commander who is versed in these nine contingencies[3] is adept
at war. A commander who cannot take advantage of these nine
contingencies is unable to take advantage of the terrain, even though
he knows it. A commander who has not mastered the art of
managing these nine contingencies is unable to fully utilize his
men, even though he is versed in the five advantages.[4]

[3] The nine contingencies are all terrain-related issues, and are fully
discussed in Essays 10. Five of the nine are mentioned in passing
in 8.1: hazardous land, cross-roads, isolated land, circumscribed
land, and deadly land.

[4] The five advantages, enumerated in 8.2 (averting some roads,
ignoring some armies, bypassing some citadels, not fighting some
lands, and not accepting the head of state's decrees), are aimed,
ostensibly, at gaining time and conserving resources en route to
the front.

8.4
是故，智者之虑，必杂于利害。杂于利，而
务可信也；杂于害，而患可解也。

An intelligent commander deliberates both the positive and negative
sides of an issue. Deliberating the positive side accomplishes the
mission; deliberating the negative side avoids disasters.

8.5

是故，屈诸侯者以害，役诸侯者以业，趋诸侯者以利。

To seek submission from other heads of state, we threaten them; to render them harmless to us, we keep them occupied; to exert control over them, we offer them advantages.

8.6

故用兵之法：无恃其不来，恃吾有以待也；无恃其不攻，恃吾有所不可攻也。

The guidelines of war are: rely not on the enemy's not coming, rely on our being ready; rely not on the enemy's not attacking, rely on our being strong to be beyond attack.

8.7

故将有五危：必死，可杀也；必生，可虏也；忿速，可侮也；廉洁，可辱也；爱民，可烦也。凡此五者，将之过也，用兵之灾也。覆军杀将，必以五危，不可不察也。

Dangerous traits in a commander, there are five: recklessness, leading to easy demise; cowardice, to easy capture; irritableness, to easy provocation; undue modesty, to easy humiliation; attachment, to easy harassment. These five dangerous traits in a commander are disastrous in the conduct of war. They are the causes of an army's destruction and its commanders' decapitation. It is not to be left uninvestigated.[5]

[5] The sentence echoes the last sentence in 1.1. The phraseology there, as here, is delicate, and suggests the need of a head of state's personal involvement in the commander-in-chief's appointment.

Case W-F   Wu-Yuè War - Sun Wu Demonstrates His Commandership (512 BCE)

[Passages referenced: 8.2, 9.21, 10.12]

Sima Qian (145-86 BCE) is one of China's great historians. Almost singlehandedly, he completed *Shi Ji* (Historical Records), a monumental work of 526,500 words in 130 chapters. The work chronicles pivotal personalities and events in Chinese history, including dynasties, emperors and kings; dynastic chronologies; political and economic systems; lords and dukes; and marquises and earls. The following is from a segment in one of the chapters. This casewriter-cum-translator's comments are added as footnotes.

Sun Tsu, Wu, was a native of the state of Chi. He presented his work on the art of war as a prelude to an audience with Hé Lü, King of Wu.

Hé Lü said: "I have read through your thirteen essays. Will you give me a brief demonstration about commanding troops?" Answered: "Yes, your excellency."

Hé Lü said: "May women be used for this demonstration?" Answered: "Yes, your excellency."

Thus, a demonstration using women was set. From the King's court, 180 beauties were selected.

Sun Tzu divided them into two teams, each captained by one of the king's favorite ladies of the court. He instructed them on how to hold halberds.

He asked: "Do you know the location of your heart, your left and right hands, your back?" The women said: "We know."

He said: "When I say 'front,' turn your head to look at your heart; 'left,' to look at your left hand; 'right,' to look at your right hand; 'back,' to look back." The women said: "We understand."

Along with these directives, an executioner's stage was set up. After that, Sun Tzu reiterated his orders three times, and explained them five times. He proceeded to beat the drum and then ordered: "Right." The women burst into laughter.

Sun Tzu said: "When directives are not clear, when orders are not explicit, the commander is at fault." So saying, he reiterated his orders three more times and explained them five more times. He then beat the drum and ordered: "Left." Again, the women laughed.[1]

Sun Tzu said: "When directives are not clear, when orders are not explicit, the commander is at fault. But, when clear directives are not followed, the officers are at fault." He wanted to behead the two captains.[2]

The King, who was sitting at the balcony observing the proceedings, was horrified to see that his two favorite ladies of the court were set to be executed. He sent an aide down with a message: "I already knew the Commander's capability in commanding soldiers. Without these two ladies by my side, food becomes tasteless. It is my wish that they not be beheaded."

Sun Tzu said: "Your subject has been appointed as the Commander. In the midst of a campaign, your excellency's decree must respectfully be declined."[3] So saying, he proceeded to behead the two captains and made their next-in-line as captains.

[1] At this juncture, Sun Wu had reasons to be concerned. He realized that he was being tested for suitability as Wu's commander-in-chief. His own writing warned him: "When the commander is indecisive and weak, when discipline is inconsistent and directives unclear, ... the result is ruin." (10.12) He realized that he had to take drastic action.

[2] While drastic action was called for, one may argue whether Sun Wu was overdoing this — Did the crime justify this harsh and irreversible punishment?

Sima Qian's narrative, necessarily terse, did not mention whether, at the time of setting up the executioner's stage, Sun Wu explained its purpose and intended use. On this point, one is reminded of another passage from Sun Wu's own work: "Penalizing men who have not been indoctrinated creates dissention; men who dissent are difficult to deploy. Men who have been indoctrinated but who will not respond to discipline are not to be deployed." (9.21)

[3] This is precisely what Sun Wu had written: "[In the midst of a campaign,] ... the head of state's decrees are not accepted" (8.2). As stated in the footnote accompanying the text, this passage is critically important; "Sun Wu wants King Hé Lü, who is reading it, to accept it, at least to acquiesce to it."

Sun Tzu began to beat the drum again. The women followed the directives with perfection: turning left, turning right, looking front, looking back, kneeling, rising — and uttering not a sound.

Sun Tzu then sent a messenger to the King: "The troops are in good order. Your excellency is invited to come down and inspect them. They are at your excellency's service, willing to confront water or fire when so directed."

The King of Wu said: "The Commander may retire to his quarters to rest. I have no desire to come down to inspect." Sun Tzu said: "Your excellency appreciates words, but is unaccustomed to seeing words put into action."[4]

Having observed that Sun Tzu can command troops, Hé Lü appointed him as the commander. He played a key role — defeating the strong Chü and invading Ying to the west; overpowering Chi and Jin to the north; and making Wu a name among the Powers.

Continuation of footnote 3 on preceding page

Thinking frivolously, it appears as if Sun Wu wanted to create this scene to dramatize this very concept, to test King Hé Lü's resolve, and, indeed, to assess whether he, Sun Wu, wanted to be appointed Wu's commander-in-chief if this concept did not prevail.

[4] Here, Sun Wu made a statement in lieu of a question suggested in the footnote accompanying passage 1.8: "Is your excellency up to it? Is the nitty-gritty of war uncomfortable to stomach?"

Case P-9   Republican Party Presidential Nomination for 2000 - The Virginia Primary

[Passages referenced: 6.6, 8.1, 8.2, 8.4, 8.7]

On February 29, 2000, Virginia and Washington hold their primaries while South Dakota has its caucus. Initially, Senator McCain plans not to enter the Virginia primary — it is simply too expensive. Television ad rates for the metropolitan Washington market (covering the District of Columbia, northern Virginia counties, and several Maryland counties) are high, 'way beyond Senator McCain's low-budget operation.

Senator McCain Decides to Contest

But, buoyed by the twin wins in Michigan and Arizona and encouraged by campaign contributions flowing in, Senator McCain decides, almost last minute, to contest it. This results in Senator McCain's campaigning in Virginia for a day and half, and buying a half-million-dollars' worth of television advertising.

For about two weeks before the Virginia primary, Governor Bush has been doing some television adverting in that state. With Senator McCain's decision to enter Virginia, Governor Bush redoubles his efforts, spending $1 million on television advertising and campaigning three days in the state.

A Win-Win Situation for Senator McCain

This last-minute decision by Senator McCain, while giving the appearance of being hasty, is, in reality, a win-win decision. To start with, it give Senator McCain a psychological advantage — Senator McCain sets the tone, and Governor Bush follows suit. Sun Wu says: "if we are determined to fight, the enemy will have to come out and fight, even though they are stationed on high grounds or behind deep channels; this is because we attack a position he must rescue." (6.6)

Senator McCain's Realistic Assessment

If Senator McCain can bring about another win, so much the better. But, realistically, with Virginia's profile similar to South Carolina's — conservative, with Governor Bush being endorsed by the establishment from the governor on down — scoring another upset win is unlikely, particularly with such short notice.

The aim is to lose by a respectable margin — any loss below the 11 percent incurred in South Carolina would be respectable — and a "moral victory." The tactics is to use Virginia to openly call attention to the difference between Governor Bush's candidacy (establishment endorsed) and Senator McCain's (voter supported).

Pre-Primary Poll

A couple of months ago, the Mason-Dixon poll shows Governor Bush leading the pack by 30 points. The latest poll, conducted after the Michigan and Arizona primaries, gives Governor Bush only a 11 point lead, 46 percent to 35 percent. By regions within the state, Senator McCain actually leads by 7 points in northern Virginia (part of metropolitan DC), and is even with Governor Bush on the Hampton Road (coastal counties, Norfolk naval base, veterans).

Senator McCain's Open Defiance

Looking ahead beyond Virginia to the Super Tuesday (see Case P-10), Senator McCain, on Sunday, February 27, decides to attack the establishment openly and boldly. The "sound bites" thus produced are sure to attract media attention.

One sound bite is to label the leadership of the governor of Virginia and the senior senator from Virginia (the latter a colleague of Senator McCain) as "machine." Another is to name the two leading religious-right leaders and label Governor Bush as their candidate.

Senator McCain as Idea-Shaper and Messenger

Sure enough. The evening news on the eve of the primary shows Senator McCain saying words such as "We are the party of Ronald Reagan, not Pat Robertson. We are the party of Theodore Roosevelt, not the party of special interests. We are the party of Abraham Lincoln, not Bob Jones." He now aims not only at winning the nomination, but also aims at changing the constituencies of the Republican Party.

What Senator McCain has done demonstrates another type of hazard in idea-messenger interaction. The first type of hazard, where idea-shaper and message-deliver are different, such as the Bush camp, is the constant *interference* of the idea-shaper. Sun Wu has cautioned against that: "[In the midst of a campaign] orders from the head of state are not accepted." (8.2)

The second type, manifested here, is where idea-shaper and message-deliver are one and the same — the hazard is the constant *revision* of the idea. Sun Wu also sees the problems — he is thus adamantly against a head-of-state's appointing himself to be the field commander.

As a start, an idea-shaper-cum-message-deliver probably does not have time to deliberate: "An intelligent commander deliberates both the positive and negative sides of an issue. Deliberating the positive side accomplishes the mission; deliberating the negative side avoids disasters." (8.4)

Sun Wu also offers the following caution: "Dangerous traits in a commander, there are five: recklessness, leading to easy demise; irritableness, to easy provocation; attachment, to easy harassment." (8.7)

Governor Bush Apologizes

In the meantime, on Sunday, February 27, Governor Bush sends a letter to Cardinal John O'Connor of New York and other Catholic officials in other states, apologizing for not "disassociating myself from the anti-Catholic sentiments and racial prejudice" when he visited Bob Jones University. Further, a major player in the religious right group whose organization made a large number of anti-Catholic calls in South Carolina is now in Mexico "on business."

These moves, when viewed as idea-messenger interaction, signal that Governor Bush bids to reestablish the agreed-upon message he agrees to deliver, and to reject uncalled-for interferences from idea-shapers. Both are bids to reclaim lost ground. "The army is not to linger in isolated land, is to negotiate a way out of circumscribed land." (8.1)

Lines Are Drawn

With Governor Bush no longer lingering on "isolated land" or "circumscribed land", with Senator McCain poised with fighting words, the lines are redrawn. On primary day, one of the two dailies serving metropolitan Washington headlines with "McCain Attacks Two Leaders of Christian Right." Another, in a four-column headline, says "McCain rides into lion's den."

Results of the Virginia Primary

The results of the Virginia primary, held on Tuesday, February 29, 2000, are shown as Exhibit 1.

Case P-9 Exhibit 1
Result of Virginia Primary
(100% of precincts reporting)
February 29, 2000

	Votes	*Percent*
Bush	350,185	53
McCain	237,888	44
Keyes	20,294	4

Pre-Primary Polls and Exit Polls

These results show the predictive power of pre-primary polls. When these pools and exit polls are taken together, all predictions seem to come true. Senator McCain indeed wins in northern Virginia, Governor Bush indeed wins statewide, and the two are indeed tied on the Hampton Road.

The 9-point margin of win in the actual vote differs from the predicted margin of win of 11 points by only two, certainly within the sampling error of ± 3 points. The single-digit margin of win also validates pre-primary polls' warning of Senator McCain's "gaining."

The fact that voters are required to sign a card stating that they do not plan to "participate in the nominating process of any other party" may have dampened independents and Democrats from participating in this Republican primary.

Exit polls also show that Republicans vote for Governor Bush over Senator McCain by a margin of 8:1, while Senator McCain receives a slight majority of votes cast by independents.

What do these mean? Where is the Republican Party headed? Only time will tell. The Super Tuesday may yet yield more clues.

Governor Bush Makes a Clean Sweep of Seven Contests

With the win in Virginia, Governor Bush picks up its entire 56-delegate block. He also wins South Dakota's 19 delegates (by vote count, 6,865 to 1,717 for McCain to 481 for Keyes; in percentages, 76, 19, and 5, respectively) and Washington's 12 delegates (in vote count, 214,611 to 141,151 to 8,955; in percentages, 58 to 38 to 2), both contested that day.

In the weekend preceding the February 29 contests, Governor Bush wins four other contests — American Samoa caucus, 4; Guam caucus, 4; Virgin Islands, caucus 4; and Puerto Rico primary, 14.

With these wins, Governor Bush makes a clean sweep of seven contests. His delegate count is now 170, a comfortable lead over Senator McCain's 105 and Mr. Keyes's 5.

On to Super Tuesday

The next battles are on Tuesday, March 7, with 13 states holding contests and 625 delegates at stake:

Case P-9 Exhibit 2
States in Super Tuesday Primary and Caucuses
(In descending order of number of delegate)
March 7, 2000
(Open = all voters ; closed = Republicans only
semi-open = Republicans + independents)

California	162 delegates	Closed
New York	101	Closed
Ohio	69	Open
Georgia	54	Open
Massachusetts	37	Semi-open
Washington	37	Open
Missouri	35	Open
Minnesota	34	Open
Maryland	31	Semi-open
Connecticut	25	Closed
Maine	14	Semi-open
Rhode Island	14	Semi-open
Vermont	12	Semi-open

9 行　军　篇

BATTLEFIELD LOGISTICS

9.1 凡处军相敌；绝山依谷，视生处高，战隆勿登，此处山之军也。

Encamping en route, take into account the enemy's position. Passing through mountains, encamp close to valleys. Encamp on high grounds, facing the sun. Refrain from moving uphill to engage in fight. These are battlefield measures involving high grounds.

9.2 绝水必远水；客绝水而来，勿迎之于水内，令半济而击之，利；欲战者，无附于水而迎客；视生处高，无迎水流，此处水上之军也。

Passing through rivers, encamp away from them. When the enemy comes by the river, refrain from meeting him in the midst of river crossing, but do so after half of his men have crossed; this is advantageous. In combat, refrain from engaging the enemy near rivers. Encamp on high grounds, facing the sun. Refrain from stationing downstream. These are battlefield measures involving rivers.

9.3 绝斥泽，惟亟去无留。若交军于斥泽之中，必依水草而背众树，此处斥泽之军也。

Passing through salt marshes, move quickly and refrain from stopping. If fighting the enemy in the midst of salt marshes, be close to water and vegetation, with back to trees. These are battlefield measures involving salt marshes.

9.4　平陆处易，而右背高，前死后生，此处平陆之军也。

Passing through plateaux, encamp, taking into account the ease of movement. Have the right and the rear backing high grounds; prepare to fight on low grounds in front of us and high grounds behind us. These are battlefield measures involving plateaux.

9.5　　凡此四军之利，黄帝之所以胜四帝也。

Emperor Huang, by taking advantage of these four groups of battlefield measures, won over the other four emperors.[1]

> [1] According to legends, Xuan Yuan was the leader of a tribe situated in an area known as You-Xiong, on the banks of Huang River (Huang = Yellow). He defeated four other tribe leaders — to the east, south, west, and north of him — to become Emperor Huang (Yellow Emperor, reign *c*2697-2597 BCE), the beginning of the Han race in China.

9.6　　　凡军好高而恶下，贵阳而贱阴，养生而处实。军无百疾，是谓必胜。

Any army would prefer ground high to low, areas sunny to shady, surroundings lively and bounteous. A precondition of a sure win is an army free of myriad diseases.

9.7　丘陵堤防，必处其阳而右背之。此兵之利，地之助也。

Encamping, face the sun, with the hillside, mound, dikes or embankments at the right and back. In war, taking advantage of the terrain is advantageous.

9.8　　上雨，水沫至，止涉，待其定也。

In a torrential rain, with water splashing at the river, stop crossing and await for the rain to stop.

9.9 绝天涧、天井、天牢、天罗、天陷、天隙，必亟去之，勿近也。吾远之，敌近之；吾迎之，敌背之。

Passing through stiff cliffs, carnivorous caverns, isolated crests, ill-defined moraines, deceptive quagmires, gripping crevices — move quickly, do not go near. Let us move away; let the enemy move in. Let us face them; let the enemy have them at his back.

9.10 军旁有险阻、潢井、葭苇、山林、翳荟者，必谨覆索之，此伏奸之所也。

Passing through spurs, meltwaters, marshes, forests, shallow ponds with undergrowths — search carefully and repeatedly. These are likely areas where enemy's spies are hiding.

9.11 敌静而近者，恃其险也；远而挑战者，欲人之进也。

When the enemy is close by but keeps quiet, he is occupying a strategic position. When the enemy is distant but provocative, he is luring us to advance. When the enemy encamps in the plains, he is tempting us.

9.12 其所居易者，利也。众树动者，来也；众草多障者，疑也。鸟起者，伏也；兽骇者，覆也。

When trees appear moving, the enemy is coming. When marshes seem to grow obstacles, the enemy is setting traps. When birds fly out in flocks, the enemy is in ambush. When beasts rush out startled, the enemy is in hiding.

9.13 尘高而锐者，车来也；卑而广者，徒来也；散而条达者，薪来也；少而往来者，营军也。

When dust soars high and sharp, chariots are coming; dust spreads low and far, foot soldiers are coming; dust scatters in a limited area, the enemy has gathered firewood; dust is spotty and recurring, the enemy has encamped.

9.14 辞卑而益备者，进也；辞强而进驱者，退也。

When the enemy talks humbly but works hard secretly, he is ready to attack. When the enemy talks harshly and moves about conspicuously, he is ready to retreat.

9.15 轻车先出，居其侧者，陈也；无约而请和者，谋也；奔走而陈兵者，期也；半进半退者，诱也。杖而立者，饥也；汲役先饮者，渴也；见利不进者，劳也。

When the enemy moves his chariots out to the two wings, he is redeploying. When the enemy offers truce unilaterally, he is scheming. When the enemy busies himself with troop movement, he is getting ready. When the enemy moves back and forth, he is luring us. When the enemy leans against his halberd, he is underfed. When the enemy sips before carrying water to the camp, he is thirsty. When the enemy is disinclined to advance to take an advantage, he is exhausted.

9.16 鸟集者，虚也；夜呼者，恐也；军扰者，将不重也；旌旗动者，乱也；吏怒者，倦也。

When birds gather in the enemy's camp, it is because the camp is uninhabited. When the enemy's men scream in the night, it is because they are scared. When the enemy's men create disturbances, it is because the commander has little discipline. When the enemy's flags move about unaccountably, it is because the battalions are in chaos. When the enemy's officers are easily angered, it is because they are weary of war.

9.17 粟马肉食，军无悬甀，不返其舍者，穷寇也。

Having no provisions and resorting to slaughtering horses as food, having no implements to prepare it, having no inclination to return to the camp, the enemy shows signs of desperation.

9.18 谆谆翕翕，徐言入入者，失众也；数赏者，窘也；数罚者，困也；先暴而后畏其众者，不精之至也。

Speaking with neither resoluteness nor authority, the enemy shows signs of insecurity. Granting repeated decorations, the enemy shows signs of purposelessness. Meting out repeated punishments, the enemy shows signs of insubordination. Disciplining his men and then being in awe of them, the enemy shows signs of incompetence.

9.19 来委谢者，欲休息也。兵怒而相迎，久而不合，又不相去，必谨察之。

Sending an envoy bearing favors, the enemy is seeking truce. After advancing in anger, but refusing to engage in combat and declining to retreat, the enemy is to be carefully watched.

9.20 兵非多益，惟无武进，足以并力、料敌、取人而已。夫惟无虑而易敌者，必擒于人。

In war, numerical superiority is not a factor. All that is needed to win is to refrain from advancing haphazardly, to consolidate resources, and to see through the enemy's plans. One who does not plan but is disdainful of his enemy is bound to be captured.

9.21 卒未亲附而罚之，则不服，不服则难用也；卒已亲附而罚不行，则不可用也。故合之以文，齐之以武，是谓必取。

Penalizing men who have not been indoctrinated creates dissention; men who dissent are difficult to deploy. Men who have been indoctrinated but who will not respond to discipline are not to be deployed. Treat men with civility; maintain accord with discipline — these are winning measures.

9.22 令素行以教其民，则民服；令素不行以教其民，则民不服。令素行者，与众相得也。

When orders are consistently applied in the training of men, they obey. When orders are not consistently applied in the training of men, they will not obey. Men obey because the officers' relationship with them is harmonious.

Case W-G   Alexander the Great at Hydaspes (326BCE)

[Passages referenced: 9.8, 9.11, 9.13, 9.14, 9.15, 9.20]

Alexander III (born 356 BCE), son of King Philip of Macedonia, was invariably referred to by historians as Alexander the Great, on account of his military accomplishments. He left his homeland early, in 334 BCE, moving eastward and gaining fame along the way, winning one battle after another.

After subduing Darius III of Persia, a most worthy opponent, in 331 BCE, Alexander marched further eastward into the Indus basin. With little resistance, he entered Taxila in 327 BCE, and considered himself an Asian monarch.

Looking still further east beyond the Jhelum River for other easy conquests, Alexander saw the plains of Punjab and the Ganges.

Punjab and Rajah Porus

Punjab was Rajah Porus's domain. Alexander sent an envoy expressing his desire to meet Porus, expecting Porus to show the same reverence as Ambhi, King of Taxila, did.

Porus, not on good terms with Ambhi, was disdainful of Ambhi's submission to Alexander. He was even more disdainful of Alexander, either as a person or as a warrior. He sent back a welcoming message, expressing his desire to meet Alexander — on the battlefield.

Alexander treated this as a declaration of war. With intelligence noting that Porus had sent word to Abhisaras, Rajah of Jammu, to come to his aid, Alexander decided to march toward the Jhelum River[1] without delay, hoping to reach Jhelum before Abhisaras did.[2]

Porus's Army at Hydaspes

Porus began marshalling his army at Hydaspes, on the east bank of the Jhelum River. Porus's strength was that shown in Exhibit 1:

[1] The Kingdom of Porus was located between the Jhelum River and Chenab; the name of its capital city was lost to history.

[2] Abhisaras's role in this episode was not clear, as he, unbeknown to Porus, had submitted himself to Alexander. In any event, though Jammu and Punjab were contiguous, Abhisaras did not come to Porus's aid until near the end.

Case W-G Exhibit 1
Strength of Porus's Army at Hydaspes

	Arrian[3]	Diodorus[4]	Wood[5]
Cavalry	4,000	3,000	2,000
Infantry	30,000	50,000	30,000
Chariots	300	1,000	unmentioned
Elephants	200	130	300

Alexander's Strength

The army Alexander amassed for this battle consisted of that shown in Exhibit 2:

Case W-G Exhibit 2
Strength of Alexander's Army at Hydaspes

	Warry[6]	Composite[7]
Infantry (Total)	*31,000-34,000*	*50,000+*
Phalanx	14,000	
Hypaspists	3,000	
Greek mercenaries	8,000-10,000	
Light troops	6,000- 7,000	
Cavalry (Total)	*7,300 10,000+*	
Companions	2,100	
Bactria	500	
Sogdiana	500	
Scythis	500	
Dahae horse archers	1,000	
Mercenaries	1,000	
Arachosia	500	
Parapahnisadae	500	
Indian allies	700	

[3] Arrian, *The Anabasis of Alexander*, recorded in 2nd century (New York: Penguin).

[4] Diodorus Siculus, *The Histories*, recorded in the 1st century BCE. Since chariots may be converted to cavalry as needed (each chariot was drawn by four horses), Diodorus's figures gave Porus's army more strength in every respect except elephants.

[5] Michael Wood, *In the Footsteps of Alexander the Great* (Berkeley: University of California Press, 1997), p. 185.

[6] John Warry, *Warfare in the Classical World* (Norman: University of Oklahoma Press, 1995), p. 84.

From Exhibits 1 and 2, it appears that the two armies were about equal in strength — Alexander was probably stronger in manpower; Porus had an edge with elephants.

Alexander Readying for the Jhelum River

To reach Punjab from the west, Alexander and his army must first cross the Jhelum River. However, there were no bridges.

Time did not permit building a flotilla. Alexander thus ordered that boats used in crossing the Indus be reused. This entailed cutting them into sections for ease in transporting to Hydaspes, with plans for reassembly at Hydaspes.

Thus prepared, Alexander and his troops marched eastward, reaching the west bank of the Jhelum River after two weeks. There, Alexander encamped to assess the situation.

Elephants in Waiting

The water level in the Jhelum River was rising due to snowmelt in the Himalayas — weather was getting warmer, and time was opportune. But the river was in the way. And on the other side of the river stood Porus and his army and cavalry — and elephants.[8]

Footnote 7 refers to Exhibit 2 on page 127

[7] To exaggerate Alexander's accomplishments, there is a tendency for historians, invariably pro-Alexander, to (1) underestimate Alexander's troop strength, (2) overestimate his opponent's, or (3) both.

Here, for example, a 5,000-strong contingent of Ambhi's allies, mentioned by Arrian, is not in Warry's list. David Eggenberger, in his *An Encyclopedia of Battles* (New York: Dover, 1967, 1985) at pp. 196-197, states Alexander's "leaving the bulk of his army (about 40,000) on the west bank of the river," and of sending "a detachment of 14,000 picked calvary and infantry" to cross river. George Bruce, in his *Dictionary of Battles* (London: Hart-Davis, 1971), at p. 117, gives a figure of "65,000 Macedonians and 70,000 Asians."

This case writer, taking into account various narratives cited, proposes a composite figure shown in Column 2 of Exhibit 2.

[8] Quintus Curtius Rufus, in his *The History of Alexander the Great* (circa 2nd century), described the scene as follows: "The Macedonians were intimidated not only by the appearance of the enemy, but by the magnitude of the river to be crossed, which

Alexander Biding Time

Alexander realized that direct crossing would be futile — the elephants were too intimidating. His horses — terrified by the elephants' sheer size and thunderous roar — would refuse to land or be mounted. Perforce, Alexander sought an alternate route — at the same time, he wanted to lull Porus into complacency.

Every night, Alexander moved a great part of his mounted troops up or down the river, making war cries and other noises as if they were ready for crossing. Porus would then bring up or down his elephants to parallel Alexander's movements on the east side of the river bank.

Beyond war cries and other noises, nothing happened. This went on for six weeks. In time, Porus felt that that was all Alexander was capable of doing — and relaxed. He no longer expected Alexander to make a sudden attempt at crossing under the cover of darkness. He stationed his troops where they were, and set up lookout posts at various points along the river.

What Alexander did was pure Sun Wu: "When the enemy moves back and forth, he is luring us." (9.15)

Alexander Moving His Camp

During this six-week period, Alexander was scouting for a ford sufficiently concealed and comfortably away from the enemy position. He succeeded. He found a ford — some 18 miles upstream from his camp — where, behind a concealed wooded bluff, the river took a sharp bend.

He then quietly moved his boats upstream — but not his camp. Then, Alexander announced his preparation for a crossing — openly — as if it were another false move.

spreading out to a width of no less than four stadia in a deep channel which nowhere opened a passage by fords, presented the aspect of a vast sea. ... The bank presented a still more formidable aspect, for, as far as the eye could see, it was covered with cavalry and infantry, in the midst of which, like so many massive structures, stood the huge elephants, which, being of set purpose provoked by their drivers, distressed the ear with their frightful roars." Quoted in Arjan Dass Malik, *Alexander the Great: A Military Study* (New Dehli: Light & Life, 1976), p. 103.

It was too bad that Rajah Porus was unaware of Sun Wu's sayings: "When the enemy is close by but keeps quiet, he is occupying a strategic position." (9.11) and "When the enemy talks humbly but works hard secretly, he is ready to attack." (9.14)

Alexander Setting Up His Plan

On the date of crossing (around May 21), Alexander left behind
- Craterus, one of Alexander's most trusted commanders
- 1,000 horse archers
- two battalions of the phalanx and
- soldiers considered dispensable — such as the 5,000 from Taxila and those from the countries surrounding India

He also instructed Craterus to cross the river should Porus move northward to face Alexander or flee the field. Else, he should stay put in the camp.

Alexander then took an advance force of 10,000 infantry and 5,000 cavalry for immediate crossing. He also left behind a rear force of 5,000 infantry and 500 cavalry, to be posted along the west bank between the Macedonian camp and the intended point of crossing, readying to cross when Alexander and the advance force began to engage in combat.

Weather

On the night of crossing, a violent storm was followed by heavy rain. Ostensibly, it hindered the plan; in actuality, it helped:
- the storm drowned all noises from arms rattling and order shouting
- the rain absorbed dust from troop movement

The first point does not contradict Sun Wu's advice ("In a torrential rain, with water splashing at the river, stop crossing and wait for the rain to stop." (9.8)), since it refers to troop movement *en route*.

The second point is a worthy extension of Sun Wu's work : "When dust soars high and sharp, chariots are coming; dust spreads low and far, foot soldiers are coming" (9.13) by adding the value of foul weather in suppressing these tell-tale signs.

Crossing

As it turned out, the land reached after crossing was an island, requiring Alexander and his troops to make another crossing (Exhibit 3). By that time, it was daybreak. One of Porus's sentries spotted the crossing and rushed to inform Porus.

Case W-G Exhibit 3
The Battle of Hydaspes[9]

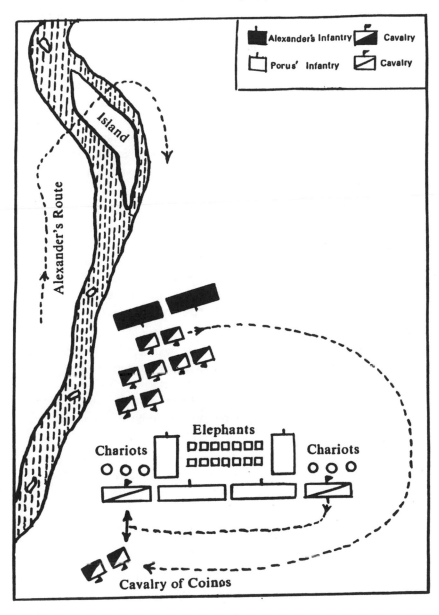

[9] Malik, *Alexander the Great: A Military Study*, p. 105.

Porus in Quandary

At first, Porus refused to believe that Alexander had forded the river; he thought it was Abhisaras coming to his aid. When convinced that it was indeed Alexander and his troops, Porus had no idea about the enemy's plan and strength.

Was it another ruse to lure Porus north? Was it merely a "ruse force" with few men? By moving north, would Alexander's main force cross from where the camp was located and strike from the rear?

Since the sentry who saw the crossing saw only a few hundred Macedonians before he rushed to inform Porus, Porus concluded that it was indeed a ruse force. He decided to stay put but send one of his sons, with 120 chariots and 2,000 cavalry, to move north to take care this ruse force.

Alexander Took Action

At first, Alexander thought the cavalry rushing toward him was Porus's advance guard. He thus stayed aside to await Porus's arrival. When informed that Porus was not in the midst, Alexander took action and routed Porus's advance force. The chariots were immobile — stuck in the mud on account of heavy rain; the weather favored Alexander on still another unanticipated front. Porus's son was killed.

Porus Made His Plans

Should Porus move north now? He was hesitant, seeing that Craterus on the other side of the river was poised to cross over. To protect his rear, Porus decided to move north with 20,000 infantry, 2,000 cavalry, most of the chariots and elephants — leaving behind 10,000 infantry to take care of Craterus should he plan to cross.

Alexander Attacking Left

With elephants conspicuously stationed in the middle of Porus's deployment (see Exhibit 3), Alexander felt that it made no sense to attack head on — again, the elephants would be too much for the horses.

At that very moment, Alexander probably did not enjoy a numerical advantage; he certainly exercised good judgment, in Sun Wu's terms: "In war, numerical superiority is not a factor. All that is needed to win is to refrain from advancing haphazardly, to consolidate resources, and to see through the enemy's plans." (9.20)

Conversely, Porus's deployment was too easy for Alexander to see through, allowing Alexander to attack Porus's right flank.

This he succeeded; Porus's troops were surrounded. A fierce battle ensued. Elephants became uncontrollable — they began to trample down Alexander's men and Porus's own men indiscriminately. Macedonians, with their superior weaponry, completely overwhelmed their Indian counterparts. Porus's troops fled.

In the meantime, Craterus and his infantry had crossed. These fresh troops easily gave the fleeing Porus's troops their last blow. It was a massacre.

Porus in Desperation

Porus, in desperation, gathered 40 elephants and fought with all his might. A powerful man, he flung javelins high and long, hitting Alexander's troops from above, beyond the protection of shields. On the other hand, Porus was also wounded.

Alexander, anxious to save the life of a great and gallant soldier, sent an intermediary, Ambhi, to the battlefield to seek Porus's surrender. By then, Ambhi was known as Taxiles, a name conferred by Alexander.

Porus Surrendered

Being enemies of long standing, Porus killed Taxiles on the battlefield; he himself was almost killed as well. It was through a second intermediary that Porus, exhausted and thirsty, dismounted from the elephant and acquiesced to a surrender.

Alexander asked Porus on how Porus should be treated. "Like a king," Porus responded. Following the Macedonian tradition, Alexander received Porus as an esteemed friend and restored him to his kingdom.

With that, the battle of Hydaspes ended — with 12,000 of Porus's men killed (including one of his sons) and 9,000 taken as prisoners. About 1,000 of Macedonians also died.

The battle of Hydaspes also scored a first and a last for the history books. It was the first battle in Indian history that was well documented; it was also the last one for Alexander anywhere.

Case WS-2   Western Chess - "Game of the [20th] Century" (1956)

[Passages referenced: 1.12, 1.13 1.14, 1.16, 4.1, 4.5, 6.4, 6.7]

The world's first war-simulation board game is Xiangqi, invented by Hán Xin in 203 BCE to entertain his officers and troops while educating them on the importance of leadership and planning in war.

Xiangqi was soon disseminated westward, by Persian merchants resident in Chang-an, the political, economic, and cultural capital of the long and prosperous Hàn dynasty (206 BCE - 220 CE).[1]

Xiangqi Disseminated to Persia, India, and the West

Royalties in Persia were indeed taken by this new invention. They also began to domesticate it and to experiment with it — an abridged Xiangqi, played on an 8x8 board, became Chatrang, later renamed as Shatranj ul Saghír (the Abridged Chess); the 11x11 Xiangqi was modified into Shatranj ul Kebír (10x11+2, the Great Chess). The abridged game became known as Chaturanga or Chatúráji when it was exported to India,[2] as Medieval Game when it reached Europe. With liberalization of moves, it became the modern western chess.

"The Game of the [20th] Century"

Illustrated below is a game played at the 1956 U. S. Open Championship, between 1953 U.S. champion Donald Byrne (1930-1976), playing White, and future world western chess champion Bobby Fischer (born 1943), a thirteen-year-old at the time, playing Black. The game is dubbed "The Game of the Century."

Donald Byrne vs. Bobby Fischer
U.S. Open Championship
1956

1	Nf3	Nf6
2	c4	g6

[1] This dissemination process is discussed in more detail in this case writer's book, *The Genealogy of Chess* (Premier: 1998, 383 pages), Chapter 14, Chess After Invention: Westward Dissemination, pp. 275-303.

[2] The long developmental process in Persia, along with diagrams and comparisons, is covered in *The Genealogy of Chess*, at pp. 282-288 and 294-296; its export to India, at pp. 288-293; the Chaturanga/Chatúráji controversy, at pp. 29-36.

3	Nc3	Bg7
4	d4	0-0
5	Bf4	d5
6	Qb3	dxc4
7	Qxc4	

By Move 5, the game is categorized as Gruenfeld Defense by transposition. After the exchange of pawns, the game is identified as the Russian Variation.

7		c6
8	e4	Nbd7
9	Rd1	Nb6
10	Qc5	Bg4
11	Bg5	Na4
12	Qa3	Nxc3
13	bxc3	Nxe4
14	Bxe7	Qb6
15	Bc4	Nxc3
16	Bc5	Rfe8+
17	Kf1	

The position at this point is shown as Exhibit 1 below.

Case WS-2 Exhibit 1

Donald Byrne vs. Bobby Fischer
U.S. Open Championship - 1956
Position after 17 Kf1

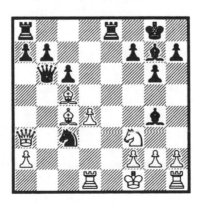

At this point, Black, instead of retrieving the Queen to safety, plays **17 ... Be6**. This moves is rated !!, the basis for labeling the game as the "Game of the [20th] Century."

17		Be6!!
18	Bxb6	Bxc4+
19	Kg1	Ne2+
20	Kf1	Nx4d+
21	Kg1	Ne2+
22	Kf1	Nc3+
23	Kg1	axb6
24	Qb6	Ra4!
25	Qxb6	Nxd1
26	h3	Rxa2
27	Kh2	Nxf2
28	Re1	Rxe1
29	Qd8+	Bf8
30	Nxe1	Bd5
31	Nf3	Be4
32	Qb8	b5
33	h4	h5
34	Ne5	Kg7
35	Kg1	Bc5+
36	Kf1	Ng3+
37	Kc1	Bb4+
38	Kd1	Bb3+
39	Kc1	Ne2+
40	Kb1	Nc3+
41	Kc1	Rc2 mate

Fischer and Sun Wu

In all probability, Bobby Fischer has never heard of Sun Wu. But, Fischer is a true student of Sun Wu.

First, Fischer is one who dedicates his waking hours to his chosen field of pursuit — studying it, working whichever way to improve his understanding of it, and earning his livelihood solely from it. This is dedication. This is professionalism. This is the mark of a leader, whether he be in war or in war simulation.[3]

Be Sure No One Can Win Over

The mark of a professional, a man adept at war, in Sun Wu's view, is to avoid defeat:

> In the past, those who knew war first made sure that no one could win over them, then sought opportunities to win over the enemy. Ensuring that no one wins over us depends upon ourselves ... (4.1)

Fischer is close to the mark. In years 1970 and 1971, in three major tournaments, his record is 57 wins, 22 draws, and only 3 losses.[4]

Feign Incompetence

The Gruenfeld Defense is not easy for Black. One writer states: "I strongly recommend that non-experts avoid this [Gruenfeld Defense] opening as Black. That center can become a steamroller if you don't have very good defensive technique, and the endgames that result require subtle handling, even in favorable circumstances."[5] But, Fischer daringly played it — at age 13, against a former U.S. Open Champion, no less.

Sun Wu has said: "War involves stratagems. Thus, when competent, feign incompetence." (1.12) What was Fischer trying to convey by playing this difficult defense? Competence? Incompetence?

Identify Many Options

Fischer studies chess day and night. He also publishes a lot. But, on this very game, intriguingly, Fischer never discussed how well he prepared for it. He kept mum and kept everyone guessing — even to this day.

---

[3] In a famous interview of Fischer by Ralph Ginzburg, published in *Harper's* (January 1962), Fischer, living alone and away from his mother at age 16 or 17, supported himself solely from playing chess, earning about $5,000 a year.

[4] Alexander Cockburn, *Idle Passion* - Chess and the Dance of Death (New York: Simon and Schuster, 1974), p. 169.

[5] Eric Schiller, *World Champion Openings*; The Definitive Guide to the Concepts and Secrets of Chess Openings as Played by the World Champions (New York: Cardoza, 1997, 373 pages), at p. 272.

Are there clues elsewhere? It so happens that, several years later, Fischer played another Gruenfeld Defense game — in 1963, against, of all people, Byrne's brother, Robert, and another U.S. Open Champion in his own right (1960). For that 1963 game, Fischer comments:

> I spent an evening just staring at the position after 14 QR-Q1, trying everything, unwilling to let my brilliancy go down the drain. The more I looked, the more I liked White's game.[6]

So, Fischer spent an *entire* evening just looking at one position — and making plans on defending that position. Marvelous. What a true student of Sun Wu Fischer is: "We can predict a win because we have identified many options through repeated top-level planning." (1.16)

For this 1963 game, White's actual move was the Kingside Rook, 14 KR-Q1 — which Fischer says is "the wrong Rook." Fischer apparently was fully prepared for *that* and began his attack. A move later, Black sacrificed a Knight for the King Bishop Pawn, and was on his way to a stunning win — and a Brilliancy Prize.

Advance Where Unexpected

In this 1963 game, Fischer, on Move 18, had a choice of using his Knight to capture either a Rook (generally more valuable) or a Bishop; in either case, that Knight would be captured. Byrne fully expected the former and says:

> And as I sat pondering why Fischer would choose such a line, because it was so obviously lost for Black, there suddenly came 18 ... NxB. This dazzling move came as the shocker ... The culminating combination is of such depth that, even at the very moment at which I resigned, both grandmasters who were commenting on the play for the spectators in a separate room believed that I had won a game.[7]

So, Fischer's play exemplifies another of Sun Wu's gems: "Attack when unprepared; advance where unexpected." (1.14)

Be Adept at Offense

In the "Game of the Century," from Move 20 onward, many checks are discovered checks. This potent move allows the attacker to redeploy playing pieces to the most advantageous locations, as the

[6] Bobby Fischer, *My 60 Memorable Games* (New York: Simon and Schuster, 1969), Game 48, at p. 299.

[7] Quoted in Fischer, *My 60 Memorable Games*, at p. 297.

defender has to busy parrying the check. This illustrates another of Sun Wu's sayings: "Thus, against one who is adept at offense, the enemy knows not how to defend." (6.4)

Divide the Enemy

The Game of the Century also has double checks in later moves. Double checks are even more potent than discovered checks, as the defense's moves are generally forced and divided. This is reminiscent of what Sun Wu has to say:

When we are consolidated and the enemy scattered in ten different positions, our attacking force is ten times that of the defending force. Even when our total man-count is inferior to the enemy's, our attacking force is numerically superior to the enemy's; this is because the enemy's force at any position must necessarily be limited. (6.7)

Bait the Enemy

The Gruenfeld Defense features baits. In the "Game of the Century," the bait is the Queen, the acceptance of which allows Black to launch an attack. In Fischer's *My 60 Memorable Games*, Grandmaster Evans gives the following introductory notes to another Gruenfeld Defense game played:

Illustrating, rather subtly, how a weaker player may be lured to his own destruction, Fischer entices his opponent to abandon his passive though solid attempts to settle for a draw. Wrongly convinced that he holds an advantage, Gudmundsson ... gives Fischer the opportunity to launch a long, unclear sacrificial combination.[8]

Fischer seems to be taking another page out of Sun Wu's work: "With the enemy seeking advantage, bait; ... displaying caution, agitate." (1.13)

Western Chess and Xiangqi

Exactly why this 1956 game is labeled "The Game of the Century" is unclear. It seems to this case writer that, in western chess, with Queen sacrifices being rare, a game featuring it, ipso facto, deserves praise. When this is accomplished by a 13-year-old, well, it deserves to be labeled "The Game of the Century."

[8] Quoted in Fischer's *My 60 Memorable Games*, Game 19, Reykjavik 1960, at p. 128.

In Xiangqi, the original war-simulation board game, the most valuable playing piece is the Chariot — and Chariot sacrifices are routine. Further, discovered checks, infrequent in western chess, are common occurrences in Xiangqi. Double checks, even rarer in western chess, come up about a dozen times in a game of Xiangqi. Xiangqi, in fact, allows triple checks and even quadruple checks.

Sun Wu says: "In the past, those who knew war won with ease. Thus, their wins were not regarded as unusual, ... They won without flaw." (4.5)

Xiangqi's matter-of-factness is clearly more in line with Sun Wu's thinking than western chess's flamboyancy.

Queenqi

All war-simulation board games in history have unique names — Weiqi and Xiangqi in China, Shatranj in Persia, Chaturanga and Chatúrájì in India, Shogi in Japan, Changgi in Korea, or even Petteia in Greece and Ludus Latrunculorum of the Romans — except the modern western chess. In honor of western chess's single-minded focus on the Queen, it is perhaps not inappropriate to suggest that its name be Queenqi.

Endnote

This case writer came across this game in an exhibition of western chess sets during the 1996 Biennial Congress of Chess Collectors International, held in Washington DC. In writing this case, he has benefitted from comments from the following, all via the internet:

"Parx," identifying the game as "The Game of the Century";

"Paul Morphy" and Dan Corbit, posting the game's moves;

Mike Scheidl in Austria, Bob Simpson in UK, and Paul Nijmeijer in the Netherlands, offering comments on moves;

Mr. Scheidl, clarifying Byrne brothers' first names;

Charles Milton Ling in Austria, PMG (Pete), Bob Musicant, Todd Durham (two messages), and Sam Sloan, commenting on the game's being labeled "The Game of the Century"; and

John Wong in Singapore and Bill Jones, commenting on tactical issues of the Gruenfeld Defense.

To those western chess masters named above, this case writer wishes to express his sincere thanks for their prompt and valuable advice.

10 地　形　篇

MANAGEMENT OF TERRAIN

10.1　地形有通者，有挂者，有支者，有
隘者，有险者，有远者。

Terrain's contours include: open, down-sloping, one-directional,
narrow, precipitous, and unfamiliar.

10.2　我可以往，彼可以来，曰通。通形者，先居高阳，利
粮道，以战则利。

Open terrain is terrain open for claiming by either us or the enemy.
Reaching it first, encamp on high ground — face the sun, ensure
movements of provisions. Open terrain is advantageous.

10.3　可以往，难以返，曰挂。挂形者，敌无备，出而胜之；
敌有备，出而不胜，难以返，不利。

Down-sloping terrain is terrain easy to get in but difficult to get
out. When the enemy is unprepared, attack and win. When the
enemy is prepared, an attack may not produce a win — and it will
be difficult for us to get out. Down-sloping terrain is not
advantageous.

10.4　我出而不利，彼出而不利，曰支。支形者，敌虽利我，
我无出也，引而去之，令敌半出而击之，利。

One-directional terrain is terrain advantageous neither to us nor to
the enemy. In a one-directional terrain, when the enemy baits us to
fight, we must decline. Yet, we must pretend we accept to lure the
enemy in. When one half of our enemy's men are in — and we can
strike them at that time — then is one-directional terrain
advantageous.

10.5   隘形者，我先居之，必盈之以待敌；若敌先居之，盈
而勿从，不盈而从之。

With narrow terrain, when we occupy it first, barricade the path
and await for the enemy. When the enemy occupies it first, if he
barricades the path, do not follow; if not, follow.

10.6   险形者，我先居之，必居高阳以待敌；若敌先居之，
引而去之，勿从也。

With precipitous terrain, when we occupy it first, stay high, face
the sun, and wait for the enemy. When the enemy occupies it first,
retreat — do not follow.

10.7   远形者，势均，难以挑战，战而不利。

With unfamiliar terrain, neither side has an advantage; it is
inadvisable to challenge the enemy to a fight. If we do, the result
will not be advantageous.

10.8   凡此六者，地之道也，将之至任，不可不察也。

These are six directives on the management of terrain. It is the
commander's responsibility to understand them. It is not to left
uninvestigated.

10.9   故兵有走者，有弛者，有陷者，有崩者，有
乱者，有北者。凡此六者，非天地之灾，将之过也。

Manifestations of defeatism: flight, slackness, chaos, collapse, ruin,
rout. These six cannot be attributed to nature's disasters, but to a
commander's ineptitude.

10.10   夫势均，以一击十，曰走。卒强吏弱，曰弛。
吏强卒弱，曰陷。

With neither side having an advantage, attacking the enemy tenfold stronger results in flight. When soldiers are energized but officers hesitant, the result is slackness. When officers are prepared but soldiers lethargic, the result is chaos.

10.11 大吏怒而不服，遇敌怼而自战，将不知其能，曰崩。

When adjunct commanders are enraged and disobedient, when they vent their indignation by engaging the enemy in combat without authorization, when their whereabouts are not reported to the commander, the result is collapse.

10.12 将弱不严，教道不明，吏卒无常，陈兵纵横，曰乱。

When the commander is indecisive and weak, when discipline is inconsistent and directives unclear, when officer-soldier communication is haphazard, when resource deployment is disorderly, the result is ruin.

10.13   将不能料敌，以少合众，以弱击强，
兵无选锋，曰北。

When a commander cannot anticipate the enemy's action, when he engages his numerically inferior men in combat with a numerically superior enemy, when he attacks the enemy's stronghold with inadequate manpower, when his forward army lacks thrust, the result is rout.

10.14   凡此六者，败之道也。将之至任，不可不察也。

These six manifestations lead to defeat. It is the commander's responsibility to understand them. It is not to be left uninvestigated.

10.15　夫地形者，兵之助也。料敌制胜，计险易、远近，上将之道也。知此而用战者必胜，不知此而用战者必败。

Terrain's contours play an important role in war. Anticipating the enemy's action contributes to winning. Estimating risks and distances are top commanders's directives. Mastering them and applying them in war produce sure wins; not knowing them and not applying them in war, sure defeats.

10.16　故战道必胜，主曰无战，必战可也；战道不胜，主曰必战，无战可也。故进不求名，退不避罪，唯民是保，而利合于主，国之宝也。

When on a path to win, fight even when the head of state decrees not to fight. When on a path to defeat, decline to fight even when the head of state decrees to fight. Advancing is not for seeking personal glory; retreating is not for shrinking from personal responsibility. A commander who concerns only with the people's welfare and who thinks only of the head of state's advantage is a treasure of the state.

10.17　视卒如婴儿，故可与之赴深谿；视卒如爱子，故可与之俱死。厚而不能使，爱而不能令，乱而不能治，譬若骄子，不可用也。

When a soldier is treated as a child, he will be willing to go to deep waters with[1] the commander. When a soldier is treated as a loving son, he will be willing to die with[1] the commander. When treated well but not accepting assignments, when loved much but not following orders, when violated rules but not receiving discipline — the soldier is a spoiled brat, and is unfit for commission.

[1] The key word in these two sentences is *with*, not *for*. That is, the soldier will follow the commander's lead.

10.18   知吾卒之可以击，而不知敌之不可击，胜之半也；知敌之可击，而不知吾卒之不可以击，胜之半也；知敌之可击，知吾卒之可以击，而不知地形之不可以战，胜之半也。

Knowing that our soldiers can fight but not knowing whether the enemy's can or cannot, the likelihood of winning is but fifty-fifty. Knowing that the enemy's soldiers can fight but not knowing whether ours can or cannot, the likelihood of winning is but fifty-fifty. Knowing that our soldiers can fight but not knowing whether the terrain's contour is advantageous to our fighting, the likelihood of winning is but fifty-fifty.

10.19   故知兵者，动而不迷，举而不穷。故曰：知彼知己，胜乃不殆；知天知地，胜乃可全。

One who knows war takes actions without hesitation, provides measures without limitation. Knowing the enemy and knowing ourselves, winning is not in doubt. Knowing nature and knowing terrain, winning is total.

Case W-H   American Civil War - The Second Bull Run (1862)

To honor Sun Tzu, the National Defense University, Ft. McNair, Washington DC, held a "Sun Tzu Art of War in Information Warfare" research competition. Award winning essays are collected in Robert E. Neilson (ed), *Sun Tzu and Information Warfare* (Washington: National Defense University Press, 1997).

One of the award-winning essays is by Colonel Adolph Carlson, United States Army. Though entitled "Information Management and the Challenge of Battle Command," his essay, in this case writer's view, deals with leadership, with leadership style, with leader-to-leader communication.

Carlson's essay covers two case studies — one is excerpted below, the other one has appeared earlier in this volume as Case W-E (Gulf War). For ease in reading, references to the other case are replaced by []; plural-to-singular correspondence is introduced as needed. Passages omitted are noted by ellipses (...). Materials augmented by this case writer are included as endnotes.

In July 1878, by order of President Rutherford B. Hayes, three distinguished U.S. Army officers were summoned to West Point, New York. The senior was Major General John M. Schofield, who had been one of Sherman's subordinate commanders during the Georgia campaign. Next was Brigadier General Alfred H. Terry, veteran of campaigns in the Carolinas and Petersburg and a key figure in the 1876 campaign against the Dakota Sioux. The third was Colonel George W. Getty, a thirty-eight year veteran who had participated in all of the Army of the Potomac's campaign from Yorktown to Appomattox.

Porter's 1863 Court Martial

These officers were directed to preside over one of the most remarkable hearings in the history of American military jurisprudence, the investigation of the "facts of the case of Fitz John Porter, late Major General of Volunteers."[1]

Fifteen years earlier, a court martial had convicted Porter for his actions during the second battle of Manassas, August 1862, when he commanded the Army of the Potomac's V Corps, attached to Major General John Pope's Army of Virginia. Porter was accused of not moving his corps in accordance to orders and of failing to attack Confederate General Jackson's forces when an attack could have prevented defeat.

Impossible Order to Execute

At the trial, Porter's defense argued that Pope's orders were impossible to execute because they were based upon an inaccurate picture of road conditions and the enemy's disposition. Porter could not have attacked Jackson without fighting Confederate General Longstreet's forces, which were concentrated in front of him when he received Pope's order. As evidence, Porter's side produced a dispatch from the commander of Union cavalry, Brigadier General John Buford, which reported Longstreet's troops pouring toward Porter almost eight hours prior to the dispatch of Pope's order. ...

Porter Convicted

Despite the flimsy case against him, Porter was convicted and sentenced to "be cashiered and forever disqualified from holding office of trust or profit under the government of the United States." Porter appealed the verdict, but it took fifteen years for the government to act on his appeal.

Review of 1863 Court Martial

The President had authorized the Schofield board to review the alleged irregularities of the 1863 court martial and to consider new evidence. Accordingly, to their great credit, ex-Confederate officers who were at the Second Battle of Manassas came forward to clarify the tactical questions on which Porter's claim rested. Most notable was General Longstreet, who revealed that at the time Porter received orders from Pope, his Confederate troops were present in strength, and that had Porter attempted to attack "we could have broken up" the Union force and "thrown everything we had in pursuit."

[1] Otto Eisenschiml, *The Celebrated Case of Fitz John Porter* (Boston: Houghton Mifflin, 1950), p. 214.

Testimony of Confederate General

Longstreet testified that Porter, by maintaining his position, had prevented him [Longstreet] from joining forces with Jackson, thereby averting a greater catastrophe on the twenty ninth of August than actually occurred on the thirtieth." Rather than censure, Porter's actions merited his commander's thanks. ...

Recommendation of 1878 Review Board

The recommendations of the Schofield board were unanimous:

In our opinion, justice requires such action as may be necessary to annul and set aside the findings and sentence of the court-martial in the case of General Fitz John Porter and to restore him to the position of which that sentence deprived him.

Rank Restored

Finally, in August 1886, twenty-three years after the original verdict, Fitz John Porter's conviction was set aside and his rank and good name were restored.

Mission Analysis

The mission of the Army of Virginia [] was to protect "Western Virginia and the National Capital" and to "attack and overcome the rebel forces under Jackson and Ewell."[2]

Strictly speaking, one component [was not] more important than the other, but [] Pope [] chose to concentrate on the enemy-oriented aspects of his mission. Pope's order of 27 August included the optimistic prediction that "We shall bag the whole crowd [i.e., Jackson's force]"

Appraisal of Enemy Capabilities

On the eve of the second battle of Manassas, Pope was under the impression that Jackson was fleeing for his life. Pope's information was based on an intercepted message and his own underestimation of enemy capabilities.

Earlier, Pope's 14 July 1862 order, calling for his command to "discard such ideas" as "taking strong positions and holding them, of

[2] Order of President Lincoln dated 26 June 1862, quoted in *The War of the Rebellion*, A Compilation of the Official Records of *the Union and Confederate Armies* (Washington: Government Printing Office, 1885), Series I, Volume XII, Part III, p. 435.

lines of retreat, and of bases of supplies"[3] was a bombastic appeal to discard a cautious style of operations in favor of bolder action.[4]

Porter, on the other hand, formed his judgments based on Buford's report, which indicated that on the morning of 29 August over 14,000 Confederates had passed through the Thoroughfare Gap and were massed in the vicinity of Union forces. Pope denied seeing this crucial piece of battlefield information until 1900 hours that evening. Thus, the two commanders made decisions based on two distinct images of the enemy situation. [See Endnote 5 for these two distinct images.]

Supervision of Operations

The manner of issuing direction [] also bears comparison. Pope's orders were vague and difficult to interpret. Porter can not be blamed for failing to deduce that he was to attack from this order:

move forward ... toward Gainsville. ... as soon as communication is established ... the whole command shall halt. It may be necessary to fall back behind Bull Run ... tonight.[5]

Appreciation of Ambient Conditions

Common to the specifications charged against Porter [] were the difficulties of night operations. In Porter's case, Pope had directed Porter to conduct a night march on 27 August, commencing at 0100 to arrive at Bristoe Station by daybreak. Porter could not obey [to] the letter of this order because of factors Pope could not appreciate: the road was narrow, Confederate forces had destroyed the bridges, and two of three thousand Union Army wagons blocked the way. Porter did not start his march until 0300 and could not reach his destination until 1000, a delay which Pope maintained had prevented him from "bagging" Jackson's forces.

Conceptual Divergence

[] Prior to the initiation of active operations, deliberate planning should produce a common vision between senior and subordinate commanders. The record shows that Pope and Porter agreed on the plan to concentrate the Army in the vicinity of Alexandria to confront Lee's threatened move north. []

[3] *The War of the Rebellion*, p. 474.

[4] Henry Gable, "The Fitz John Porter Case: Politics and Military Justice" (City University of New York Ph.D. Thesis, 1979), p. 52.

[5] Eisenschiml, *Case of Fitz John Porter*, p. 55.

After the senior and subordinate reach consensus, each begins a process of subsequent decision making independent of the other. Once a combat operations commence, decision must be made at a rate that does not permit the formal, fully-staffed process, especially when the demands of supervision compete with the demands of decision making. Accordingly, commanders involve a smaller number of staff officers and make decisions using an abbreviated procedures.

Abbreviated Procedures of Decision Making

These procedures will vary according to the commanders' personalities, but will include the following analytical processes:

· detailed planning, to ensure that each of the mission's component tasks is assigned to the most capable element

· fine tuning, to provide refined guidance to subordinate units based upon the most detailed data available.

· contingency analysis, so that the organization is prepared to respond effectively to possible changes in the enemy or friendly situation or to unpredictable variations in terrain or weather.

· disaster avoidance, to avoid catastrophic defeat in the event of the worst case.

· updating, to ensure that actions underway or contemplated are still appropriate to the current situation.

Decision Making With Data From Different Sources

In the absence of any other variable, there is already a likelihood that a subordinate commander's concept of operations will diverge from his superior's, because regardless how much we enhance the collection and dissemination of data, the ability to arrive at a decision based on that data cannot be automated.

If the two are making their assessments based on data from different sources, that divergence is likely to be more pronounced. because the commanders will view each piece of data in different contextual settings.

Role of Intermediate Commanders

In Porter's case, Major General Irwin McDowell, who was senior to Porter, assumed command of his own and Porter's corps, in accordance with the custom of the day. McDowell had been with Pope since the Army of Virginia was created, and enjoyed his confidence.

As McDowell positioned the two corps, Porter looked to him for clarification of Pope's intent. "What do you want me to do?" Porter asked McDowell at a critical point. McDowell only waved his hand and rode off, leaving Porter to rely on his own judgment. [This order is reproduced as Endnote 2; for "mistakes" in this order, see Endnote 3; for General Robert E. Lee's reaction, see Endnote 4.]

McDowell's absence was a subject of testimony at Porter's court martial. Porter stated that: "From about 10 a.m. ... till after 6 p.m., I received no instructions from him [i.e., Pope] or General McDowell, though I had sent many messages to both of them."

Blaming Subordinates for Failure

This practice of blaming scapegoats caused much bad feeling among the officers of the Army of the Potomac. [] Blaming failure on subordinates was one of the least appealing characteristics of the Army during the Civil War, but while we may not condone it, we can at least appreciate that it was a result of repeated defeats.

Endnotes

1 A battlefield map of Second Bull Run is shown as Exhibit 1 on page 152.

2 A key point in the court martial proceedings seems to be a document known as the "4.30 p.m. order." It reads, in part, as follows:

HEAD-QUARTERS IN THE FIELD,
August 29, 1862 (4.30 p.m.)

Your line of march brings you in on the enemy's right flank. I desire you to push forward into action at once on the enemy's flank, and if possible, on his rear, keeping your right in communication with General Reynolds. ...

JOHN POPE,
Major-General commanding
Major-General PORTER.

From Theodore A. Lord, *A Summary of the Case of General Fitz-John Porter* (San Francisco, 1883), p. 59.

Case W-H Exhibit 1
Battlefield Map of Second Bull Run
August 1862

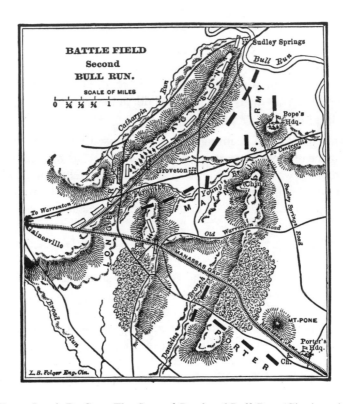

From Jacob D. Cox, *The Second Battle of Bull Run* (Cincinnati: Thompson, 1882), p. 31

3   The order (shown in Endnote 2) "was not delivered to Porter until sundown, too late to execute it." It also contained two "mistakes." One, "The flank and rear which Pope intended should be attacked were of course Jackson's. But ... it brought him directly upon Longstreet's front, where 25,000 men were ready to receive him." Two, "Reynolds ... was at least two miles from Porter, with ... impassable country between them. Porter could not connect with Reynolds, and there was no flank or rear of any enemy that could be attacked. Longstreet outflanked Porter, and Jackson was too far off and too well defended." (Lord, p. 60)

4 "On this point General [Robert E.] Lee says: 'We flanked him. He could not flank Jackson. I suppose we should have cut Porter to pieces if he had attacked to get at Jackson's flank.'" (Lord, p. 61)

5 "The situation on the 29th of August may be represented approximately thus (Lord, p. 62):

What Pope assumed it to be:

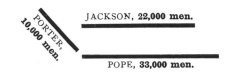

What it actually was:

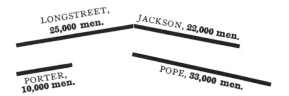

6 It seemed that McDowell took away 15,000 men from Porter, leaving Porter with 10,000. Lord, who appeared to be the defense counsel, deduced as follows:

"Can it be supposed that McDowell would order an immediate attack with 10,000 men, when he thought it was too far out, and no place to fight in, with 25,000 men?

"When McDowell declined to make an attack in that position with 25,000 men, and took away 15,000 of them into the wilderness, Porter supposed, as it was reasonable to suppose, that he did so for the purpose of bringing the whole army into communication, in accordance with the intent of the Joint Order, and with sound military judgment. Porter did not and could not suppose, that he was expected to attack, or would be justified in attacking, before that communication was established, and McDowell was in a position to co-operate with him. As war is not a conjectural science, he was right in waiting until he *knew* whether that co-operation was assured or not."
(Lord, pp. 43-44)

Case P10 Republican Party Presidential Nomination for 2000 - Super Tuesday

[Passages referenced: 1.9, 10.13]

After contests in Virginia, Washington, and South Dakota on February 29, 2000, the next important date is one week following, March 7, 2000. On that date, with 13 states holding primaries or caucuses, it is likely to be a make-or-break day for candidates still in the running for the presidential nomination. Because of its importance, it is dubbed by the media as Super Tuesday.

Super Tuesday

The states holding contests on March 7, 2000, along with the stakes in each, are shown in Exhibit 1 below.

Case P-10 Exhibit 1
States Holding Primary and Caucus
on Tuesday, March 7, 2000
(In descending order of number of delegates)
(Open = all voters; closed = Republicans only
semi-open = Republicans + independents)

California	162 delegates	Closed
New York	101	Closed
Ohio	69	Open
Georgia	54	Open
Massachusetts	37	Semi-open
Washington	37	Open
Missouri	35	Open
Minnesota	34	Open
Maryland	31	Semi-open
Connecticut	25	Closed
Maine	14	Semi-open
Rhode Island	14	Semi-open
Vermont	12	Semi-open

March 1, Unanticipated Harsher Reaction

On March 1, one day after the Virginia and Washington primaries and the South Dakota caucus — with Governor Bush winning all three and claiming all delegates — Senator McCain realizes that his tactics to denounce the religious right has backfired. Party members' reaction to his lashing out is much harsher than he anticipates.

Sun Wu has this to say: "When a commander cannot anticipate the enemy's action, when he engages his numerically inferior men in combat with a numerically superior enemy, when he attacks the enemy's stronghold with inadequate manpower, when his forward army lacks thrust, the result is rout." (10.13)

Apologies Demanded and Clarification Issued

Whether Sun Wu's word has any predictive power only time will tell — and it is but a week away. In any case, on March 1, prominent members of the Republican Party begin to speak out against Senator McCain, claiming that his tactics — splitting the Party along religious lines — is ill advised, to say the least.

Gary Bauer, a religious conservative who dropped out of the race before the South Carolina primary and threw his support to Senator McCain, is particularly displeased. He suggests that Senator McCain issue an apology.

An apology Senator McCain does not issue; still defiant, he does issue a clarification, stating that he does not consider leaders of Christian right "evil," and that he regrets that "my flip remark may have mistakenly created that impression."

March 2, Ad Campaign in New York

On Super Tuesday, New York, with 101 delegates at stake, is a critical battleground. Early on, Governor Bush has the endorsement of its governor and the New York establishment. Pre-primary poll in late 1999, barely three months ago, shows Governor Bush leading Senator McCain by a lop-sided 61 percent to 3 percent.

But, the latest pre-primary poll, released just five days before primary, tells a different story — it gives Senator McCain a slight lead of 2 points. One reason might be the public's reaction to the state's earlier ruling disallowing Senator McCain's name to appear on ballots of many congressional districts — a ready-made campaign issue for Senator McCain. While this ruling is later reversed, the sympathy for Senator McCain's underdog role of fighting the establishment lingers.

Because of the tightness of this race, both candidates spend time campaigning. On March 2, a group called Republicans for Clean Air attacking Senator McCain begin to appear in New York (also in California and Ohio), spending $2.5 million (over $1 million in New York). This lavish outlay, later traced to two close Texas friends of

Governor Bush, perhaps lends further support to Senator McCain's campaign finance reform issue.

Hsia Verdict

On March 2, a verdict concerning political fund-raiser Maria Hsia is announced. For channelling some $100,000 "illegal" contributions, including some $65,000 "tainted" money, to Democratic candidates in 1996, she is convicted and is to serve a 25-year sentence.

The amount raised pales in the face of the $2.5 million ad campaign on "Republicans for Clean Air" just launched — the difference appears to be one between "tainted" money (whatever that means) and billionaires' own money (clearly "untainted"). But, for raising money enough for probably one 30-second ad in New York, Ms. Hsia gets 25 years.

California Debate

That evening, March 2, the three Republican candidates have a televised debate in California — Governor Bush and Mr. Keyes in person, Senator McCain via satellite from New York.

Given the format (television personalities asking questions and candidates answering), and an eye on ratings (entertainment value as evidence of viewer interest), questions asked are mainly on tactics ("Bob Jones University", "Catholic voter alert"). Given the time limit (only one hour), there are but brief discussions on policy issues such as education.

Direction vs. Victory

When it is time for candidates to summarize, Mr. Keyes wonders out loud — even though his message is the sanest among the three (against "moral decline"), even though he conducts himself beyond reproach, even though he offers himself as the alternative to the other two, his vote-getting percentage remains in the single digit.

These are good questions even Sun Wu would have trouble answering. According to Sun Wu, "Which head of state has the Direction" is a key factor determining "victory or defeat" (1.9). Perhaps this has to be qualified with *in due course* and *under the right circumstances*.

March 4-5, Pundits' Forecasts

The weekend before the Super Tuesday is pundits' field day. Their forecast is that Governor Bush will take California, Georgia, Washington, and Missouri, while Senator McCain seems to be ahead in New England states (Connecticut, Maine, Rhode Island, and Vermont). New York is too close to call, but they all agree that Senator McCain must win here to remain a viable candidate.

An interesting point discussed by pundits is California's two-tier voting system — independents may vote, but their votes do not count toward the delegate-selection process. Thus, it would be embarrassing were Senator McCain to win the "beauty contest," as this popular vote is dubbed, while Governor Bush claims the entire winner-take-all 162 delegates.

Since Governor Bush is reemerging as the favorite and the likely Republican standard bearer, these pundits speak with care. The $2.5 million "Clean Air" ad campaign is obviously a topic unsuited for discussion. On the other hand, the fact that candidates, during their debate, makes no mention of the Hsia verdict is lamented. She is referred to, by several commentators as a "small fry". Very much so.

Sunday, March 5, March in Selma

Thirty-five years ago the first Sunday in March, March 7, 1965, Rev. Martin Luther King Jr. and about 600 others marched in Selma, Alabama, to protest the state's refusal to allow most blacks to register to vote. Brutality ensued — it was dubbed a "Bloody Sunday." Belatedly, the 1965 Voting Rights Act was passed — 189 years after the founding of the United States of America.

Today, President Clinton joins the crowd in a ceremony, marches across the Edmund Pettus Bridge, where shocking actions against the marchers took place, and gives a speech. Greeted by a sea of Confederate flags, an issue at the South Carolina primary, President Clinton remarks: "As long as the waving symbol of one American's pride is the shameful symbol of another American's pain, we have another bridge to cross."

On to Super Tuesday

It is in this ambivalent atmosphere — you may have the right to vote but you cannot register to vote, you may vote but your vote does not count, you may participate in the voting process but you risk going to jail — that the drama of voting on Super Tuesday unfolds.

Results of Super Tuesday

Results of votes cast in the Super Tuesday are as shown in Exhibit 2 (page 158).

Case P-10 Exhibit 2
Results of Primaries and Caucuses
Held on Tuesday, March 7, 2000
(In descending order of number of delegates)
(100% counted unless otherwise noted)
(Winner shown boldfaced)

	Delegates	Bush	McCain	Keyes
California	162	**1,542,110**	885,255	100,173
*New York	101	**355,958**	306,443	25,118
Ohio	69	**796,848**	507,943	54,094
Georgia	54	**431,201**	179,439	29,754
Massachusetts	37	158,208	**320,617**	12,561
Washington	37	**80%**	15%	4%
Missouri	35	**275,412**	167,962	27,284
***Minnesota	34	**10,914**	3,004	3,505
Maryland	31	**206,425**	132,618	24,603
*Connecticut	25	82,386	**86,484**	5,803
**Maine	14	**47,669**	41,379	2,929
Rhode Island	14	12,888	**21,456**	907
*Vermont	12	28,702	**48,870**	2,154
Delegates to date		**617**	**231**	**12**

*	=	99% counted
**	=	93%
***	=	68%

Senator McCain Suspends Campaigning

On Thursday, March 9, two days after the Super Tuesday, Senator McCain announces that he is suspending his race for Republican presidential nomination for Year 2000.

11 九 地 篇

DEPLOYMENT OF FIELD FORCES

11.1 用兵之法，有散地，有轻地，有争地，有交地，有衢地，有重地，有圯地，有围地，有死地。

In war, we have leave-tempting land, peripheral land, contested land, neutral land, cross-road land, core land, hazardous land, circumscribed land, and deadly land.

11.2 诸侯自战其地者，为散地。入人之地而不深者为轻地。我得则利，彼得亦利者，为争地。我可以往，彼可以来者，为交地。诸侯之地三属，先至而得天下之众者，为衢地。入人之地深，背城邑多者，为重地。

Leave-tempting land is our home territory; peripheral land, outer regions of the enemy's territory; contested land, area for control for advantage; neutral land, open area accessible to us as well as to the enemy. Cross-roads are areas common to various states; one who arrives first is likely to receive their support. Core land is enemy's population and trade centers.

11.3 山林、险阻、沮泽，凡难行之道者，为圯地。所由入者隘，所从归者迂，彼寡可以击吾之众者，为围地。疾战则存，不疾战则亡者，为死地。

Hazardous land is land with treacherous passes, precarious cliffs, unspecified rivers and streams — difficult passageways in general. Circumscribed land is land offering narrow paths getting in and circuitous routes getting out, an area where our large army may subject to attack by a small enemy force. Deadly land is land that requires quick combats for survival — protracted engagements result in annihilation.

11.4   是故散地则无战，轻地则无止，争地则无攻，交地则无绝，衢地则合交，重地则掠，圮地则行，围地则谋，死地则战。

Thus, do not engage in combat on leave-tempting land, do not stop on peripheral land, do not attack contested land, do not barricade neutral land. Rendezvous at cross-roads, appropriate provisions on core land, hasten through hazardous land, negotiate out of circumscribed land, fight our way out of deadly land.

11.5   所谓古之善用兵者，能使敌人前后不相及，众寡不相恃，贵贱不相救，上下不相收，卒离而不集，兵合而不齐。

In the past, those who knew war dislodged the enemy's front from his rear, isolated the enemy's main force from his flanks, interfered the enemy officers' support from their men, cut off the enemy commander's communication with his staff, separated the enemy's men from their groups, and disrupted the enemy's force from being unified.

11.6   合于利而动，不合于利而止。敢问："敌众以整，将来，待之若何？"曰："先夺其所爱，则听矣。"

Act when the scenario is advantageous, wait when it is not. When asked: "How do we act when the enemy, well organized and en masse, is coming at us?" Answer: "Capture what is precious to him, and he will listen."

11.7 兵之情主速，乘人之不及，由不虞之道，攻其所不戒也。

War demands quick action — act before the enemy is ready, march through routes he does not suspect, attack positions he does not guard.

11.8 凡为客之道：深入则专，主人不克；掠于饶野，三军足食；谨养而勿劳，并气积力；

Attacking inside the enemy territory, move deep and in unison to overpower the enemy. Appropriate materiel from town and country to fortify our army's supply. Rest and be at ease to elevate our men's physical condition and morale.

11.9 运兵计谋，为不可测。

War is planning. Plan beyond the enemy's ability to anticipate.

11.10 投之无所往，死且不北。死，焉不得士人尽力？兵士甚陷则不惧，无所往则固，

Placed in a circumscribed position, death is preferred to desertion. Faced with death, would one not fight to one's utmost best? Placed in a deadly position, fear is absent; placed in a circumscribed position, morale is high.

11.11 入深则拘，不得已则斗。是故不修而戒，不求而得，不约而来，不令而信，

Deep in enemy territory, move with care, and fight only when forced. Without being warned, our men will be on guard. Without being coached, our men will be at ready. Without being advised, our men will help one another. Without invoking rules, our men will exercise self-restraint.

11.12 禁祥去疑，至死无所之。

Subscribe not to irrational beliefs and listen not to questionable views. Retreat not from death.

11.13 吾士无余财，非恶货也；无余命，非恶寿也。令发之日，士坐者涕沾襟，卧者涕交颐。投之无所往者，诸、刿之勇也。

Our men may not possess much, but it is not because they disdain affluence. They may not live long, but it is not because they spurn longevity. When an order [to fight their way out of a circumscribed position] is issued, those who are standing[1] might weep; those who are lying[1] might cry. Being circumscribed, they would fight as bravely as did Chu[2] and Gui[3].

[1] *Standing* is an euphemism for *healthy*; *lying*, for *wounded*.

[2]   Zhan Chu, of Wu, on the staff of Prince Guang, assassinated King Liao, in 515 BCE, thus allowing the prince to assume the throne to become King Hé Lü, the very person reading these thirteen essays in 512 BCE. See also Appendix A, Chronology, for entry under 515 BCE.

[3] Cao Gui, of Lü, assassinated Duke Huan of Chi (reign 685-643 BCE), a Power in the early phase of the Spring and Autumn Period (770-476 BCE), for the Duke's refusal to return land, captured earlier from Lü, back to Lü.

11.14 故善用兵者，譬如率然；率然者，恒山之蛇也。击其首则尾至，击其尾则首至，击其中则首尾俱至。

One who knows war may be likened to a *so-ran* snake[4] of Mountain Heng. Hitting a so-ran snake's tail, its head comes to the rescue. Hitting its head, its tail comes to the rescue. Hitting its middle, both its head and its tail come to the rescue.

[4] A species of snake known for its quick movement and alert reaction. *So-ran*, here rendered phonetically, means, literally, *instantaneous action*.

11.15

敢问：兵可使如率然乎？曰：可。夫吴人与越人相恶也，当其同舟而济，其相救也，如左右手。

Question: Can an army act like a so-ran snake? Answer: Yes. Although Wu and Yuè are at odds with each other, were the two in the same boat during a river-crossing, one would come to the aid of the other as if the left hand were to the right hand.

11.16
是故方马埋轮，未足恃也；齐勇若一，政之道也；刚柔皆得，地之理也。故善用兵者，携手若使一人，不得已也。

Thus, to motivate our men by roping in horses and burying chariot wheels[5] is ineffective. It is Direction that inspires our men to act with bravery in unison. It is the advantage from terrain that yields both steeliness and resiliency. Thus, one who knows war can direct an army to act as if one man — it has to be so.

[5] Roping in horses and burying chariot wheels are actions to indicate a determination to fight.

11.17
将军之事，静以幽，正以治。能愚士卒之耳目，使民无知。易其事，革其谋，使民无识；易其居，迂其途，使民不得虑。

A commander's role is to deliberate with calmness, and govern with fairness. Make plans difficult to understand; our men will be unable to discern. Reassign missions and revise plans; our men will be unable to detect. Change camping grounds and use different routes; our men will be unable to deduce.[6]

[6] In these passages, Sun Wu seems to be excessively concerned with spies in his midst.

11.18
帅与之期，如登高而志其梯；帅与之深入诸侯之地，而发其机；

Readying for combat, induce our men to move ahead as if removing the ladder after reaching the top. Advancing deep into enemy territory, encourage our men to move forward as if firing an arrow from a bow-firing machine.[7]

[7] In the first sentence, instilling bravery and independence is intended; the second, swiftness and adventurousness. Both use analogies suggesting one-way no-return scenarios comparable to circumscribed positions in 11.10 and 11.13.

11.19   若驱群羊，驱而往，驱而来，莫知所之。聚三军之众，投之于险，此谓将军之事也。

The army must be led, as a flock of sheep, going here, going there, without being told the reason. Gathering men for a three-battalion army for combat and risking their lives are the commander's responsibilities.[8]

[8] To counteract the impression that the first sentence exhibits arrogance, the second sentence provides the underlying reason: combat is hazardous; the men must not have the opportunity to show hesitancy — and possible dissension — thereby ruining the oneness concept so important to building morale, concerted action. and win.

11.20   九地之变，屈伸之利，人情之理，不可不察也。

Knowledge of the nine types of terrain, their effect on attack and retreat, and their effect on our men's morale are not to be left uninvestigated.

11.21

凡为客之道，深则专，浅则散。去国越境而师者，绝地也；四彻者，衢地也；入深者，重地也；入浅者，轻地也；背固前隘者，围地也；无所往者，死地也。

When in enemy territory, moving deep promotes unison; move peripherally tempts leaves without absences.[9] Enemy territory reachable through crossing other states is isolated land. Areas reachable from all four sides are cross-roads. Core land requires penetration; peripheral land may be slighted. Areas with stiff cliffs at back and narrow paths in front are circumscribed land. Land with no exits is deadly.

[9] This sentence suggests that the enemy territory is contiguous to the invading army's home territory, allowing features of the leave-tempting land to come into play.

11.22 是故散地，吾将一其志；轻地，吾将使之属；争地，吾将趋其后；交地，吾将谨其守；衢地，吾将固其结；重地，吾将继其食；圮地，吾将进其途；围地，吾将塞其阙；死地，吾将示之以不活。

On leave-tempting land, we must solidify our willingness to fight. On peripheral land, we must attempt to annex. On contested land, we must go after it. On neutral land, we must be guard our movement. On cross-roads, we must strengthen our ties. On core land, we must appropriate our provisions. On hazardous land, we must pass through quickly. On circumscribed land, we must barricade the remaining openings. On deadly land, we must show our willingness to not live.

11.23 诸侯之情：围则御，不得已则斗，过则从。

The enemy's inclination is to resist when circumscribed, fight when forced, and surrender when overwhelmed.

11.24 是故，不知诸侯之谋者，不能预交；不知山林、险阻、沮泽之形者，不能行军；不用乡导者，不能得地利。

Seek no alliance without knowledge of other states' plans. Move no troops without knowledge of contours of mountains and forests, passes and obstacles , and marshes and swamps. Without the services of local intelligence, we gain no advantage from terrain.

11.25 四、五者，一不知，非王霸之兵也。

Of the four plans [about others][10] and five factors [about ourselves][11], even if we are ignorant of but one, we are unlikely to become a Power[12].

[10] Three of the four plans about others refer to the enemy's inclinations (in 11.23): resist when circumscribed, fight when forced, and surrender when overwhelmed. The fourth refers to other states' plans (in 11.24).

[11] Of the five factors about ourselves, three relate to combat strategy (in 11.20): knowledge of the nine types of terrain, terrain's effect on attack and retreat, and terrain's effect on our men's morale. The remaining two relate to troop deployment (in 11.24): knowledge of terrain in troop deployment and use of local intelligence to gain terrain advantage.

[12] With this passage, winning a war over a *single* state is summarized. The last sentence is very tempting. Sun Wu assumes that King Hé Lü of Wu, by then the *only* reader of his essays, will *not* be satisfied after winning over his arch-enemy, Yuè, but will entertain even grander plans — to be a Power and, perhaps, even the Head of the League of Powers. On the state of Wu's being a Power, see Appendix A, Chronology, entries under 485 BCE et seq.

11.26　　夫王霸之兵，伐大国，则其众不得聚；威加于敌，则其交不得合。是故，不事天下之交，不养天下之权，信己之私，威加于敌，故其城可拔，其国可隳。

The army of a Power, in attacking a major state, moves swiftly before she can mobilize her army. With that major state subdued, her allies are unlikely to come to rescue. Thus, there is no need to seek alliance with other states, there is no need to share influence with them. All that is needed is to strengthen ourselves to overpower our enemies, capture their citadels, and destroy their sovereignty.

11.27 施无法之赏，悬无政之令，犯三军之众，若使一人。

By offering extraordinarily generous rewards, by giving unquestionably effective orders, we can command a three-battalion army as if a single man.

11.28　　犯之以事，勿告以言；犯之以害，勿告以利。

Give the men assignments, but do not discuss reasons; give them missions, but do not discuss risks.

11.29　　投之亡地然后存，陷之死地然后生。
故众陷于害，然后能为胜败。

Put them in a lost position; let them seek survival. Put them in a deadly position; let them seek life. Only when an army is in danger does it fight its way out for a victory.

11.30   故

为兵之事，在于顺详敌之意，并敌一向，千里杀将，此谓巧能成事者也。

Thus, the conduct of war is to carefully evaluate the enemy's intentions, concentrate our forces, and take the enemy's commander a thousand miles away. This is the intelligent approach to conducting war.

11.31   是故，政举之日，夷关折符，无通其使；厉

于廊庙之上，以诛其事。

On the decision day, seal all ports and void all travel documents, constrain envoys' movements. At the headquarters, go over plans and finalize a course of action.

11.32 敌人开阖，必亟入之。先其所爱，微与之期。践墨随

敌，以决战事。

When the enemy gives us an opening, seize it immediately. Seek out the head of state's confidants and reach private understandings with them. Follow the enemy unexpectedly; annihilate him when the time comes.

11.33

是故，始如处女，敌人开户；后如脱兔，敌不及拒。

Thus, at the beginning, behave as if a demure maiden, luring the enemy to open his doors. Following that, act as if an untamed hare, advancing beyond the enemy's ability to defend.

Case W-I   The Chü-Hàn Conflict - Hán Xin and Sun Tzu's *Art of Leadership* (203 BCE)

[Passages referenced: 1.14, 3.2, 5.3, 6.6, 7.13, 8.1, 9.1, 11.4, 11.7, 11.9, 11.21, 11.22, 11.28, 11.29]

The Duke of Qin, After conquering six other principalities to unify China for the first time, founded the Qin dynasty in 221 BCE and declared himself Qin Shihuangdi (the founding emperor of the Qin dynasty). A ruthless ruler, his death (reign 221-210 BCE), prompted many peasant groups to revolt.

While the throne was succeeded by one of Qin Shihuangdi's sons to become the Second Emperor of Qin, his reign lasted but five years; he was assassinated (reign 210-206 BCE).

Country in Turmoil

With that regicide, the Qin dynasty (221-206 BCE) came to an end, putting the country in a turmoil. Groups, some peasant and others aristocratic, vied for power, land, and alliance — with the eventual aim at supremacy, at reuniting the country and founding a new dynasty.

In short order, there were but two major alliances — one led by Liu Pang, the Prince of Hàn; the other by Xiang Qi, the Prince of Chü. Their fight for supremacy became known in Chinese history as the Chü-Hàn Conflict (206-202 BCE).

Chü-Hàn Conflict

Of the two principals in this Chü-Hàn Conflict, Xiang Qi, the Prince of Chü, was by far the superior — an all-winning warrior, strong, brave. In contrast, Liu Pang was more a scholar than a warrior — he was thrust into the leadership role more for his intelligence than for his battlefield prowess. Indeed, practically every battle under his command resulted in defeat.

Thus, in this Chü-Hàn Conflict, Chü, based in the west, was gaining. Moving eastward, Xiang Qi, the Prince of Chü annexed more ground and secured more allies. In time, a direct head-to-head confrontation between these two princes became unavoidable, with the Prince of Chü almost sure to prevail.

Hàn's Commander-in-Chief

Thus, the need for Liu Pang, the Prince of Hàn, to remove himself and appoint a commander-in-chief became apparent. One of his ministers, Xiao Ho, recommended Hán Xin.

Hán Xin was an orphan (thus, his year of birth was unknown), but came from an aristocratic family. Self-taught, he knew Sun Wu's *Art of Leadership* by heart. Still, he had no real battlefield experience. It was Liu Pang's confidence in Xiao Ho — and not his confidence in Hán Xin — that led Liu Pang to appoint Hán Xin, reluctantly, to be Hàn's commander-in-chief.[1] The year was 205 BCE.

Hán Xin's Military Successes

Since his appointment as Hàn's commander-in-chief, Hán Xin produced one military success after another. His achievement is considered unparalleled in Chinese military history.[2]

Win Over Princes of Wei and Dai

May - August 205 BCE - Hán Xin produced a win over Bao, the Prince of Wei and an ally of the Prince of Chü. Hán Xin took over Prince of Wei's principality. In this campaign, Hán Xin followed a strategy in Sun Wu's *Art of Leadership* — a sudden strike.[3] "Attack when unprepared; advance where unexpected." (1.14)

September 205 BCE - Hán Xin produced a win over the principality of Dai, another ally of the Prince of Chü.

On to the Principality of Chao

October 204 BCE - In the month immediately following Hán Xin's win over the Prince of Dai, Hán Xin was directed by Liu Pang to confront the Prince of Chao, another of Prince of Chü's allies. (At the time, the country followed the Qin calendar; the beginning of a new year was the first day of the tenth new moon.)

[1] Sima Qian (145-86 BCE), *Shi Ji* (Historical Records), a monumental work of 526,500 words in 130 chapters, chronicled pivotal personalities and events in Chinese history, one of which is on Hán Xin. In Chinese.

[2] Yuan Wei (ed), *Encyclopedia of Chinese Military Campaigns - Volume 1: 3000 BC - 1919* (Beijing: Museum of Chinese Military Affairs, 1994), pp. 133-141. In Chinese.

[3] Harro von Senger, a Swedish sinologist, in his *The Book of Stratagems: Tactics for Triumph and Survival* (New York: Viking, 1991), cites this campaign, at pp. 79-80, as an illustration of a stratagem from a Chinese classic known as *The 36 Stratagems*. His translation, into Swedish, covers 18. Translating from Swedish into English is by Myron B. Gubitz.

Exhausted, Hán Xin nevertheless redeployed his troops across Tai-Hang Mountain to the vicinity of Jing-xin, Chao's stronghold on the right bank of Mian-Màn River (the light curved double lines bisecting the map in Exhibit 1).

Case W-I Exhibit 1
The Battle of Jing-xin (204 BCE)

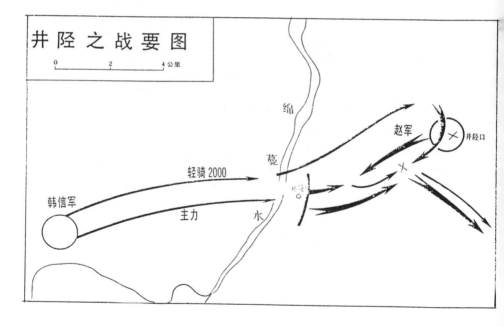

Yuan Wei (ed), *Encyclopedia of Chinese Military Campaigns - Volume 1: 3000 BC - 1919* (Beijing: Museum of Chinese Military Affairs, 1994)

Hán Xin first set up his camp some distance from the left bank, giving his troops some needed rest. Indeed, moving into the enemy's headquarters area with fatigued troops that were far outnumbered, Hán Xin was in no mood to initiate any offensive action.

Enemy Troops Numbered 200,000

The troops of the Prince of Chao, augmented by those from the Prince of Dai (who fled from his principality to join Chao's), totaled 200,000. Their home base was on high grounds of Jing-xin, on the right side of the Mian-Màn River.

Proposal to Surround Not Accepted

A strategist in the Chao-Dai camp, knowing that Hán Xin's troops were substantially outnumbered, proposed to the Prince of Chao that 30,000 of Prince of Dai's very best be sent to Hán Xin's back side to cut off his supply line and weaponry route — in effect, to surround him, allowing him neither a route to advance nor one to retreat.

The Prince of Chao rejected that proposal, on the ground that "a virtuous army does not employ deceptive plans nor unorthodox strategies."

Hán Xin Encamped With Back to River

Hán Xin's intelligence brought back this piece of good news. Elated, Hán Xin decided to move his troops close to the Mian-Màn River, encamping only thirty miles from the enemy's headquarters (represented by the larger of two circles near the lower left corner of the map in Exhibit 1) — "When in enemy territory, moving deep promotes unison." (11.21)

There, Hán Xin encamped and began a reciprocal surveillance to await the spring's arrival for a decisive battle.

Hán Xin Had a Strategy

One spring night, Hán Xin selected 2,000 cavalry, each given a red flag (the color of the Principality of Hàn), and directed them, by using obscure roads and sheltered terrain, to move toward the vicinity of enemy headquarters without being detected — and wait. He also gave them the following instructions:

As the combat begins, the Chao army, seeing our army in retreat, will come out from their base *en masse* in pursuit. Seeing this happening, you are to advance to the enemy headquarters, remove their flags, and replace them with the ones you are given.

Hán Xin offered no explanations — following exactly what Sun Wu said: "Give the men assignments, but do not discuss reasons." (11.28)

In the meantime, Hán Xin gave the other troops very little food, stating that "We'll have a feast tonight after we defeat the Chao army." The troops, unconvinced, gave only a perfunctory vote of appreciation.

Hán Xin Set Up His Headquarters

Hán Xin then said to his officers: "The Chao army encamps on high ground. Before they will come out to fight our advance force, they would like to know where our headquarters are located, which is where our flag is hoisted. They fear that we might retreat at critical moments."

Thus, Hán Xin sent 10,000 of his troops to set up camp on the east bank of the Mian-Màn River (represented by a small circle just to the right of the river in Exhibit 1). This meant that the camp would be set with the river behind them, a practice frowned upon by Sun Wu — "Encamp on high grounds, facing the sun." (9.1), "not to encamp in hazardous land" (8.1), and "hasten through hazardous land" (11.4, 11.22)

Thus, Hán Xin's set-up caused the Chao army to snicker.

Hán Xin Began His Attack

The next morning, Hán Xin set up the commander-in-chief's flag, led his troops to advance toward Jing-xin with great fanfare. The Chao army opened their camp gate and proceeded to meet Hán Xin and his troops.

After a suitably long combat action, Hán Xin and his other generals pretended defeat, dropped their commander-in-chief's flags and other baits, and retreated toward the river bank, with the Chao army in hot pursuit. (Here, Hán Xin again followed Sun Wu: "if we are determined to fight, the enemy will have to come out and fight, even though they are stationed on high grounds" (6.6))

By the riverside, Hán Xin's army opened the camp door to let them in and then engage them in combat. (Here, Hán Xin again followed Sun Wu: "with the enemy coming down from high grounds, do not intercede frontally." (7.13)) In the meantime, other men in the Chao army who vacated their base to collect the discarded flags and other baits were forced to participate in the combat.

With the river behind them, Hán Xin's army had no way to retreat but fight. And fight they did, as the numerically superior Chao army were unable to subdue them. (Here, Hán Xin also applied Sun Wu; this was discussed by Hán Xin himself (see below).)

Hán Xin's Cavalry Moved In

In the meantime, with the Chao army's camp vacant, the 2,000 cavalry hiding in its vicinity charged in. They removed Principality of Chao's flags and replaced them with those they carried with them — all 2,000 of them.

With fighting at a stand still, the Chao army decided to retreat to their base. Nearing it and seeing the 2,000 Principality of Hàn's flags hoisted all over the camp, the troops thought that the camp had been overtaken and that the Prince of Chao had surrendered. The troops were entrapped and began to flee, causing chaos.

Chao Army Uttered Defeated

This enabled Hán Xin's troops to attack from the west (heavy arrows in the eastward direction in Exhibit 1) and his calvary to attack from the east (heaving arrows in the southwest direction), the Chao army was utterly defeated. The Prince of Wei was decapitated; the Prince of Chao was captured.

At the feast Hán Xin promised that evening, officers honored Hán Xin with the decapitated head of the Prince of Wei. They asked: "*The Art of Leadership* calls for encampment with high ground to the right and at back, and with water to the left and in front. This time, our commander-in-chief asked us to set up camp with water at our back. We were also told that we would have a feast after defeating Chao's army. At the time, we were not convinced. Still, we won. What is the strategy?"

Strategy Is in *The Art of Leadership*

Hán Xin answered: "This strategy also comes out of the *Art of Leadership*; perhaps you did not pay much attention. Does the *Art of Leadership* not say: 'Put them in a lost position; let them seek survival. Put them in a deadly position; let them seek life'? (11.29)

"Also, I had little occasion to comfort and train our officers and men — analogous to sending people on the street to fight. In such a scenario, unless I 'put [them] in danger' (11.29), they are unlikely to fight for their lives. Given an exit, they are likely to flee. They are unlikely to 'fight [their] way out for a victory.'" (11.29)

The officers answered in unison: "That is exactly right. Our commander-in-chief's planning is 'way above our comprehension." Indeed, this was what Hán Xin excelled. In Sun Wu's words, "War is planning. Plan beyond the enemy's ability to anticipate." (11.9)

Hán Xin Achieved the Ultimate

After this win over the Prince of Chao, Hán Xin sent an envoy to the Prince of Yen, persuading the prince to surrender without a fight. The prince surrendered — thereby allowing Hán Xin to score another win *without a fight*. This is the ultimate, as Sun Wu said: "engaging in 100 wars and winning 100 is not the best of the best; winning the enemy's army without engaging in war is." (3.2)

Hán Xin an Ardent Student of Sun Wu's *Art of Leadership*

Unquestionably, Hán Xin was Sun Wu's most ardent student. He applied Sun Wu's other strategies to score two additional memorable wins.

Immediately after the Prince of Yen's surrender, in November 204 BCE, Hán Xin, using unorthodoxy, scored a win over the combined forces of the Princes of Chi and Chü — "use orthodox formations to engage the enemy, but use unorthodox formations to win." (5.2)

In a long intermittent engagement lasting some 17 months (from April 205 BCE to August 203 BCE), with the assistance of troops directed by Liu Pang (from the west), those directed by Pang Yue (from the east), and those Hán Xin directed himself (from the north), they surrounded the Prince of Chü's troops and inflicted the latter with heavy losses. The strategy used was surrounding — "On circumscribed land, we must barricade the remaining openings." (11.22)[4]

Hán Xin Ended the Chü-Hàn Conflict

This 17-month long intermittent engagement, known as the Battle of Cheng Gao, was the turning point in the Chü-Hàn Conflict.

A few months later, in December 202 BCE, Hán Xin engaged in a decisive battle against troops personally led by the Prince of Chü. With numerical superiority on his side, Hán Xin easily cornered the Prince of Chü.

[4] von Senger, in his *Stratagems*, cites, at p. 116, another instance where Hán Xin used Sun Wu's "march through routes he [the enemy] does not suspect" (11.7) to transport his troops.

At the bank of Ou River, Xiang Qi, the Prince of Chü, could have retreated to his homeland by crossing the river on a boat moored at the dock for his use. But, he said: "I left with 8,000 of the finest young men in my state. They are all lost. How can I return to face their elders?" Thereupon, using his own sword, he took his life.

With that, the years-long Chü-Hàn Conflict (206-202 BCE) came to an end. A new dynasty, the Hàn dynasty, was founded, retroactive to 206 BCE, when the Qin dynasty ended. Liu Pang was proclaimed as its first king (reign 206-195 BCE).[5]

[5] A biographical sketch of Hán Xin is in David H. Li, *The Genealogy of Chess* (Bethesda: Premier, 1998), pp. 143-147. Hán Xin, during the siege in 204-203 BCE, invented XiangQi (Chinese Chess) as a means of entertaining as well as educating his troops in war management. This invention is discussed in Case WS-1, as one of the case studies at the back of Essay 7.

Case P-11   Politics. Democratic Party Presidential Nomination for 2000

[Passages referenced: 3.7, 3.9]

The occupant of the White House since January 20, 1993, has been President William Jefferson Clinton, a Democrat. Having served two 4-year terms, he can no longer stand for reelection. Thus, the Democratic Party needs a new presidential nominee for Year 2000.

The Clinton Administration

Under President Clinton, the United States has enjoyed an unprecedented 40-month economic prosperity. All economic and social indicators are at their post-war best — inflation rate at 2 percent, unemployment rate at 4 percent, crime rate trending downward. People, thus, are generally happy — as evidenced by the record high consumer confidence index.

A blemish in the Clinton administration is, perhaps, his personal indiscretions that prompted an impeachment inquiry in the Congress in 1999. He overcame that, despiteRepublican majority in both the House of Representatives and the Senate, since impeachment requires a two-thirds majority vote, which Republicans could not muster.

The Gore Candidacy

Given the unprecedented economic prosperity, the Clinton administration's Vice President, Al Gore, Jr., would be the Democratic Party's logical choice as its presidential nominee. Grooming him for this role, President Clinton has given Vice President Gore many special assignments for which Vice President Gore serves with distinction. So, for practical purposes, the nomination of Vice President Gore as the Democratic Party's standard bearer is merely a formality — with no challenge expected.

The Bradley Challenge

But, in comes Bill Bradley, former senator from New Jersey and a former professional basketball player. More idealistic, he wants health insurance extended to everyone — currently, some 12 million are uninsured. Improving education, revamping campaign finance, and tightening gun control are also high on his list.

With these as his campaign issues, Mr. Bradley began his quest for the Democratic Party's nomination in January 1999, in New Hampshire — exactly one year before that state's primary.

The issues clearly resonate with voters. Mr. Bradley is thus able to assemble a war chest almost matching Vice President Gore's — not a mean feat. Various pre-primary polls also show Mr. Bradley gaining ground on Vice President Gore as time passes.

Iowa Caucus and New Hampshire Primary

In Iowa, the pre-caucus poll shows Mr. Bradley lagging behind Vice President Gore. But, in New Hampshire, the reverse is so. In the week preceding the New Hampshire primary, thinking that he has a win there, Mr. Bradley spends more time campaigning in Iowa to shore up support and reduce the gap. This proves to be unsuccessful, as Vice President Gore wins Iowa handily.

This strategy also backfires on Mr. Bradley in New Hampshire. The pre-primary lead he has evaporates on primary day:

Case P-11 Exhibit 1
Results of New Hampshire Primary
February 1, 2000

	Votes	Percent	Delegates to date
Gore	76,527	50	42
Bradley	70,295	46	27

Be Selective and Be Prepared

While the loss in Iowa is not unexpected, losing in New Hampshire certainly hurts. Here, Sun Wu may offer some counsel. Of Sun Wu's "five ways to winning," two come readily to mind: "Knowing when to fight and when not to fight"; "being ready and rested while waiting for tired enemy troops." (3.7) Indeed, on both points, Senator McCain — Mr. Bradley's counterpart in the Republican party's presidential nomination race — understands well. Senator McCain elects to bypass the Iowa caucus to concentrate on the New Hampshire primary — and produces stunning results.

Another passage by Sun Wu is, perhaps, even more pertinent and commands Mr. Bradley's attention: "with knowledge of our enemy and knowledge of ourselves, we will not be in a precarious position — not even once in 100 battles. Knowing not our enemy but only ourselves, we are as likely to win a battle as to lose one. Knowing neither our enemy nor ourselves, we will lose every battle." (3.9)

A Four-Week Drought

After the New Hampshire primary, the next contest for Democrats is Washington's primary on February 29. This is a long stretch. During this four-week period, Bradley has nothing tangible to show — and nothing for the media to talk or write about.

This long drought is demoralizing by itself. But, in the meantime, other developments beyond Mr. Bradley's control are beginning to overwhelm him.

During this four-week period, Republican primaries are generating a lot of excitement, mainly Senator McCain's ups and downs, and his being in the center of a religion-politics controversy — his winning New Hampshire, losing South Carolina, winning again in Michigan and Arizona, and fighting furiously in Virginia, South Dakota, and Washington. Thus, Republican primaries are grabbing all the headlines, crowding Mr. Bradley's candidacy from the front page.

Unfortunate Timing

When Mr. Bradley starts his campaign, he is the lone voice — in both parties — citing campaign finance reform as a key issue. Though Senator McCain advocates campaign finance reform in his campaign in the Republican Party, at the beginning, his voice is too faint to be heard. When the two, early on, in a joint appearance, shook hands to pledge campaign finance reform, it was Mr. Bradley's stature that carried the day.

But, with Republican contests grabbing the headlines, it is now Senator McCain's view on campaign finance reform that gets the media attention. Senator McCain has the spotlight, while Mr. Bradley's campaign is reported, if at all, only in inconspicuous inside pages.

It seems that the public can accept at most one reformer at any given time. With Senator McCain in the spotlight and the darling of the media, Mr. Bradley's reform views are either slighted or ignored. Mr. Bradley, in short, has lost the timing advantage to Senator McCain.

Washington Primary

As to the Washington primary, Mr. Bradley works very hard — investing five days campaigning there. But the results are disappointing — trailing Vice President Gore by a score of 27 percent to 73 percent.

Looking Forward to New York

With this poor showing, key supporters advise Mr. Bradley to withdraw. With Super Tuesday but six days away, Mr. Bradley decides to continue, hoping to win one or two states — in particular, New York, in which he has a strong name recognition, and led its 1999 pre-primary polls. Indeed, Mr. Bradley continues to do well there.

One reason is that Mr. Bradley, at one time, was a star professional basketballer playing for the New York franchise. His elegant fund-raising party, held in New York earlier in 2000 featuring fellow basketball stars, was the talk of the town — unique, memorable, and highly successful, both financially and publicity-wise.

March 1 Debate

On March 1, Democratic candidates have their final televised debate before the Super Tuesday. During the debate, Mr. Bradley is more conciliatory and accommodating, signaling his intention to bow out on a high note and on good terms with Vice President Gore.

Results of Super Tuesday

Results of votes cast in the Super Tuesday are as shown below.

Case P-11 Exhibit 2
Results of Primaries and Caucuses
Held on Tuesday, March 7, 2000
(In descending order of number of delegates)
(100% counted unless noted with *)

	Delegates	Gore		Bradley	
California	367	**1,965,515**	81%	437,897	18%
*New York	243	**698,833**	65	359,981	33
Ohio	146	**717,389**	74	241,298	25
Massachusetts	93	**337,175**	60	210,132	37
Georgia	77	**239,015**	84	46,215	16
*Washington	75		**68**		29
Missouri	75	**171,528**	65	89,094	34
Maryland	68	**334,405**	67	141,445	28
Connecticut	54	**97,151**	55	72,864	42
*Maine	23	**33,726**	54	25,900	41
Rhode Island	22	**25,975**	57	18,614	41
Hawaii	22	NA		NA	
Idaho	18		**63**		33
*Vermont	15	**26,719**	55	21,561	44
*North Dakota	14		**78**		22
Delegates to date		**1,424**		**412**	

Mr. Bradley Withdraws

On Thursday, March 9, two days after the Super Tuesday, Mr. Bradley withdraws from the race for Democratic presidential nomination for Year 2000.

12 火 攻 篇

USE OF INCENDIARY

12.1 凡火攻有五，一曰火人，二曰火积，
三曰火辎，四曰火库，五曰火队。

Targets of incendiary are five: officers and men, food storage facilities, chariots and weaponry, armories, and transportation equipment and routes.

12.2 行火必有因，因必素具。
发火有时，起火有日。时者，天之燥也；日者，月在箕、
壁、翼、轸也。凡此四宿者，风起之日也。

Doing incendiary requires special supplies; they must be stored and be at ready. Time to instigate incendiary is the dry season, on days when the moon position is at the Sieve, Wall, Wing, and Cross Bar[1] — these are likely to be windy days.

[1] When the 28 lunar positions are divided into four quarters of seven positions each, Sieve occupies the last one of the first quarter; Wall, last one of the second quarter; Wing, the sixth one of the third quarter; and Cross Bar, the last one of the fourth quarter. Days with these moon positions are said to be windy days.

12.3 凡火攻，必因五火之变而应之。火发于内，则
早应之于外。火发其兵静，待而勿攻；极其火央，可从而
从之，不可从而止之。

In using incendiary to support an attack, what to do is based on the fire's path. When a fire is initiated inside the enemy camp, be ready at the outside. When a fire is initiated but the enemy is calm, wait and take no action. When the fire turns violent, attack when the situation seems ripe; otherwise, refrain from attacking.

12.4   火可发于外，无待于内，以时发之。

When incendiary may be instigated from outside, there is no need to instigate it inside the enemy camp; just make sure that the timing is right.

12.5   火发上风，无攻下风。昼风久，夜风止。

When a fire is moving up-wind, do not attack from the down-wind. When wind is blowing strong during the day, it is likely to stop during the night.

12.6   凡军必知有五火之变，以数守之。

An army must understand these five fire variations, seize opportunities, and take appropriate action.

12.7   故以火佐攻者明，以水佐攻者强。水可以绝，不可以夺。

Using incendiary as support, the attack is furious; using water as support, the attack is violent. Water may isolate the enemy, but cannot destroy them.

12.8   夫战胜攻取，而不修其功者，凶，命曰费留。故曰：明主虑之，良将修之。

After winning the war and capturing the enemy's land, it does not bode well when the defeated are not care for.[2] Otherwise, the effort is wasted.[3] Thus, it may be said that a sagacious head of state is cognizant of this, and a conscientious commander acts upon this.

[2] From this sentence onward to the end of this essay, Sun Wu begins to offer his philosophical views on war. While this seems to be an odd place to present these views, Sun Wu really has no alternative. What follows is profound, but he does not want to infuriate his royal reader nor give his excellency the impression that he, Sun Wu, is ambivalent about war. Thus, Sun Wu offers these views without undue emphasis nor undue importance — the original, from this sentence down to the end, has but 104 words.

This very first sentence is most profound. Ostensibly, it discusses postwar reconstruction, but this discussion is based on an unstated premise: that the war just concluded was a just war, that the war fought was to allow Direction to prevail — over an evil head of state. Thus, Sun Wu seems to say, the people are innocent. Though their head of state is defeated, they are nevertheless innocent. They should not be abused (above all, they should not be enslaved, not uncommon in Sun Wu's time), but, rather, be cared for — be allowed to regain their footing and become useful members of the community, now an integral part of the winning state.

[3] This is a delicate statement euphemistically presented. What Sun Wu wants to say, it seems, is this. If a head of state initiates a war on the pretense that it is to have Direction prevail, but, upon winning this self-claimed just war, takes actions that are beneath this very Direction, then, this head of state is no better than the one just disposed. "The effort is wasted."

Indeed, what will be the pretense the next time this winning head of state initiates another war? Can his excellency recruit a commander who, absent the enthusiasm of a just war, will risk his life to lead in such an enterprise? Can the commander, in turn, recruit men who would risk their lives to fight in such a war? Sun Wu's own assessment: "it does not bode well."

12.9   非利不动，非得不用，非危不战。

Where there is no advantage, move not. Where there is no gain, act not. Where there is no danger, fight not.

12.10
主不可以怒而举军，将不可以愠而致战。合于利而动，不合于利而止。怒可复喜，愠可复悦，亡国不可以复存，死者不可以复生。

A head of state is not to authorize war just to even a grudge. A commander is not to initiate fight just to avenge a slight. Act only when the reason to act is on our side; resist from acting when it is not. Anger may turn into joy, displeasure into pleasure, but a conquered state cannot bring back her statehood, and the dead cannot be bought back to life.

12.11　故明君慎之，良将警之，此安国全军之道也。

Thus, a sagacious head of state exercises care [in deciding whether to engage in war], and a conscientious commander reminds himself [of the devastations of war]. This is the Direction — for a state to have peace and for an army to be whole.

Case W-J　World War I - The World's First Tank Battle (1917)

In Sun Wu's time, incendiary devices represent new technology. New technology in World War I (1914-1918) is the tank.

During World War I, fighting a war across the vast span of continental Europe was a major problem in logistics. How to move an attacking force through swampy "no man's land" to the enemy side without succumbing to its artillery surveillance was a real challenge.

A Technological Leap

Seeing a caterpillar tractor in Antwerp in July 1914 by a friend, a British military engineer Lt. Col Ernest D. Swinton envisaged its potential in military use.[1] Experimenting with a small number of these tractors shipped to England by October, Swinton and his colleagues made the technological leap — wedding an armored body (then in use on scout cars) to caterpillar traction to form a fully tracked combat machine. It was tested in secret in England's countryside, practicing driving and maintenance.[2]

[1] Anne Cipriano Venzon in *The United States in the First World War: an Encyclopedia* (New York: Garland, 1995), entry under "Tanks," pp. 590-592.

[2] Lyn Macdonald, 1914-1918: Voices and Images of the Great War (London: Michael Joseph, 1988), entry under "Corporal A. E. Lee, A Battalion, of Tank Corps," pp. 167-168.

Deployment of This New Combat Machine

While still under development, the field people debated its proper deployment. Winston Churchill[1], Britain's First Lord of the Admiralty, visualized it as an armored infantry carrier[3] — its War Office still called it *amoured car.*

The General Staff, on the other hand, intended to use it as an infantry support weapon, with each unit receiving a few. Swinton, its developer, saw it as a weapons platform — with its semi-immunity to small-arms fire, it could swiftly cross no man's land, subdue trench strongpoints, and arrive in advance of the attacking infantry.

When Britain's General Douglas Haig took over the overall field commandership from the French on December 19, 1915, and learned of plans to construct this weapon — its name was still under wraps — he was full of enthusiasm. He planned to use a large number of these armored vehicles in his mid-1916 offensive on the Somme.

Conflicting Demands on the New Weapon

These conflicting demands certainly added pressure on the new vehicle's development — and, later, its production. As a troops carrier, the machine needed to be load-bearing and spacious. As an infantry support weapon, it needed to be agile and versatile. As a weapons platform, it needed to withstand artillery shelling and swampy terrain. And, as a major force in combat, it needed industrial muscle in the homeland to produce them in large numbers at a fast clip and superior quality.

All the while, the weapon was still under development and experimentation. Questions such as: Can it withstand enemy shell fire? Can it negotiate difficult terrain? How is its maneuverability? Its reliability? Maintainability?

World's First Massed Tank Attack

The world's first massed tank attack was mounted on November 20, 1917, on a two-miles-deep Hindenburg Line west of Cambrai. Field Marshal Haig's objective was to end the trench-warfare stalemate by penetrating the enemy line, then take it in reverse westward and northward.[4]

[3] Cited by Robin Prior and Trevor Wilson in *Passchendaele: the Untold Story* (New Haven: Yale University Press, 1996), p.16.

[4] George Bruce (ed), *Harbottle's Dictionary of Battles* (London: Hart-Davis, 1971), entry under "Cambrai - *World War I,*" p. 55.

Case W-J Exhibit 1
Cambrai, Belgium, November 1917

New Line Won by the Great British Drive on Cambrai

The broken line indicates approximately the position reached by Field Marshal Haig's advance, which began early Tuesday morning and has penetrated at one point (Cantaing) to within less than three miles of Cambrai The drive at Cambrai imperils the entire Hindenburg line from St. Quentin to the sea.
The inserted map shows the general configuration of the western front.

New York Times, November 22, 1917

Field Report of Cambrai Attack

The Cambrai attack, on November 20, 1917, is reported as an across-the-page headline and cover story by the *New York Times* on November 22. The headline, all caps on three lines, states:

HAIG HURLS HIS ARMY AT CAMBRAI, GAINING FIVE MILES;
HUNDREDS OF TANKS LEAD DRIVE, CAVALRY CAPTURES GUNS
8,000 PRISONERS TAKEN, FOE'S LAST DEFENSES REACHED

Column-wide subheadings add the following:

TANKS INSURE THE VICTORY
Masses of Them Open Way for
  British Infantry's Charges
DESTROY WIRE DEFENSES
Giant Machines Screened by Smoke
  to Baffle the German Gunners
HAIG HID HIS PREPARATIONS
Moved Tanks and Guns at Night and
  Few Officers Knew His Real Plans
First Stage of the Battle

Order Tanks to Do Their "Damnedest"

A second dispatch, after secrecy was lifted, reports, in part, as follows:

These squadrons of tanks were led into action by the General commanding their corps, who carried his flag on his own tank .... To every officer and men of the tanks he sent this order of the day before the battle:

"The Tank Corps expects that every tank this day will do its damnedest."

They did. As the pilot of one of them told me, they "played merry hell." They moved forward in small groups, several hundreds of them, rolled down the German wires, trampled down its lines, and then crossed the deep gulf of the Hindenburg main line ....

The German troops knew nothing of the fate that awaited them until out of the gloom of dawn they saw these great numbers of gray inhuman creatures roaring down upon them, crushing down their wire, crossing their impregnable lines, firing fiercely from their flanks, and sweeping the trenches with machine gun bullets.

Infantry Penetration Lacking

For this battle, a total of 434 tanks were involved, of which 378 were used in combat and the remainder for specialized support. These tanks were backing up six infantry divisions and 40,000 cavalry. By 11 a.m. on November 20, the entire six-mile Hindenburg front (main, reserve, and final systems) was broken.

The road to Cambrai was thus open, but the calvary, with a bridge down, was unable to cross the Scheldt canal at Masnières. Using another bridge, one mile east at Marconing, was not explored. Without this attempt, the chance to exploit the tanks' historic breakthrough was totally lost.[5]

German Counter-attack

From the next day onward, many tanks, for one mechanical reason or another, were out of action. Perforce, the infantry had to resume playing the main role.

Ten days later, on November 30, General Ludendorff, with 16 fresh divisions, ordered a counter-attack against the British lines, leading the way with gas shells. Soon, much of the gains were lost, and Haig ordered a withdrawal to shorten the salient.

Thus, what could have been a decisive battle ended with little gain for the Allies.

Ninety Thousand Lost, No Gain

The Cambrai operation was said to be Haig's hope to counterbalance the dismal results of the Third Battle of Ypres. [See Endnote below.] Still, with both timing (a surprise attack) and new technology (tanks) on his side, General Haig produced no gains but another 40,000 dead or wounded of his own countrymen.[6]

Two reasons account for this no-gain end result: (1) failing to use light tanks to exploit but relying instead on the cavalry, and (2) poor generalship. [For reason 2, see Endnote beginning on page 188.]

---

[5] "Cambrai" in *Dictionary of Battles*, p. 55.

[6] "Cambrai" in *Dictionary of Battles*, p. 55. The German's losses were 50,000 killed and wounded, and 11,000 taken prisoners.

Endnote

Douglas Haig rose quickly, owing to his marriage to Dorothy Crespigny, maid-of-honour to both Queen Victoria and Queen Alexandria — from staff to Director of Military Operations, to Commander of I Corps of the British European Front in 1914, and to being in charge of overall command on December 19, 1915.

Cool, aloof, unimaginative, Haig was not overly receptive to new ideas. His tactics were marked by an "attack at all costs" mentality.[7]

Battles at the Somme and at Passchendaele, both under Haig's commandership, produced heavy losses[8,9] — for which he was persistently blamed, and with which he earned the nickname of "the butcher."[10]

[7] Philip J. Haythornwaite, *The World War One Source Book* (London: Arms & Armour, 1992), entry under "Haig, Sir Douglas, 1st Earl Haig of Bemersyde," at pp. 328-330.

[8] The battle at the Somme lasted from July 1 to November 18, 1916, with the Allies advancing seven miles along a 20-mile front. British casualties were 418,000 killed or wounded; French, 195,000; Germans, 650,000. "Somme I" in *Dictionary of Battles*, p. 238.

[9] The battle at Passchendaele, from October 30 to November 10, 1917, the last operation in the Third Battle of Ypres, which began on July 31, fell "significantly short of his [Haig's] original goals of advancing inland beyond Ghent and freeing the Belgian coast." British losses: 80,000 killed, 230,000 wounded, and 14,000 taken prisoners; German losses: 50,000, 113,000, and 37,000, respectively. David H. Burg and Edward Purcell, *Almanac of World War I* (Louisville: University Press of Kentucky, 1998), entry under "10 November 1917," p. 188.

[10] "Haig" in *World War One Source Book*, p. 329.

Case P-6 Republican Party Presidential Nomination for 2000 - The South Carolina Primary; Momentum vs. Firewall

[Passages referenced: 5.2, 5.3, 12.2, 12.3]

Coming out of New Hampshire, with a win — and a larger-than-expected win at that — Senator McCain clearly has momentum.

Senator McCain Has Momentum

This momentum is evidenced by two entirely different phenomena. One, without setting foot in Delaware, Senator McCain is honored with 25 percent of total votes cast. Though this is behind Governor Bush's 51 percent, it is ahead of Mr. Forbes's 20, even though Mr. Forbes campaigns heavily there — this is heartening.

Two — even more heartening — is the inflow of spontaneous campaign contributions, coming in through the internet — unsolicited, at the rate of $250,000 a day, and mainly in small amounts.

This much needed infusion of money is doubly welcome — it not only augments the almost depleted treasury, spent to counter the negative advertising from the Bush camp, but also gets the federal matching funds almost dollar for dollar. (An individual contributing $350 or below is matched, dollar for dollar, with federal funds.)

Coming through the internet unsolicited also suggests that these contributors are younger, better educated, and more knowledgeable in current affairs — attributes of voters whose support Senator McCain very much wants to attract. And they are doing so, not only by votes, but by money as well.

Great news all around. But reality beckons.

Senator McCain in Inhospitable Territory

Senator McCain first visited South Carolina on August 1, 1999, in the same, now-famous "Straight Talk Express" bus. It was a lonely journey; he was able to attract but a handful people's attention in each stop he made en route.

During that 1999 visit, he was made painfully clear that South Carolina is a conservative state. A state that prides itself in "heritages," in flying the Confederacy flag on the dome of its State House.

Needless to say, South Carolina is also a state that follows its leaders without question. South Carolina was the first state to secede the Union to form the Confederate States of America. South Carolina supports the candidate its leadership endorses.

For Year 2000, the leadership of South Carolina endorses Governor Bush. South Carolina is Bush territory — Governor Bush has a definite location advantage.

Senator McCain's Strategy

But, Senator McCain has the momentum. And momentum means a lot. It can overcome a lot; even Sun Wu says so: "Water rushing down can move stones; this is momentum." (5.3)

But to move stone with water takes a while, even with momentum on water's side. Coming out of New Hampshire, Senator McCain has momentum, but has 18 days to turn the tide. A new quick-working strategy to complement with momentum is needed.

How? How about another page from Sun Wu? "Use expected formations to engage the enemy, but use unexpected formations to win." (5.2) How do we apply this concept here? Call upon the independents and the Democrats.

Independents and "Reagan Democrats"

Senator McCain has used this strategy in New Hampshire — but only in part. There, with the primary open to registered Republican voters and independents, Senator McCain appealed to the latter group — with great success.

South Carolina is an "open" primary — any registered voter may vote, irrespective of party registration. Courting independents is probably okay — but courting Democrats?

What is the alternative? With South Carolina's registered Republican voters overwhelmingly in the Bush corner, with the establishment building a firewall to protect Governor Bush, appealing to independent votes will not be enough.

Democrats must be courted. We need them to win in the general election in November. Why not now?

Sun Wu Advises Caution

In using incendiary, Sun Wu suggests caution: "In incendiary, special supplies are needed; they must be stored and be at ready." (12.2) Is the McCain camp ready? "Time to instigate incendiary is the dry season." (12.2) Is timing right?

How will the Bush camp react? "When a fire is initiated but the enemy is calm, wait and take no action." (12.3) Only time will tell.

The Establishment Reacts

The Bush camp — or, more precisely, the establishment — reacts with a vengeance.

The religious right calls the fellow faithfuls to come out and vote. And vote for Governor Bush.

And the faithfuls certainly do what they always do — support the leadership. The turnout for the 2000 primary is thus the largest ever — twice the 1996 turnout. And they cast their votes for Governor Bush.

Results of the South Carolina Primary

The results of the South Carolina primary, held on Saturday, February 19, 2000, are shown as Exhibit 1.

Case P-6 Exhibit 1
Result of South Carolina Primary
February 19, 2000
(99% of precincts reporting)

	Votes	*Percent*	*Delegates*	
			Added	*ToDate*
Bush	301,050	53	34	61
McCain	237,888	42	3	14
Keyes	25,510	4	-	4

On to Michigan

Well, the appeal-to-Democrat strategy has not worked. Or, perhaps, it works but simply not well enough.

Before New Hampshire, the pre-primary poll in South Carolina shows Governor Bush leading by some 30 points. The final results shows that Governor Bush wins by but 11 points.

Though Governor Bush's win in South Carolina is by but 11 points — highly satisfying but certainly not a "blowout" as many pundits describe it — Senator McCain's momentum seems to have been arrested.

There is talk that Michigan, three days away, will be Senator McCain's last hurrah. In any case, this time, the media embrace Governor Bush and put his photo on newsmagazine covers.

What a difference a primary makes. On to Michigan.

13 用 间 篇

USE OF INTELLIGENCE

13.1　　凡兴师十万，出征千里，百姓之费，公家之奉，日费千金；内外骚动，怠于道路，不得操事者，七十万家。

Raising an army of 100,000 and sending it 1,000 miles away are burdensome to the people as well as to the state treasury — spending 1,000 pieces of gold per day, creating disequilibrium inside and out, diverting 700,000 households to care for soldiers en route and enduring dislocations at home.

13.2　　相守数年，以争一日之胜，而爱爵禄百金，不知敌之情者，不仁之至也，非民之将也，非主之佐也，非胜之主也。

Preparation for war takes years; fighting a war takes but one day. A commander who is more concerned with his emolument and the state treasury than with seeking information about his enemy is ignoble to the utmost. He is not a worthy commander for the people. He is not a worthy advisor to the head of state. He is not in command for a win.

13.3

故明君贤将，所以动而胜人，成功出于众者，先知也。先知者，不可取于鬼神，不可象于事，不可验于度，必取于人，知敌之情者也。

The reason a sagacious head of state or an intelligent commander acts and wins, succeeds beyond the conventional expectation, is foreknowledge. Foreknowledge is based not on oracles, not on analogies, not on astrology, but on men who have information on the enemy.

13.4 故用间有五：有乡间、有内间、有反间、有死间、有生间。五间俱起，莫知其道，是为神纪，人君之宝也。

Sources of intelligence are five: local intelligence, insider intelligence, double intelligence, counterintelligence, and live intelligence. When all five are used concurrently, their work is wizardry beyond anyone's comprehension. These sources of intelligence are to be treasured by head of states.

13.5 乡间者，因其乡人而用之。内间者，因其官人而用之。反间者，因其敌间而用之。

Local intelligence is provided by ordinary people in the enemy's midst but in· our employ; insider intelligence, by officers in the enemy's court but in our employ; double intelligence, by the enemy's own intelligence working for us.

13.6 死间者，为诳事于外，令吾间知之，而传于敌间也。生间者，反报也。

Counterintelligence[1] is misinformation, flowing about in our camp with seeming credibility, intended to induce enemy intelligence in our midst to transmit as intelligence to the enemy. Live intelligence is in-person reporting by our own intelligence returning from behind enemy lines.

[1] The term used by Sun Wu means, literally, *dead intelligence*, with, perhaps, a double meaning. One, the enemy, upon acting on the misinformation, is likely to incur heavy casualties. Two, realizing that the intelligence gathered is but misinformation, the enemy may take drastic action against the person(s) supplying same.

13.7 故三军之亲，莫亲于间，赏莫厚于间，事莫密于间。

In a three-battalion army, no one needs accorded more confidence than intelligence, no one needs rewarded more heavily than intelligence, nothing needs guarded more secretively than intelligence.

13.8 非圣不能用间，非仁不能使间，非微妙不能得间之实。

No one except those who are righteous and intelligent knows whom to employ for intelligence work. No one except those who are noble knows how to motivate people in intelligence. No one except those who are discerning knows what to make out of intelligence.

13.9　　　微哉微哉，无所不用间也。

What a delicate matter! What a delicate matter! There is no time nor place where intelligence cannot be employed.

13.10　　　间事未发，而先闻者，间与所告者皆死。

Where intelligence is leaked before it has served its purpose, the provider and recipient of such intelligence are at risk and are to die.

13.11　　凡军之所欲击，城之所欲攻，人之所欲杀，必先知其守将、左右、谒者、门者、舍人之姓名，令吾间必 索知之。

Before our army strikes, before a citadel is attacked, before a dignitary is assassinated, we must know the names of the commander who is defending, his aides-de-camps, his visitors, and members of his inner circles. We must ask our intelligence to seek these out.

13.12　　必索敌人之间来间我者，因而利之，导而舍之，故反间可得而用也。

In order to seek information from enemy intelligence caught in our camp, we need to induce him, enlighten him, and then send him back to his home camp. This is how we secure the services of double intelligence.

13.13　　　因是而知之，故乡间、内间可得而使也；

Through double intelligence, we secure the services of local intelligence and insider intelligence.

13.14   因是而知之，故死间为诳事，可使告敌；

Through double intelligence, our misinformation gains credibility, inducing enemy intelligence in our midst to transmit it as intelligence to the enemy.

13.15   因是而知之，故生间可使如期。

Through double intelligence, our own intelligence in the enemy's midst can return to report with regularity.

13.16   五间之事，主必知之。知之必在于反间。
故反间不可不厚也。

The head of state must be made aware of these five sources of intelligence. Among these, double intelligence is critically important. Thus, double intelligence must be heavily rewarded.

13.17   昔殷之兴也，伊挚在夏；周之兴也，吕牙在
殷。故惟明君贤将，能以上智为间者，必成大功。此兵之
要，三军之所恃而动也。

For Yin to come into being, one reason is I Zhe in Xia[2]; for Zhou to come into being, one reason is Lü Ya in Yin[3]. Thus, when a sagacious head of state or an intelligent commander has a person with superior intellect to provide intelligence, big success awaits[4]. This is the essence of war — on intelligence the actions of a three-battalion army depend.

[2] I Zhe was a minister in the court of Jie, the last monarch of the Xia dynasty (2140-1711 BCE). Known for his tyrannical acts, his extravagant personal life, and his neglect of state affairs, there was widespread dissatisfaction of his reign, including many in his court, of which I Zhe was one. With I Zhe providing intelligence to an insurgent force, the Xia dynasty was overthrown. Upon the establishment of the Yin dynasty (1711-1066 BCE), I Zhe was

made the prime minister. He and his descendants were all well treated by the royal family in the Yin dynasty.

[3] Lü Ya was a minister in the court of Zhou, the last monarch of the Yin dynasty (reign 1099-1096 BCE). His lack of Direction, along with cruel acts, personal indulgences, and negligence of state affairs, caused many ministers to leave his court, including Lü Ya. Recruited by an insurgent group, rulers of a nearby principality, Lü Ya assisted two leading members, a father-son duo, to topple the Yin dynasty and establish the Zhou dynasty (1066-256 BCE). The son assumed the throne as King Wu (reign 1066-1064 BCE); his father was retroactively and posthumously accorded the title as King Wen and the founder of the Zhou dynasty.

[4] Though unstated, Sun Wu again euphemistically makes reference to a head of state's having Direction. A person with superior intellect will only support a head of state whose Direction he endorses, as the examples of I Zhe and Lü Ya clearly demonstrate.

Case W-K   The American Revolution - Washington and the Intelligence Community

[Passages referenced: 7.5, 9.7, 10.8, 10.19, 11.24]

George Washington (1732-1799), the first president of the United States (1789-1797), began his public service as official surveyor of Culpeper County, Virginia, in 1749. During the French and Indian (Seven Years') War, he was a brigadier in the Virginia militia.

Later, he was a member of the House of Burgesses, and served as a Virginia delegate to the Continental Congress in 1774-1775. While there, Washington advocated military preparedness against Britain.

Intelligence Network in the Colonies

About the time the British Parliament enacted the Stamps Act of 1765, a secret society, known as *Sons of Liberty*, was set into motion. The purpose of the Act was to levy taxes on commerce in the American colonies; that of the society was to sabotage its implementation.

The Stamps Act was repealed in 1766, a year after its enactment, but the society did not disband. It continued to function — as a Patriot underground, and as intercolonial communications networks — to mold public opinion and disseminate Patriot views against the British.

Intelligence in the Initial Phase of Revolution

About one third of the colonies' population was loyal to Britain. Known as Loyalists, they — mostly members of the privileged class such as crown officials, members of the cloth, physicians, teachers, merchants, landowners, gentleman farmers — served as Britain's secret intelligence agents.

It was one of the Loyalists' intelligence agents in Concord that prompted the British troops, stationed in Boston, to raid Patriots' military stores in the villages. This was mid-April, 1775. But, before this could be carried out, the Patriots' Boston-based intelligence network detected British preparations and sent a courier — the famed Paul Revere — to Lexington to warn of the imminent British operation, resulting in a timely removal of these supplies.

These intelligence and counter-intelligence so infuriated the British that they brought about the battles of Lexington and Concord — and triggered the Revolution.

Commander-in-Chief of Continental Army

In June 1775, shortly after battles of Lexington and Concord, Washington was unanimously appointed the commander-in-chief of the Continental Army.

Washington realized that the British army was superior in every respect — larger, better trained and equipped, more mobile. He also understood, drawing from his background as a surveyor, that the war involved the movement of troops over long distances. Washington fully appreciated the importance of location — and knowledge of terrain — in the course of planning his campaigns. On this, Sun Wu has offered the following: "In war, taking advantage of the terrain is advantageous" (9.7); "It is the commander's responsibility to understand them [the management of terrain]. It is not to be left uninvestigated" (10.8); "Knowing nature and knowing terrain, winning is total" (10.19)

Factoring in the need to know the enemy's location and strength, Washington, early on, decided to neutralize the enemy's tangible superiority with intelligence. Here, Sun Wu has offered the following: "Knowing the enemy and knowing ourselves, winning is not in doubt" (10.19)

Early Successful Use of Military Intelligence

With the outbreak of war with Britain in 1775, successors to Sons of Liberty (as Committee on Correspondence and Committee on Safety) began supplying military intelligence to Washington and his Continental Army. Washington, appreciating its value, also took a personal interest in recruiting intelligence agents.

Washington attributed his victory in the Battle of Trenton (December 1776) to a secret reconnaissance carried out by one of his personally recruited agents. Another New York-based agent, also personally recruited by Washington, was instrumental in saving Washington — twice — from kidnapping and assassination attempts by the British.

In 1776, Washington set up an intelligence and reconnaissance unit to institutionalize this function. The unit is the forerunner of U.S. Army intelligence.

Washington as Master Counterintelligence Agent

Washington was a master counterintelligence agent — using misinformation calculated to reach the intended ear.

In early 1777, with his greatly depleted army in Morristown, Washington manufactured grossly inflated reports of his troop strength — and fed them to two British agents working independently and a third to a double agent. These three reports found their separate ways to General Howe, the commanding general of the British Army. Convinced of their authenticity, since each came to him independently but confirming, General Howe was dissuaded from attacking him.

Washington executed a similarly elaborate scheme the following winter, when his army was badly beaten by British troops at Brandywine and Germantown and was recuperating at Valley Forge. Washington sent word that he was ready to attack Philadelphia and New York simultaneously.

Disinformation at Yorktown

Washington scored a great breakthrough at Yorktown, in August 1781. Again, through disinformation, the British commander Clinton got wind that Washington was amassing troops for an assault on New York City. Clinton's plan to reinforce Cornwallis at Yorktown was abandoned, allowing Washington to effect a siege of Yorktown.

Washington's Intelligence Shortfalls

In the Battle of Brandywine Creek in September 1777, Washington's basic intelligence on the terrain was inaccurate. He suffered a serious defeat — and nearly lost his entire army. Sun Wu, earlier, cautioned as much: "Without knowing contours of hazards and blockades, we cannot move troops" (7.5, 11.24)

In June 1778, Washington learned that Clinton was moving his army from Philadelphia to New York City — but the intended route was a mystery. After learning that the British had reached Bordentown, New Jersey, Washington again had no clues as to the subsequent route.

Perforce, Washington spread his troops over several routes, and was unable to initiate a major engagement, allowing the British troops to reach Monmouth. At Monmouth, a major battle ensued, with both sides suffering heavy losses.

Had Washington had better intelligence, he could have inflicted heavy damages on the British troops while they were en route from Bordertown to Monmouth. Had this taken place, particularly on the heels of the British surrender at Saratoga, the Revolution could have ended then and there.

British Intelligence in Washington's Camp

One of the Loyalists serving as Britain's secret intelligence agents was Washington's personal physician, Dr. Benjamin Church. Washington, despite his experience as a master spy, never suspected the doctor, even the latter flaunted wealth, including the purchase of a fancy home.

The doctor was exposed, inadvertently, by his mistress, who indiscreetly entrusted the delivery of an enciphered letter, written by the doctor to a general in Britain, to one of her earlier benefactors. When that letter was deciphered, it gave Continental Army's strength in detail, though exaggerated, not unlike what Washington would have done himself as disinformation.

In laws they drew up, the Patriots failed to include provisions on how spies in their midst were to be prosecuted. The doctor also argued that he was actually feeding the British misinformation.

In any event, the doctor's life was spared. He was merely jailed and later released.

References

G. J. A. O'Toole, *The Encyclopedia of American Intelligence & Espionage* (New York: Facts on File, 1988)

John Bakeless, *Turncoats, Traitors, and Heroes* (Philadelphia: Lippincott, 1959), Chapter 1, The Case of the Dangerous Doctor, pp. 9-23.

WS-3   Kriegspiel - A War-Simulation Game for the New Millennium

[Passages referenced: 1.13, 1.16, 3.9, 9.20, 13.4, 13.5, 13.6]

Xiangqi was intended as a vehicle to teach Sun Wu's maxims. Invented by Hán Xin, an all-winning commander-in-chief, in 203 BCE, he used playing pieces with different move patterns to represent different types of combat personnel. His invention became the world's first war-simulation game and, later, the world's most played board game as well.

Xiangqi was also adapted to become other games — Changgi in Korea, Shogi in Japan, Shatranj in Persia, Chaturanga in India, the Medieval Game in Europe, and the modern western chess in the west.

Board Games as War Simulation

As entertainment devices, Xiangqi et al are unqualified successes. As education vehicles to impart sound military advices, they are also excellent — to a certain extent. Playing face to face or across the board, each player knows what the opponent's formation is. The fog-of-war element is missing.

In comes Kriegspiel.

Kriegspiel

Kriegspiel[1] uses the same board, the same playing pieces, and the same rules as western chess — and makes but one change: Each player can see *only* his/her own playing pieces on the board. The opponent's moves are hidden — the opponent's position must be *deduced*.

Kriegspiel as War Simulation

Although Kriegspiel introduces but one modification, visibility, it changes the game of western chess *completely*. No longer can a player rely on rote to make moves, on frequent-playing familiarity to overwhelm the opponent.

[1] Although the game has a German name (*Krieg* = war; *spiel* = game), Kriegspiel was invented in London, in 1898, between the two Boer Wars (1890-96, 1899-1902).

Kriegsspiel (spelled with two *s*) is an entirely different game. Invented by the Prussian military, it uses a big three-dimensional board showing contours of the battlefield terrain and miniature soldiers and officers; that game is known as *war gaming*.

In Kriegspiel, a player has to use his/her mind — to deduce, to think. If "Excellence in chess is commonly regarded as the attribute of a powerful mind,"[2] as one writer on chess contends, it is time for that player to show that he/she wins by superior deductive reasoning, by superior analysis — and not by regurgitation.

Kriegspiel as Intelligence Gathering Exercise

The object of Kriegspiel is the same as that of any across-the-board war-simulation game — to capture the opponent's commander. But, since the opponent's playing pieces are not visible, a Kriegspiel player must use all his/her faculties to gather intelligence. What is the opponent's formation? How does the opponent plan to capture *our* commander? Where is the opponent's commander?

Mechanics of Playing Kriegspiel

Kriegspiel is played with three sets of playing pieces and three boards: White has a set and a board, Black has another set and another board, and a referee has the third set and the third board. White uses his/her set to play White pieces and "model" the opponent's, and vice versa for Black.

The referee replicates both players' moves. Only the referee's board shows correct positions of *both* players.

The three boards are screened off, so that a player does not see the opponent's board nor the referee's.

Intelligence Gathering in Kriegspiel

Kriegspiel is a game that tests a player's ingenuity in gathering intelligence. Intelligence is dispensed by only person: the referee, in the form of announcements (the *exact* wording in each is shown under quotation marks):

(1) whose turn it is to move — e.g., "White to move";

(2) whenever an attempted move is illegal — e.g, White makes a Bishop sweep, from b2 to h8, hoping to capture Black's Rook at h8, but Black's g-pawn is in the way — "No" (the reason is not dispensed; there may be other Black pieces on the path);

(3) whenever a move produces a capture — "White captures a piece at xy", "White captures a pawn at xy" (x = file; y = rank; piece = Queen, Rook, Bishop, or Knight; the identity of piece is not dispensed, the square on which a capture takes place is);

[2] Alexander Cockburn, *Idle Passion* - Chess and the Dance of Death (New York: Simon and Schuster, 1974), at p. 12.

(4) whenever a move produces a check — "Black is in check on the vertical", "Black is in check on the horizontal", "Black is in check on the diagonal", or "Black is in check by a Knight" (only the Knight's identity is revealed because of its difficult-to-describe move pattern);

Intelligence Gathering by Pawn

In western chess, pawn moves forward except when in a capture, then it moves diagonally. Kriegspiel makes use of this unique feature for intelligence gathering purposes.

Before a player makes a move, he/he may ask: "Are there any pawn capture opportunities?" which is shortened to "Are there any?" or, simply "Any?" The referee must then respond.[3]

If the referee's answer is "Try," this means that (1) "Yes," there is (at least) one such opportunity, and (2) the player *must* make one attempt at capturing with a pawn. (This is further explained in the illustrative game following.)

Kriegspiel Trains Intelligence Gathering

Kriegspiel is an excellent vehicle for training intelligence gathering techniques. Not surprisingly, its inventor was a member of a profession keen on intelligence gathering — Michael Henry Temple (1862-1928), a Fleet Street newspaper reporter (Fleet Street = Wall Street in "The City" [of London]).

In World War I, German generals were fond of playing Kriegspiel. In World War II, many top cryptoanalysts gathered in Bletchley Park near London were Kriegspiel players.[4] In the post-war era, Kriegspiel is embraced by information professionals — research professors, intelligence officers, computer analysts, newspaper reporters.

---

[3] This is the original U.K. rule. The U.S. rules are different, and involves different playing (and intelligence gathering) strategy. See comments in the Endnote.

[4] The relationship between Kriegspiel and code-cracking is more than coincidental. The German Enigma codes changed every 15 minutes, which is similar to changes in a Kriegspiel game after every move. Changes in German codes were incremental, which is again similar to incremental changes in a Kriegspiel game after a move.

Nobel Laureate Plays Kriegspiel

Illustrated below is a Kriegspiel game[5] played by Sir Robert Robinson around the time he was awarded the Nobel Prize.[6] His opponent was the husband of former Women's World Western Chess Champion Vera Menchik and, at the time of this game, manager of National Chess Centre in London.

Sir R. Robinson - R. H. S. Stevenson
London, 1940s
(Questions and responses in quotes;
Announcements on moves and captures not shown;
Attempted moves in light face; Actual moves in boldface)

1	**e4**		**e5**
2	"Any?" "No" **c4**		"Any?" "No" **d5**
3	"Any?" "Try" **cxd5**	**Qxd5**	

3 ... Qxd5, recapturing a pawn, is extremely dangerous; the Queen is subject to immediate capture by White's e-pawn. The position at this point is shown as Exhibit 1.

Case WS-3 Exhibit 1
R. Robinson vs. R. H. S. Stevenson
Position after 3 ... Qxd5

---

[5] From the premier issue (August 1995) of *Kriegspiel Connoisseur*, a quarterly journal published by this case writer. This game later appeared as an article, "Kriegspiel," in the October 1995 issue of *Chess* magazine (UK).

[6] Sir Robert Robinson (1886-1975), in addition to being a Nobel laureate in Chemistry (1947) and Professor of Chemistry at Oxford University (1930-1955), was also a two-term President of the British Chess Federation (1950-1953). He openly stated that he preferred to play Kriegspiel over regular western chess.

Black Queen Subject to Capture

      4 "Any?" "Try"
      exf5 "No" **Nc5**

White's query of "Any?" before his fourth move indicates that another of his pawns is in a position to recapture, at d5. Giving more credit to Black than he deserves, White thinks that Black has used a pawn for his third move, and decides not to recapture it.

Thus, White makes a perfunctory attempt, 4 exf5, knowing fully well that that attempt will produced a "No" (since f5 is clearly vacant). With the obligatory attempt out of the way, White plays 4 Nc5.

Black Survives

To Black, White's query of "Any?" before his fourth move is bad news — Black's Queen is in danger of immediate capture. But, hearing *only* "Black to move," Black knows that the Queen has survived. He retreats it to safety, 4 ... Qe6.

      4   **Qe6**
      5 "Any?" "No"

The "No" response to White's query of "Any?" indicates that the d5 square is now vacant. This means: (1) the pawn, sitting on d5 on the last move, has been pushed forward, or (2) a piece, used in capturing in Move 3, has escaped.

White tests with 5 d4, expecting to hear a "No". But, to his surprise, the move is allowed to stand.

      5 d4

Now, it is Black's turn to move. But, that is no reason for White to sit still. He must gather his thoughts and digest this piece of intelligence — Black did use a piece to capture White's pawn in Move 3.

Looking at the board, that piece has to be the Queen. What a risk taker Black is!

Black Retaliates

      5   "Any?" "Try" **exd4**

White's 5 d4 move, intended as an intelligence-gathering attempt, now puts that pawn at risk. When it is Black's turn to move, that pawn is immediately removed. The exciting life of intelligence work is fully reflected on a Kriegspiel board.

The position at this point is shown as Exhibit 2.

Case WS-3 Exhibit 2
R. Robinson vs. R. H. S. Stevenson
Position after 5 ... exd5

White Sees an Opportunity

At this point, White can do what Black did earlier: using the Queen to recapture. But, not knowing where Black has retreated his Queen to, risks are high. In any case, White sees a move that is both safer and more enterprising, 6 Bg6.

6 Bg6

Black Cannot Resist the Temptation

With White's 6th move, Black can proceed to capture the Knight. By deliberately not moving that Knight but playing 6 Bg6, White offers a bait. Sun Wu would indeed applaud at this scheme — "With the opponent seeking advantage, bait" (1.13)

6   "Any?" "Try" dxc3

When it is Black's turn to move, he wastes no time and captures the Knight — "Black captures a piece at c3; White to move."

White Charges in for the Kill

So, Black falls for the bait. Now, except for the location of the Black Queen, White knows Black's position exactly. The actual position is shown as Exhibit 3.

Calmly, White plays 7 Qd8 for a checkmate.

7 Qd8++

Case WS-3 Exhibit 3
R. Robinson vs. R. H. S. Stevenson
Position after 6 ... dxc3

Know Our Enemy, Know Ourselves

It must be mentioned that White's 7th move is not as risky as it seems. Were 4 ... d6 or 4 ... d7 played, attempting to play 7 Qd8 would produce a "No", since the path is blocked. Were 4 ... d8 played, playing 7 Qd8 captures the Black Queen and executes the checkmate in the same move.

The only way to thwart this checkmate is when the Queen is at e7 or f6 (when so, the d8-g5 diagonal would be blocked, preventing the Bishop from maintaining surveillance over d8). But neither location was possible (from d5 to reach either e7 or f6 would require a Knight move).

Thus, with risk-benefit greatly in his favor, White's playing 7 Qd8 is an odds-on preposition.

Sun Wu has said: "With knowledge of our enemy and knowledge of ourselves, we will not be in a precarious position — not even once in 100 battles." (3.9)

Kriegspiel and Sun Wu

Sun Wu mentions five sources of intelligence. Their approximate equivalency in Kriegspiel is tabulated as Exhibit 4 (page 208).

Case WS-3 Exhibit 4
Sources of Intelligence in Sun Wu
and Their Approximation in Kriegspiel

In Sun Wu	*Through Kriegspiel*
Local (13.4, 13.5)	An isolated attempt (such as the Bishop sweep discussed in the case)
Insider (13.4, 13.5)	The referee's announcements
Double (13.4, 13.5)	Any query or announcement (audible to both players)
Counter (13.4, 13.6)	Any attempt at confusing the opponent (In the Robinson-Stevenson game, 1 e4 and 2 c4 is an attempt at misinformation. Were a Black pawn at d5 and getting a "Try", Black would not necessarily know that both c4 and e4 are occupied)
Live (13.4, 13.6)	Any move or announcement that produces intelligence but does not cause the loss of a playing piece or, better yet, not the loss of tempo (e.g., when moving the King, say from e1 to d1, receives a "No," White knows that d1 is under surveillance)

Options and Winning

The Robinson-Stevenson game offers an opportunity to illustrate another important point in Sun Wu.

On White's mating move, 7 Qd8++, the annotation states that for the Black Queen to move from d5 to either e7 or f6 is not possible; this is indeed so. But, what happens if the Black Queen were at either e7 or f6?

Were this so, White's playing of 7 Qd8 results in the *net* loss of a Bishop — provided all options are covered. Assuming we are White, we might move and hear the following:

White　　　　**7 Qd8**

Ref: "Black is in check on the horizontal" (Black must parry the check, thus "Black to move" is understood and not announced)

Black [makes a move]

Ref: "Black captures a piece at d8. White to move."

White   **8 Be7**

Ref: "Black to move."

What happens after 8 Be7? Why does the referee not also announce "White captures a piece at e7. Black is in check on the diagonal?"

Simple. After 7 Qd8+, Black has two options to parry the check. White's play of 8 Be7 takes into account only one option — 7 ... Kdx8, using the King to capture the Queen to parry the check — but not the other. Poor commandership — not identifying all options.

Black's other option is 7 ... Qdx8, playing the Queen back to its own square, capturing the White Queen, and parrying the check. So, to cover both options, White must attempt 8 Bd8. Two scenarios are possible. Let us witness both.

Scenario 1

White 8 Bd8

Ref: "White captures a piece at d8. Black to move."

Black [makes a move]

Ref: "Black captures a piece at d8. White to move."

So, Black indeed used the Queen in **7 ... Qxd8**. So, after 8 Bxd8 Kxd8, White captures the Black Queen, and Black retaliates by capturing the White Bishop. White has a net loss of a Bishop for this venture.

Scenario 2

White 8 Bd8

Ref: "No"

White 8 Be7

Ref: "No"

White 8 Bf6

Ref: "White captures a piece at f6. Black is in check on the diagonal."

Black [makes a move][7]

Ref: "Black captures a piece at d8. White to move."

Here, White attempts with the same 8 Bd8, but receives a "No." This indicates that, for his 7th move, Black used the King, **7 ... Kxd8**, to parry the check. The Queen is unmoved   it is still at either e7 or f6; its presence still blocks the g5-d8 diagonal.

[7] When a player is in check, the top priority is to parry the check. Thus, asking "Any?" at this time is out of order. In any event, asking "Any?" is not mandatory.

What next? White must then attempt 8 Be7 — and *not* Bf6.[8]
Were the Black Queen at e7, after 8 Be7, the referee would
announce: "White captures a piece at e7. Black is in check in
the diagonal." So the Black Queen was at e7.

At that point, White is indeed down. But, out? No. The game
is still young, and White must have a positive attitude and play
on. With a positive attitude, White may recover.

When the referee again announces "No" to 8 Be7, this means
that the short diagonal g5-e7 is still blocked — the Queen is at
f6.

So, White next attempts 8 Bf6, and hears the referee's
announcement as shown under Scenario 2. So, make moves
that would maximize options.

Numerical Superiority Not a Factor

This case writer's 1994 book (see Endnote) annotates an actual
game where Black, with but two pawns, manages to check the
opponent with Queen, Rook, and two pawns.

In Kriegspiel, the motto is: Play on. That game illustrates
beautifully what Sun Wu has said: "In war, numerical superiority is
not a factor. All that is needed to win is to refrain from advancing
haphazardly, to consolidate resources, and to see through the enemy's
plans. One who does not plan but is disdainful of his enemy is bound
to be captured." (9.20)

Cover All Options

To cover all options is clearly what Sun Wu has in mind when he
says:

We can predict a win because we have identified many options
through repeated top-level planning. We cannot predict a win
because we have identified few options through little top-level
planning. With many options, one wins; with few options, one
does not win. With no options, how can one win? (1.16)

With this statement from Sun Wu, it is time for this case as well as
this book to close. *Qing bao zhong* - please take good care of yourself.

---

[8] This is because, were the Black Queen at e7, the move 8 Bf6 is
legal, since the g5-f6 path is clear. When 8 Bf6 is allowed to stand,
that Bishop is subject to pawn capture. With that capture, White
would be down by the Queen and a Bishop.

Endnote

There is a dearth of books on Kriegspiel. To this case writer's knowledge, up until the mid-1990s, there are but two such books, both in German, published in the 1910s. They are in the collection of Bibliotheca van der Linde - Niemeijeriana of Koninklijke Bibliotheck, at the Hague.

As to works in English, there is a 48-page pamphlet, published in U.K. in 1910, and a collection of Kriegspiel problems, privately-printed by a renowned western chess composer, Gerald F. Anderson, *Are There Any?*, published in 1945. Both are out of print; the first one is absent even in the van der Linde collection.

In 1994, this case writer produced the very first book-length work on Kriegspiel in English: *Kriegspiel - Chess Under Uncertainty* (Bethesda: Premier, 1994, 144 pages). Encouraged by the book's reception, he produced, the following year, another book, *Chess Detective - Kriegspiel Strategies, Endgames and Problems* (Bethesda: Premier, 1995, 196 pages). He has also ventured into publishing a quarterly, *Kriegspiel Connoisseur.*

In this case writer's 1994 book, U.S. rules are used. (All games in the book are played by faculty members at the University of Washington, Seattle, where this case writer held the rank of Professor.) U.S. rules expose counterintelligence more readily than U.K. rules, making camouflaging more difficult. To play Kriegspiel with U.S. rules well requires, in this case writer's view, more ingenuity and, thus, more difficult.

In this case writer's 1995 book, both U.K. and U.S. approaches are discussed. That book uses the case study approach, and includes many games from leading players on both sides of the Atlantic, compares their approaches, and discusses their amusing consequences.

A SUN WU'S (SUN TZU'S) LIFE
A CHRONOLOGY

(Background information is given sans serif)

(In China, a person's surname is shown first)

Age BCE

1 535 Born, given the name of *Wu* (= martial), during the second half of the tumultuous Spring and Autumn Period (770-476 BCE), son to Chen (later Sun) Píng, a member of the court in the State of Qi; grandson to Chen (later Sun) Shu, a man-of-martial-letters

2 534 Wu was nominally 2 on Lunar New Year's Day; generally, the age of a person born in China (then, as now) is overstated, on average, by a year and half

3 533

4 532

5 531

6 530

7 529

8 528

9 527

10 526

11 525

12 524

13 523 • Duke of Qi, in recognition of Chen Shu's role in conquering the nearby State of Ju, made him a vassal and granted him the surname of Sun — Chen Shu thus became Sun Shu

• Wu, now Sun Wu, moved with his father, now Sun Píng, to his grandfather's vassalage [Because the word *Wu* appears in several contexts in this chronology (a state, a prominent official, and Sun Wu's given name), although all different in Chinese characters, to reduce confusion, Sun Wu's full name is used hereinafter]

• Sun Wu began schooling in his grandfather's vassalage

14 522

15 521

16 520

17 519

18 518

19 517 Migrated to the State of Wu, as infighting among members of the court in his home state of Qi became unbearable

20 516 Gained the acquaintance of Wu Yun, an emigré from the State of Chü, who harbored the hope that Wu would invade Chü to

revenge for his father's and elder brother's assassination by members of the Chü court

21 515 • King Liao decided to invade Chü; Wu Yun played no part in this decision

• Prince Guang took the opportunity of Wu's invasion of Chü to commit a regicide, using the services of an assassin, Zhan Chu, arranged by Wu Yun [Sun Wu made a reference to Zhan Chu and his act in 11.13]

• Prince Guang assumed the throne, became King Hé Lü, and appointed Wu Yun as *xin ren* (Minister of External Affairs); he also appointed Bai Pei, another emigré from the State of Chü, as minister; following their advice, King Hé Lü began to build up his state in earnest

22 514 Began writing his essays, sensing Wu as an up-and-coming state with a bright future and hoping to play a role in it

23 513 Continued preparing the Thirteen Essays, with the hope that his one-time acquaintance, now an important member of the court, Wu Yun, could arrange an audience with King Hé Lü

24 512 • After seven attempts, Wu Yun succeeded in having King Hé Lü read Sun Wu's essay(s) [In this chronicler's estimation, only Essay 1 was first submitted to King Hé Lü]

• Sun Wu's essay(s) struck a cord with King Hé Lü, as King Hé Lü sought revenge against the State of Yuè, a foe of long-standing (*inter alia,* in 544 BCE, King Yu Ji of Wu was assassinated by a prisoner of war, a former Yuè soldier)

• King Hé Lü read additional, and, eventually, all, of Sun Wu's thirteen essays [Wu- or Yuè-specific references appear only from Essay 6 onward]

• Had audience with King Hé Lü

• Obliged King Hé Lü to a demonstration of his competence [for details, see Case W-F after Essay 8]

• Was appointed Wu's commander-in-chief, having demonstrated his competence to King Hé Lü's satisfaction

• Convinced King Hé Lü of frugality to self and generosity to people to gain their confidence and support

• Captured Su, an ally of Chü, as commander-in-chief, after King Hé Lü, Wu Yun, and Bai Pei decided that time was ripe to take aim at Chü by annoying her allies; the trio participated in the campaign

• King Hé Lü captured Xu, another Chü ally, forcing two princes of Wu (King Hé Lü's uncles), who earlier fled to Xu when their brother, King Liao, was assassinated, to flee again, this time to Chü

· Persuaded King Hé Lü, overjoyed by his successes, not to march to Chü's capital, pleading that the troops were tired and needed rest

25 511 • Captured Yi, another Chü ally

• Designed a strategy aimed at wearing Chü down — marched toward Qian and Liu, two other allies of Chü, and retreated when a Chü general came to the rescue

• Marched toward Xian, another Chü ally, and retreated when another Chü general came to the rescue

26 510 On the pretense that Yuè did not follow Wu's lead in attacking Chü, King Hé Lü invaded Yuè, furthering the animosity between these two states

27 509

28 508 • Persuaded the State of Tong to rebel against Chü, using the strategy of winning by diplomacy (3.2)

• Defeated Chü army at Yu-chang, using the strategy of attacking the unprepared (1.14)

• Conquered Chao, still another Chü ally, and captured Chao's Prince Pó

29 507

30 506 • Led Wu army of 30,000 and crushed the Chü army of 200,000 — strategies used: attacking the enemy when half of his men have crossed (9.2); satisfying the army's sustenance needs from the enemy (2.3)

• Marched into Chü capital in November

• With Sun Wu's counsel unavailing, King Hé Lü, Wu Yun, Bai Pei, and others ransacked the capital, creating anguish among Chü citizenry

•Yuè, Wu's long-time foe, taking advantage of Wu army's being in Chü, attacked Wu, causing substantial damage, retreating only when Prince Fu Gai's troops returned (see entry immediately below)

• Shen Pao-xi, a Chü minister, with assistance from Qin, counterattacked Wu's troops in Chü, defeating those led by Prince Fu Gai (King Hé Lü's younger brother), who retreated to Wu and declared himself King

• The combined forces of Chü (led by Shen Pao-xi) and Qin also inflicted repeated losses on Wu's troops in Chü led by King Hé Lü

31 505 King Hé Lü retreated to Wu, defeated Prince Fu Gai, and regained the throne

32 504 King Hé Lü sent Prince Zon Re, one of his sons, to invade Chü, defeating Chü army, forcing Chü to move her capital

33 503 Suggested that citadels and way stations be built along the common border of Wu and Yuè to reduce repeated skirmishes between these two states

34 502 Requested, and granted, an advisory role from his line function on account of (1) his inability to influence the action of King Hé

Lü, Wu Yun, et al at Chü (entry 3 under 506 BCE above), and
(2) his lack of field-marshal authority due to King Hé Lü's
unceasing personal involvement in war making

35 501

36 500

37 499

38 498

39 497

40 496 • King Yuen Chang, of Yuè, passed away, succeeded by young
King Gou Jian, prompting King Hé Lü to invade Yuè
• Aimed at shocking Wu army into bewilderment, young King
Gou Jian, after a few skirmishes, arranged to have Yuè prisoners
forming three lines and committing suicides in front of Wu army;
succeeding, Yuè troops penetrated Wu's formation and cut off
King Hé Lü's toe, who retreated and died en route
• Young King Gou Jian, knowing that his army was outnumbered, did
not pursue, but claimed victory and retreated to home territory
• Prince Fu Cha succeeded Hé Lü as King of Wu and vowed revenge

41 495

42 494 • In a preventive strike, King Gou Jian invaded Wu, and was met by a
100,000-strong Wu army
• Took a more active role in view of the new king's inexperience;
decided to use incendiary (12.4) — divided the troops into two
flanks to initiate an unexpected night attack, routing Yuè army
• Directed Wu army in pursuit of retreating Yuè troops, using
incendiary to again rout Yuè army
• Surrounded King Gou Jian and his 5,000 troops, who retreated
to a mountain top
• King Gou Jian decided to surrender
• Wu Yun suggested to King Fu Cha not to accept King Gou Jian's
surrender but to terminate him and annihilate Yuè
• King Fu Cha temporized by ordering King Gou Jian to serve three
years of servitude in his palace
• Wu minister Bai Pei, heavily bribed by King Gou Jian, suggested to,
and accepted by, King Fu Cha that King Gou Jian be set free and
returned to his homeland after three years of servitude

43 493

44 492

45 491

46 490

47 489

48 488
49 487
50 486
51 485 • King Fu Cha, attempting to fulfill the unrealized dream of his father, King Hé Lü, of becoming the Head of League of Powers, invaded Qi, a power, but was defeated
52 484 • King Fu Cha, with assistance from Lü, invaded Qi again, and won
         • Wu Yun, anticipating an invasion by Yuè, whose King Gou Jian, upon his release, quietly built up his state's resources, and foreseeing a Wu defeat, sent his son to a family in Qi
         • King Fu Cha, upon returning from his successful campaign in Qi and hearing what Wu Yun had done, decreed that Wu Yun take his own life
         • Decided to retire, seeing that his best friend, Wu Yun, ended his life so miserably
?   ?   The year of Sun Wu's death is not in recorded. Historians estimate that it was in 483 BCE or no more than a couple of years thereafter.

Subsequent Events
    482 • King Fu Cha met other heads of state at Yellow Pond, and succeeded in having Wu acknowledged as the Head of League of Powers
         • During King Fu Cha's meeting at Yellow Pond, King Gou Jian, of Yuè, invaded Wu, taking her capital and ransacked it
    475 Yuè invaded Wu again, defeating Wu army, and surrounded her capital with King Fu Cha in it; this siege continued for a year and half
    474 Yuè's siege of Wu's capital continued
    473 • King Fu Cha fled the capital to a nearby mountain top, was captured, and committed suicide
         • With King Fu Cha's death, the State of Wu was annihilated, and her territory became a part of Yuè

References (all in Chinese):

Yang Shan-qun, *Sun Tzu: A Critical Biography* (Nanjing: Nanjing University Press, 1995), 562 pp.
Yuan Wei (ed), *Encyclopedia of Chinese Military Campaigns - Volume 1: 3000 BC - 1919* (Beijing: Museum of Military Affairs, 1994), pp. 70 et seq
Registry of Major Chinese Military Campaigns (Shanghai: Shanghai Dictionary Press, 1996), pp. 23 et seq
Huang Xiu-wen (ed), *Dictionary of Chinese Chronology* (Shanghai: Shanghai Dictionary Press, 1997), entry under Sun Wu

B RECAPITULATION OF TEXT IN ENGLISH

1   TOPMOST-LEVEL PLANNING

1.1   War is a major affair of the State, a domain deciding life and death, a direction defining existence and extinction. It is not to be left uninvestigated.

1.2   For better understanding, it needs to be delineated into five factors and analyzed separately. They are:

> One, Direction
> Two, *Tian*
> Three, Location
> Four, Commandership
> Five, Support

1.3   Direction refers to a common goal that molds the subordinates' with the superior's — making them willing to die, to fight, to be unafraid of risks.

1.4   *Tian* refers to *yin* and *yang*, to wintery and summery climates, to changes in seasons.

1.5   Location refers to land high and low, to land close by and distant, treacherous and plain, easily accessible and not easily accessible, deadly and lively.

1.6   Commandership refers to intelligence, trustworthiness, nobleness, courage, and discipline.

1.7   Support refers to military organization, administrative direction, and fiscal appropriation.

1.8   A commander-in-chief is knowledgeable in all these five factors. One with such knowledge wins; one without does not win.

1.9   When factors as delineated are analyzed separately, the issues become:

> Which head of state has the Direction?
> Which commander is more capable?
> Which side has natural and geographical advantages?
> Which side has better support?
> Which army is numerically superior?

Which army is better trained?

Which side's reward-penalty system is more equitable? With answers to these, I can predict a victory or defeat.

1.10   For a commander who will follow my plan, using his services results in a sure win — keep him. For a commander who will not follow my plan, using his services results in a sure loss — release him.

1.11   A well formulated plan well received builds up momentum; momentum has a significant effect on those in the field. Momentum necessarily changes as conditions change.

1.12   War involves stratagems. Thus, when competent, feign incompetence; when active, feign inaction; when close in, feign distance; when distant, feign proximity.

1.13   With the enemy seeking advantage, bait; in disarray, take; showing strength, prepare; parading power, elude; prone to anger, provoke; displaying caution, agitate; at ease, make work; exhibiting unity, divide.

1.14   Attack when unprepared; advance where unexpected.

1.15   Tactics for winning are as stated; they cannot be predesignated.

1.16   We can predict a win because we have identified many options through repeated top-level planning. We cannot predict a win because we have identified few options through little top-level planning. With many options, one wins; with few options, one does not win. With no options, how can one win?

1.17   Viewed this way, I can readily predict victory or defeat.

2   TOTAL-RESOURCE PLANNING

2.1   In general, a war campaign requires 1,000 four-horse chariots, 1,000 heavy-armored chariots, 100,000 weapon-carrying soldiers, provisions to last 1,000 miles, expenditures at home and in the field, stipends for advisors and envoys, parts for chariot maintenance, and feed for horses. To marshal a 100,000-member army needs the daily outlay of 1,000 measures of gold.

2.2   In campaigns, aiming for a protracted win dulls the soldiers and lowers their morale, leaving little to attack the city, but thrusting the army's extended needs upon an inadequate treasury. Dull soldiers, lowered morale, feeble force and depleted treasury allow heads of other states to take advantage and take action. When so, even the intelligent cannot come up with a good solution. Thus, one hears about clumsy but quick wins, but never clever and protracted wins. There is no instance where a state benefits from a protracted war.

2.3   One who does not fully understand the negative side of war is incapable of fully understand**ing** its positive side. One who knows war knows not to draft men more than once nor to seek provisions more than thrice. Bring in weaponry from the state, but satisfy the army's sustenance needs from the enemy.

2.4   Long-distance transport of provisions for the troops is the cause of a state's impoverishment. To take care of long-distance transport, people are pushed to poverty. To take care of local troops' demands, prices go up. Paying high prices depletes people's savings and prompts the state to hasten the collection of land taxes. With feeble force and depleted treasury in the field, with reduced abundance at home, people's resources are squandered seven out of ten. With fractured chariots and tired horses, with damaged armor and split arrows, with spent halberds and broken shields, the state's resources are consumed six out of ten.

2.5   Thus, an intelligent commander seeks provisions from the enemy. Consuming one bushel of enemy provisions is the equal of consuming twenty bushels of our own; appropriating one ton[4] of enemy supplies is the equal of appropriating twenty tons of our own.

2.6   Hatred destroys enemies; rewards encourage boldness. In combats involving chariots, when ten or more chariots are seized, reward the leader, change their flags, and blend them in deployment. For soldiers captured, treat them well. With wins, we grow stronger.

2.7   Thus, in war, quick wins are valued, while protracted ones are not. A commander who knows war [is aware that he] is responsible for people's destiny and the state's security.

3   STRATEGIC PLANNING

3.1   In war, taking the enemy's state whole is superior to taking it disintegrated, taking the enemy's army whole is superior to taking it splintered, taking the enemy's battalion whole is superior to taking it shattered, taking the enemy's squadron whole is superior to taking it smashed, taking the enemy's company whole is superior to taking it crushed, taking the enemy's unit whole is superior to taking it demolished.

3.2   Thus, engaging in 100 wars and winning 100 is not the best of the best; winning the enemy's army without engaging in war is. Winning a war is best accomplished by planning; the next best, by diplomacy; the next best, by combat in open field; the worst, by invading the citadel.

3.3   Invade the citadel only when there is no alternative. Repairing weaponry, readying chariots, and preparing equipment take three months. Deploying them with proper support takes another three months. Impatient and restless, the commander orders the troop to climb walls and invade the citadel. The result is the deaths of one third of his men, yet the citadel is still not taken. These are the perils of invading the citadel.

3.4   Thus, one who knows war takes the enemy's army without engaging in combat, takes the enemy's citadel without invading it, and takes the enemy's state without sieging it. He takes them whole and readies to contest for leadership in the world. These are the results of strategic planning — the troops are not fatigued and resources are intact.

3.5   Deploy troops thus: when we are superior by tenfold, siege; superior by fivefold, attack; superior by twofold, divide; even, fight; inferior, withdraw; much inferior, elude. An inferior force, regardless of how strenuously they fight, become but prisoners of the superior force.

3.6   The commander assists the state. Proper assistance strengthens the state; inadequate assistance weakens it.

3.7   A head of state harms his troops three ways. Ordering the troops to advance not knowing that they should not, or ordering them to retreat not knowing that they should not — the troops are misengaged. Involving in troops administration not knowing military affairs — the troops are perplexed. Participating in troops command not knowing military hierarchy — the troops are suspicious. Perplexed and suspicious troops cause disasters, as they invite heads of other states to invade. A disorganized army allows the enemy to win.

3.8   On win indicators, there are five. Knowing when to fight and when not to fight wins. Knowing how to handle numerical superiority and inferiority wins. Molding superiors and subordinates to the same goal wins. Waiting for tired troops while rested and at ready wins. Being capably commanded without constraint from the head of state wins. These are the five ways to winning.

3.9   Therefore, with knowledge of our enemy and knowledge of ourselves, we will not be in a precarious position — not even once in 100 battles. Knowing not our enemy but only ourselves, we are as likely to win a battle as to lose one. Knowing neither our enemy nor ourselves, we will lose every battle.

4   FORMATION PLANNING

4.1   In the past, those who knew war first made sure that no one could win over them, then sought opportunities to win over the enemy. Ensuring that no one wins over us depends upon ourselves, seeking to win over the enemy depends upon the enemy. Thus, he who knows war can be sure that no one wins over him, but cannot be sure of a win over the enemy.

4.2   Thus, winning may be predicted but cannot be **forced**. Unable to win, defend. Capable of winning, attack. Defend because we are inferior. Attack because we are superior.

4.3   He who knows how to defend conceals as if hiding in nine levels below. He who knows how to attack bursts as if descending from nine levels above. Thus, he protects himself while winning totally.

4.4   A not-unexpected win that is foreseen by the populace is not the best of the best; a hard-fought win that is praised by the world is not the best of the best. One who can lift a feather is not acknowledged as a man of great strength; one who can see the sun and moon, not a man of clear vision; one who can hear thunder and storm, not a man of sharp hearing.

4.5   In the past, those who knew war won with ease. Thus, their wins were not regarded as unusual, their intelligence was not praised, and their bravery was not recognized. They won without flaw. Their measures were winning measures, applied to an enemy who had already lost. Thus, he who knows war takes a position that cannot be defeated, and takes on an enemy that is already defeated. A winning war takes a winning position and then takes action, a losing war takes action and then expects to win.

4.6   One who knows war is vigilant on Direction and protective of support. Direction and support govern win or loss.

4.7   Support is gauged in five steps: step 1, gauge length; step 2, gauge volume; step 3, gauge quantity; step 4, gauge weight; step 5, gauge winning. Land yields length; length yields volume; volume yields quantity; quantity yields weight; weight yields win.

4.8   In war, [support received by] a winning army is like a kilogram to [the enemy's] gram; [support received by] a losing army is like a gram to [the enemy's] kilogram.

4.9   In war, the winning army may be likened to water rushing down from a mile-and-half-high mountain to the stream. This is formation.

5   MOMENTUM PLANNING

5.1   Managing a large army is no different from managing a small army; the key is divisional organization. Giving directives to a large army is no different from giving directives to a small army; the key is command hierarchy. A three-battalion army surrounded by the enemy may suffer no loss; the key is orthodox and unorthodox formations. A superior army overpowers, as if throwing stones at eggs; the key is a firm formation against a façade formation.

5.2   In war, use orthodox formations to engage the enemy, but use unorthodox formations to win. One who is adept can produce unorthodox formations as infinitely as sky and earth and as inexhaustibly as oceans and rivers — repeating as day and night, regenerating as the four seasons.

5.3   In tone there are but five; still, the variation of these five tones can produce melodies beyond anyone's ability to assimilate. In color there are but five; still, the combination of these five colors can produce paintings beyond anyone's ability to appreciate. In taste there are but five; still, the combination of these five tastes can produce cuisines beyond anyone's ability to associate.

5.4   In formations, there are but two, orthodox and unorthodox; still, their variations are endless. Orthodox and unorthodox formations evolve in infinite cycles. Who can exhaust them?

5.5   Water rushing down can move stones; this is momentum. Falcons charging in can crush their preys; this is swiftness.

5.6   Thus, one who knows war builds momentum as if spontaneous, readies for swiftness as if instantaneous. Spontaneous momentum is like a bow completely extended; instantaneous swiftness is like weaponry fully ready.

5.7   In the midst of turmoil and tumult, fight chaos but avoid being chaotic. In the midst of confusion and commotion, form into circles to avoid loss. [The enemy's] Chaos is the result of [our] discipline; [the enemy's] cowardice, the result of our courage; [the enemy's] weakness, the result of [our] strength. The difference between discipline and chaos is organization; between courage and cowardice, formation; between strength and weakness, momentum.

5.8   Thus, one who can outmaneuver the enemy creates [illusory] formations for the enemy to follow; creates [empty] opportunities for the enemy to take. Thus outmaneuvered, our men are ready.

5.9   Thus, one who knows war makes use of momentum but does ont blame his men; he deploys men in the light of momentum. Momentum, in relation to deploying men, may be likened to propelling wood and stones. Wood and stone remain stationary on a plane, but move about on a slope; remain still as squares, but become mobile when round. Thus, one who knows how to deploy men deploys them as propelling round stones from a mile-and-half-high mountain. This is momentum.

6   PREPAREDNESS PLANNING

6.1   One who arrives at the battlefield to await for the enemy's arrival is at ready. One who arrives at the battlefield to meet the enemy is not at ready. One who knows war outmaneuvers the enemy but is not outmaneuvered by him.

6.2   Maneuvering the enemy so that he comes to where we want him is the result of our bait. Maneuvering the enemy so that he cannot go to where he wants is the result of our blockade. We make him occupied instead of at ease, make him hungry instead of well fed, make him move about instead of at ready. We attack where he must come out to defend.

6.3   Marching a thousand miles and not feeling tired, it is because the march is through unpopulated land; attacking a position and producing a sure win, it is because the attack is on the undefended; defending a position and ensuring a secure hold, it is because the defense is against an expected attack.

6.4   Thus, against one who is adept at offense, the enemy knows not how to defend; against one who is adept at defense, the enemy knows not how to attack. Being minuscule and approaching infinitesimal, we are almost invisible. Being elusive and approaching imaginary, we are almost inaudible. We are thus in control of the enemy's destiny.

6.5   Advancing as to be beyond defense, it is because we smash the façade. Retreating as to be beyond pursuit, it is because we move with swiftness.

6.6   Thus, if we are determined to fight, the enemy will have to come out and fight, even though they are stationed on high grounds or behind deep channels; this is because we attack a position he must rescue. If we are determined not to fight, the enemy will not engage us in a fight, even though our defense is but a line on the ground; this is because we compel him to deploy his forces elsewhere.

6.7   Thus, when the enemy is visible and we are invisible, we are consolidated but the enemy is scattered. When we are consolidated and the enemy scattered in ten different positions, our attacking force is ten times that of the defending force. Even when our total man-count is inferior to the enemy's, our attacking force is numerically superior to the enemy's; this is because the enemy's force at any position must necessarily be limited.

6.8   Where we plan to fight is not to be known to the enemy. Without this knowledge, the enemy has to guard many positions. With the enemy guarding many positions, wherever we attack, the defending force will be numerically inferior to ours.

6.9   Thus, [the enemy's] guarding his front exposes his back, guarding his back exposes his front, guarding his left exposes his right, guarding his right exposes his left. Guarding his every position exposes his every position.

6.10   Being exposed is the result of guarding many positions. Being numerically superior is the result of forcing the enemy to guard many positions.

6.11   Knowing where and when to fight, the battle line may be as long as a thousand miles. Not knowing where and when to fight, even though the battle line is but a few score miles, or perhaps but a few miles, the left cannot rescue the right, the right cannot rescue the left, the front cannot rescue the rear, the rear cannot rescue the front.

6.12   In my estimation, while the army of Yuè has an advantage in number, that is not necessarily an advantage in winning a war. Winning is the result of planning. Although the enemy is more numerous, it can be rendered non-combative.

6.13   With planning, we identify strategies for winning and losing. With provocation, we deduce the enemy's movement and deployment. With formation, we explore terrains the enemy thrives and disdains. With skirmishes, we assess our preparedness and deficiencies.

6.14   The ultimate of formation is formless. Being formless, it is beyond the cleverest intelligence were they in our innermost, and beyond the most intelligent planners were they in the enemy's employ.

6.15   The masses do not understand why a particular formation wins. All they know is that a specific formation wins, but do not know what causes that formation to win. Formations are specific to a specific enemy; they do not recur. They adapt endlessly.

6.16   Formations may be likened to water. Water formation avoids the high ground but seeks the low plain; military formations bypass the firm but attack the façade. To flow, water accommodates the terrain; to win, formations accommodate the enemy. In war, momentum is not set, formation is not constant.

6.17   One who is all-winning over an enemy in all kinds of maneuvers is a wizard. This is because, among the five elements, none is always predominant; of the four seasons, none is ever-present; of days, some are long and others short; the moon waxes and wanes.

7   BATTLEFIELD MANEUVERS

7.1   Among the processes of war — the commander's receiving his commission from the head of state, the commander's gathering men to form the army, the armies' engaging in combat — none is more demanding than maneuvering. Maneuvering is demanding because one must **regard** the circuitous as straight-forward, the disadvantageous as advantageous.

7.2   [The enemy] must be persuaded to take a circuitous route by tempting him with advantages. Thus, even though we begin later than the enemy, we arrive at the battlefield ahead of him. This is using straight-forwardness and circuitousness in planning.

7.3   Maneuvering is to seek advantage — and maneuvering is hazardous. Seeking advantage by moving an entire army results in falling behind in arrival; seeking advantage by moving only men results in leaving behind weaponry. Seeking advantage 100 miles away by taking weaponry and by advancing day and night without rest, the commanders of all three battalions are likely to be captured; among men, one in ten might arrive, robust ones first, and tired ones lagging behind. Seeking advantage 50 miles away, the commander of the front battalion is likely to be captured; among men, one in two might arrive. Seeking advantage 30 miles away, two men in three might arrive.

7.4   An army without weaponry is lost. An army without provisions is lost. An army without supplies is lost.

7.5   Thus, without knowing other heads of state's plans, we cannot seek alliance. Without knowing contours of mountains and forest, of hazards and blockades, of channels and rivers, we cannot move troops. Without local guides, we cannot take advantage of the terrain.

7.6   Thus, war is built on stratagems, acts on advantages, adapts with formations. Moving swiftly, the thrust is like gust; moving deliberately, the pace is like forest. In attack, the energy is like fire; in defense, the sturdiness is like mountain; unknowable as the moon; unstoppable as thunder. In exploiting the countryside, split men; in expropriating land, control advantageous points. Weigh alternatives before redeploying.

7.7   One who knows the straight-forward from the circuitous wins. This is battlefield maneuvering.

7.8   According to *Military Practices*: "When words cannot be heard, use gongs and drums; when positions cannot be seen, display banners and flags." Use gongs and drums for night-time battles, use banners and flags for day-time battles. Gongs, drums, banners, and flags set the pace for the men. With men moving in unison, the brave cannot advance by himself, and the timid cannot retreat by himself. These are ways to manage men.

7.9   Destroy the morale of enemy's three-battalion army; demolish their commanders' resolve. During the day, the morale is high; in the evening, low. Thus, to one who knows war, avoid when the enemy's morale is high and attack when his morale is low. These are ways to manage morale.

7.10   Be at ready and await for the disorganized; be quiet to await for the boisterous. These are ways to manage resolve.

7.11   Be close by and await for the distant. Be at ease to await for the exhausted. Be fed to await for the hungry. These are ways to manage strength.

7.12   Cross not well-displayed flags; attack not well-deployed formation. These are the ways to manage unexpectedness.

7.13   Thus, in maneuvers, with the enemy situated on high grounds, do not advance uphill; with the enemy coming down from high grounds, do not intercede frontally; with the enemy's feigning defeat, do not pursue; with the enemy's best troops, do not attack; with the enemy's bait, do not accept; with the enemy's retreating, do not block; with the enemy's being surrounded, do leave an opening; with the enemy's fleeing, do not press. These are ways to manage maneuvers.

8   BATTLEFIELD CONTINGENCIES

8.1   Guidelines of war are: the commander is to receive his commission from the head of state; the commander is to gather men to form the army; the army is not to encamp in hazardous land, is to rendezvous with allied forces at cross-roads, is not to linger in isolated land, is to negotiate its way out of circumscribed land, and to fight its way out of deadly land.

8.2   [In the midst of a campaign,] Some roads are deliberately averted, some armies are purposely ignored, some citadels are voluntarily bypassed, some lands are intentionally not fought, the head of state's decrees are not accepted.

8.3   A commander who is versed in these nine contingencies is adept at war. A commander who cannot take advantage of these nine contingencies is unable to take advantage of the terrain, even though he knows it. A commander who has not mastered the art of managing these nine contingencies is unable to fully utilize his men, even though he is versed in the five advantages.

8.4   An intelligent commander deliberates both the positive and negative sides of an issue. Deliberating the positive side accomplishes the mission; deliberating the negative side avoids disasters.

8.5   To seek submission from other heads of state, we threaten them; to render them harmless to us, we keep them occupied; to exert control over them, we offer them advantages.

8.6   The guidelines of war are: rely not on the enemy's not coming, rely on our being ready; rely not on the enemy's not attacking, rely on our being strong to be beyond attack.

8.7   Dangerous traits in a commander, there are five: recklessness, leading to easy demise; cowardice, to easy capture; irritableness, to easy provocation; undue modesty, to easy humiliation; attachment, to easy harassment. These five dangerous traits in a commander are disastrous in the conduct of war. They are the causes of an army's destruction and its commanders' decapitation. It is not to be left uninvestigated.

9   BATTLEFIELD LOGISTICS

9.1   Encamping en route, take into account the enemy's position. Passing through mountains, encamp close to valleys. Encamp on high grounds, facing the sun. Refrain from moving uphill to engage in fight. These are battlefield measures involving high grounds.

9.2   Passing through rivers, encamp away from them. When the enemy comes by the river, refrain from meeting him in the midst of river crossing, but do so after half of his men have crossed; this is advantageous. In combat, refrain from engaging the enemy near rivers. Encamp on high grounds, facing the sun. Refrain from stationing downstream. These are battlefield measures involving rivers.

9.3   Passing through salt marshes, move quickly and refrain from stopping. If fighting the enemy in the midst of salt marshes, be close to water and vegetation, with back to trees. These are battlefield measures involving salt marshes.

9.4   Passing through plateaux, encamp, taking into account the ease of movement. Have the right and the rear backing high grounds; prepare to fight on low grounds in front of us and high grounds behind us. These are battlefield measures involving plateaux.

9.5   Emperor Huang, by taking advantage of these four groups of battlefield measures, won over the other four emperors.

9.6   Any army would prefer ground high to low, areas sunny to shady, surroundings lively and bounteous. A precondition of a sure win is an army free of myriad diseases.

9.7   Encamping, face the sun, with the hillside, mound, dikes or embankments at the right and back. In war, taking advantage of the terrain is advantageous.

9.8   In a torrential rain, with water splashing at the river, stop crossing and await for the rain to stop.

9.9   Passing through stiff cliffs, carnivorous caverns, isolated crests, ill-defined moraines, deceptive quagmires, gripping crevices — move quickly, do not go near. Let us move away; let the enemy move in. Let us face them; let the enemy have them at his back.

9.10   Passing through spurs, meltwaters, marshes, forests, shallow ponds with undergrowths — search carefully and repeatedly. These are likely areas where enemy's spies are hiding.

9.11   When the enemy is close by but keeps quiet, he is occupying a strategic position. When the enemy is distant but provocative, he is luring us to advance. When the enemy encamps in the plains, he is tempting us.

9.12   When trees appear moving, the enemy is coming. When marshes seem to grow obstacles, the enemy is setting traps. When birds fly out in flocks, the enemy is in ambush. When beasts rush out startled, the enemy is in hiding.

9.13   When dust soars high and sharp, chariots are coming; dust spreads low and far, foot soldiers are coming; dust scatters in a limited area, the enemy has gathered firewood; dust is spotty and recurring, the enemy has encamped.

9.14   When the enemy talks humbly but works hard secretly, he is ready to attack. When the enemy talks harshly and moves about conspicuously, he is ready to retreat.

9.15   When the enemy moves his chariots out to the two wings, he is redeploying. When the enemy offers truce unilaterally, he is scheming. When the enemy busies himself with troop movement, he is getting ready. When the enemy moves back and forth, he is luring us. When the enemy leans against his halberd, he is underfed. When the enemy sips before carrying water to the camp, he is thirsty. When the enemy is disinclined to advance to take an advantage, he is exhausted.

9.16   When birds gather in the enemy's camp, it is because the camp is uninhabited. When the enemy's men scream in the night, it is because they are scared. When the enemy's men create disturbances, it is because the commander has little discipline. When the enemy's flags move about unaccountably, it is because the battalions are in chaos. When the enemy's officers are easily angered, it is because they are weary of war.

9.17   Having no provisions and resorting to slaughtering horses as food, having no implements to prepare it, having no inclination to return to the camp, the enemy shows signs of desperation.

9.18   Speaking with neither resoluteness nor authority, the enemy shows signs of insecurity. Granting repeated decorations, the enemy shows signs of purposelessness. Meting out repeated punishments, the enemy shows signs of insubordination. Disciplining his men and then being in awe of them, the enemy shows signs of incompetence.

9.19   Sending an envoy bearing favors, the enemy is seeking truce. After advancing in anger, but refusing to engage in combat and declining to retreat, the enemy is to be carefully watched.

9.20   In war, numerical superiority is not a factor. All that is needed to win is to refrain from advancing haphazardly, to consolidate resources, and to see through the enemy's plans. One who does not plan but is disdainful of his enemy is bound to be captured.

9.21   Penalizing men who have not been indoctrinated creates dissention; men who dissent are difficult to deploy. Men who have been indoctrinated but who will not respond to discipline are not to be deployed. Treat men with civility; maintain accord with discipline — these are winning measures.

9.22   When orders are consistently applied in the training of men, they obey. When orders are not consistently applied in the training of men, they will not obey. Men obey because the officers' relationship with them is harmonious.

10   MANAGEMENT OF TERRAIN

10.1   Terrain's contours include: open, down-sloping, one-directional, narrow, and precipitous.

10.2   Open terrain is terrain open for claiming by either us or the enemy. Reaching it first, encamp on high ground — face the sun, ensure movements of provisions. Open terrain is advantageous.

10.3   Down-sloping terrain is terrain easy to get in but difficult to get out. When the enemy is unprepared, attack and win. When the enemy is prepared, an attack may not produce a win — and it will be difficult for us to get out. Down-sloping terrain is not advantageous.

10.4   One-directional terrain is terrain advantageous neither to us nor to the enemy. In a one-directional terrain, when the enemy baits us to fight, we must decline. Yet, we must pretend we accept to lure the enemy in. When one half of our enemy's men are in — and we can strike them at that time — then is one-directional terrain advantageous.

10.5   With narrow terrain, when we occupy it first, barricade the path and await for the enemy. When the enemy occupies it first, if he barricades the path, do not follow; if not, follow.

10.6   With precipitous terrain, when we occupy it first, stay high, face the sun, and wait for the enemy. When the enemy occupies it first, retreat — do not follow.

10.7   With unfamiliar terrain, neither side has an advantage; it is inadvisable to challenge the enemy to a fight. If we do, the result will not be advantageous.

10.8   These are six directives on the management of terrain. It is the commander's responsibility to understand them. It is not to left uninvestigated.

10.9   Manifestations of defeatism: flight, slackness, chaos, collapse, ruin, rout. These six cannot be attributed to nature's disasters, but to a commander's ineptitude.

10.10   With neither side having an advantage, attacking the enemy tenfold stronger results in flight. When soldiers are energized but officers hesitant, the result is slackness. When officers are prepared but soldiers lethargic, the result is chaos.

10.11   When adjunct commanders are enraged and disobedient, when they vent their indignation by engaging the enemy in combat without authorization, when their whereabouts are not reported to the commander, the result is collapse.

10.12   When the commander is indecisive and weak, when discipline is inconsistent and directives unclear, when officer-soldier communication is haphazard, when resource deployment is disorderly, the result is ruin.

10.13   When a commander cannot anticipate the enemy's action, when he engages his numerically inferior men in combat with a numerically superior enemy, when he attacks the enemy's stronghold with inadequate manpower, when his forward army lacks thrust, the result is rout.

10.14   These six manifestations lead to defeat. It is the commander's responsibility to understand them. It is not to be left uninvestigated.

10.15   Terrain's contours play an important role in war. Anticipating the enemy's action contributes to winning. Estimating risks and distances are top commanders's directives. Mastering them and applying them in war produce sure wins; not knowing them and not applying them in war, sure defeats.

10.16   When on a path to win, fight even when the head of state decrees not to fight. When on a path to defeat, decline to fight even when the head of state decrees to fight. Advancing is not for seeking personal glory; retreating is not for shrinking from personal responsibility. A commander who concerns only with the people's welfare and who thinks only of the head of state's advantage is a treasure of the state.

10.17   When a soldier is treated as a child, he will be willing to go to deep waters with the commander. When a soldier is treated as a loving son, he will be willing to die with[1] the commander. When treated well but not accepting assignments, when loved much but not following orders, when violated rules but not receiving discipline — the soldier is a spoiled brat, and is unfit for commission.

10.18   Knowing that our soldiers can fight but not knowing whether the enemy's can or cannot, the likelihood of winning is but fifty-fifty. Knowing that the enemy's soldiers can fight but not knowing whether ours can or cannot, the likelihood of winning is but fifty-fifty. Knowing that our soldiers can fight but not knowing whether the terrain's contour is advantageous to our fighting, the likelihood of winning is but fifty-fifty.

10.19   One who knows war takes actions without hesitation, provides measures without limitation. Knowing the enemy and knowing ourselves, winning is not in doubt. Knowing nature and knowing terrain, winning is total.

11   DEPLOYMENT OF FIELD FORCES

11.1   In war, we have leave-tempting land, peripheral land, contested land, neutral land, cross-road land, core land, hazardous land, circumscribed land, and deadly land.

11.2   Leave-tempting land is our home territory; peripheral land, outer regions of the enemy's territory; contested land, area for control for advantage; neutral land, open area accessible to us as well as to the enemy. Cross-roads are areas common to various states; one who arrives first is likely to receive their support. Core land is enemy's population and trade centers.

11.3   Hazardous land is land with treacherous passes, precarious cliffs, unspecified rivers and streams — difficult passageways in general. Circumscribed land is land offering narrow paths getting in and circuitous routes getting out, an area where our large army may subject to attack by a small enemy force. Deadly land is land that requires quick combats for survival — protracted engagements result in annihilation.

11.4   Thus, do not engage in combat on leave-tempting land, do not stop on peripheral land, do not attack contested land, do not barricade neutral land. Rendezvous at cross-roads, appropriate provisions on core land, hasten through hazardous land, negotiate out of circumscribed land, fight our way out of deadly land.

11.5   In the past, those who knew war dislodged the enemy's front from his rear, isolated the enemy's main force from his flanks, interfered the enemy officers' support from their men, cut off the enemy commander's communication with his staff, separated the enemy's men from their groups, and disrupted the enemy's force from being unified.

11.6   Act when the scenario is advantageous, wait when it is not. When asked: "How do we act when the enemy, well organized and en masse, is coming at us?" Answer: "Capture what is precious to him, and he will listen."

11.7   War demands quick action — act before the enemy is ready, march through routes he does not suspect, attack positions he does not guard.

11.8   Attacking inside the enemy territory, move deep and in unison to overpower the enemy. Appropriate materiel from town and country to fortify our army's supply. Rest and be at ease to elevate our men's physical condition and morale.

11.9   War is planning. Plan beyond the enemy's ability to anticipate.

11.10   Placed in a circumscribed position, death is preferred to desertion. Faced with death, would one not fight to his utmost best? Placed in a deadly position, fear is absent; placed in a circumscribed position, morale is high.

11.11   Deep in enemy territory, move with care, and fight only when forced. Without being warned, our men will be on guard. Without being coached, our men will be at ready. Without being advised, our men will help one another. Without invoking rules, our men will exercise self-restraint.

11.12   Subscribe not to irrational beliefs and listen not to questionable views. Retreat not from death.

11.13   Our men may not possess much, but it is not because they disdain affluence. They may not live long, but it is not because they spurn longevity. When an order [to fight their way out of a circumscribed position] is issued, those who are standing might weep;

those who are lying might cry. Being circumscribed, they would fight as bravely as did Chu and Gui.

11.14 One who knows war may be likened to a *so-ran* snake of Mountain Heng. Hitting a so-ran snake's tail, its head comes to the rescue. Hitting its head, its tail comes to the rescue. Hitting its middle, both its head and its tail come to the rescue.

11.15 Question: Can an army act like a so-ran snake? Answer: Yes. Although Wu and Yuè are at odds with each other, were the two in the same boat during a river-crossing, one would come to the aid of the other as if the left hand were to the right hand.

11.16 Thus, to motivate our men by roping in horses and burying chariot wheels is ineffective. It is Direction that inspires our men to act with bravery in unison. It is advantage from terrain that yields both steeliness and resiliency. Thus, one who knows war can direct an army to act as if a man — it has to be so.

11.17 A commander's role is to deliberate with calmness, and govern with fairness. Make plans difficult to understand; our men will be unable to discern. Reassign missions and revise plans; our men will be unable to detect. Change camping grounds and use different routes; our men will be unable to deduce.

11.18 Readying for combat, induce our men to move ahead as if removing the ladder after reaching the top. Advancing deep into enemy territory, encourage our men to move forward as if firing an arrow from a bow-firing machine.

11.19 The army must be led, as a flock of sheep, going here, going there, without being told the reason. Gathering men for a three-battalion army for combat and risking their lives are the commander's responsibilities.

11.20 Knowledge of the nine types of terrain, their effect on attack and retreat, and their effect on our men's morale are not to be left uninvestigated.

11.21 When in enemy territory, moving deep promotes unison; move peripherally tempts leaves without absences. Enemy territory reachable through crossing other states is isolated land. Areas reachable from all four sides are cross-roads. Core land requires penetration; peripheral land may be slighted. Areas with stiff cliffs at back and narrow paths in front are circumscribed land. Land with no exits is deadly.

11.22   On leave-tempting land, we must solidify our willingness to fight. On peripheral land, we must attempt to annex. On contested land, we must go after it. On neutral land, we must be guard our movement. On cross-roads, we must strengthen our ties. On core land, we must appropriate our provisions. On hazardous land, we must pass through quickly. On circumscribed land, we must barricade the remaining openings. On deadly land, we must show our willingness to not live.

11.23   The enemy's inclination is to resist when circumscribed, fight when forced, and surrender when overwhelmed.

11.24   Seek no alliance without knowledge of other states' plans. Move no troops without knowledge of contours of mountains and forests, passes and obstacles, and marshes and swamps. Without the services of local intelligence, we gain no advantage from terrain.

11.25   Of the four plans [about others] and five factors [about ourselves], even if we are ignorant of but one, we are unlikely to become a Power.

11.26   The army of a Power, in attacking a major state, moves swiftly before she can mobilize her army. With that major state subdued, her allies are unlikely to come to rescue. Thus, there is no need to seek alliance with other states, there is no need to share influence with them. All that is needed is to strengthen ourselves to overpower our enemies, capture their citadels, and destroy their sovereignty.

11.27   By offering extraordinarily generous rewards, by giving unquestionably effective orders, we can command a three-battalion army as if a single man.

11.28   Give the men assignments, but do not discuss reasons; give them missions, but do not discuss risks.

11.29   Put them in a lost position; let them seek survival. Put them in a deadly position; let them seek life. Only when an army is in danger does it fight its way out for a victory.

11.30   Thus, the conduct of war is to carefully evaluate the enemy's intentions, concentrate our forces, and take the enemy's commander a thousand miles away. This is the intelligent approach to conducting war.

11.31   On the decision day, seal all ports and void all travel documents, constrain envoys' movements. At the headquarters, go over plans and finalize a course of action.

11.32   When the enemy gives us an opening, seize it immediately. Seek out the head of state's confidants and reach private understandings with them. Follow the enemy unexpectedly; annihilate him when the time comes.

11.33   Thus, at the beginning, behave as if a demure maiden, luring the enemy to open his doors. Following that, act as if an untamed hare, advancing beyond the enemy's ability to defend.

12   USE OF INCENDIARY

12.1   Targets of incendiary are five: officers and men, food storage facilities, chariots and weaponry, armories, and transportation equipment and routes.

12.2   Doing incendiary requires special supplies; they must be stored and be at ready. Time to instigate incendiary is the dry season, days when the moon position is at the Sieve, Wall, Wing, and Cross Bar — days with the moon on these poistions are likely to be windy.

12.3   In using incendiary to support an attack, what to do is based on the fire's path. When a fire is initiated inside the enemy camp, be ready at the outside. When a fire is initiated but the enemy is calm, wait and take no action. When the fire turns violent, attack when the situation seems ripe; otherwise, refrain from attacking.

12.4   When incendiary may be instigated from outside, there is no need to instigate it inside the enemy camp; just make sure that the timing is right.

12.5   When a fire is moving up-wind, do not attack from the down-wind. When wind is blowing strong during the day, it is likely to stop during the night.

12.6   An army must understand these five fire variations, seize opportunities, and take appropriate action.

12.7   Using incendiary as support, the attack is furious; using water as support, the attack is violent. Water may isolate the enemy, but cannot destroy them.

12.8   After winning the war and capturing the enemy's land, it does not bode well when the defeated are not care for. Otherwise, the effort is wasted.[3] Thus, it may be said that a sagacious head of state is cognizant of this, and a conscientious commander acts upon this.

12.9   Where there is no advantage, move not. Where there is no gain, act not. Where there is no danger, fight not.

12.10   A head of state is not to authorize war just to even a grudge. A commander is not to initiate fight just to avenge a slight. Act only when the reason to act is on our side; resist from acting when it is not. Anger may turn into joy, displeasure into pleasure, but a conquered state cannot bring back her statehood, and the dead cannot be bought back to life.

12.11 Thus, a sagacious head of state exercises care [in deciding whether to engage in war], and a conscientious commander reminds himself [of the devastations of war]. This is the Direction — for a state to have peace and for an army to be whole.

13   USE OF INTELLIGENCE

13.1   Raising an army of 100,000 and sending it 1,000 miles away are burdensome to the people as well as to the state treasury — spending 1,000 pieces of gold per day, creating disequilibrium inside and out, diverting 700,000 households to care for soldiers en route and enduring dislocations at home.

13.2   Preparation for war takes years; fighting a war takes but one day. A commander who is more concerned with his emolument and the state treasury than with seeking information about his enemy is ignoble to the utmost. He is not a worthy commander for the people. He is not a worthy advisor to the head of state. He is not in command for a win.

13.3   The reason a sagacious head of state or an intelligent commander acts and wins, succeeds beyond the conventional expectation, is foreknowledge. Foreknowledge is based not on oracles, not on analogies, not on astrology, but on men who have information on the enemy.

13.4   Sources of intelligence are five: local intelligence, insider intelligence, double intelligence, counterintelligence, and live intelligence. When all five are used concurrently, their work is wizardry beyond anyone's comprehension. These sources of intelligence are to be treasured by head of states.

13.5   Local intelligence is provided by ordinary people in the enemy's midst but in our employ; insider intelligence, by officers in the enemy's court but in our employ; double intelligence, by the enemy's own intelligence working for us.

13.6   Counterintelligence is misinformation, flowing about in our camp with seeming credibility, intended to induce enemy intelligence in our midst to transmit as intelligence to the enemy. Live intelligence is in-person reporting by our own intelligence returning from behind enemy lines.

13.7   In a three-battalion army, no one needs accorded more confidence than intelligence, no one needs rewarded more heavily than intelligence, nothing needs guarded more secretively than intelligence.

13.8   No one except those who are righteous and intelligent knows whom to employ for intelligence work. No one except those who are noble knows how to motivate people in intelligence. No one except those who are discerning knows what to make out of intelligence.

13.9   What a delicate matter! What a delicate matter! There is no time nor place where intelligence cannot be employed.

13.10   Where intelligence is leaked before it has served its purpose, the provider and recipient of such intelligence are at risk and are to die.

13.11   Before our army strikes, before a citadel is attacked, before a dignitary is assassinated, we must know the names of the commander who is defending, his aides-de-camp, his visitors, and members of his inner circles. We must ask our intelligence to seek these out.

13.12   In order to seek information from enemy intelligence caught in our camp, we need to induce him, enlighten him, and then send him back to his home camp. This is how we secure the services of double intelligence.

13.13   Through double intelligence, we secure the services of local intelligence and insider intelligence.

13.14   Through double intelligence, our misinformation gains credibility, inducing enemy intelligence in our midst to transmit it as intelligence to the enemy.

13.15   Through double intelligence, our own intelligence in the enemy's midst can return to report with regularity.

13.16   The head of state must be made aware of these five sources of intelligence. Among these, double intelligence is critically important. Thus, double intelligence must be heavily rewarded.

13.17   For Yin to come into being, one reason is I Zhe in Xia; for Zhou to come into being, one reason is Lü Ya in Yin. Thus, when a sagacious head of state or an intelligent commander has a person with superior intellect to provide intelligence, big success awaits. This is the essence of war — on intelligence the actions of a three-battalion army depend.

C   SUBJECT INDEX

This index covers text and footnotes. Index on war-related cases is in Annex D; index on cases related to the Year 2000 Presidential nomination process is in Annex E.

Entries indexed are (1) attributes of the physical environment; (2) attributes of human behavior; (3) issues on governance, planning, and management; (4) issues on war; (5) heads of state; (6) past dynasties; and (7) classics. Not indexed are (a) individuals other than heads of state; (b) geographical names, weights, and measures; (c) analogies and metaphors.

Citations are to passage numbers. *n* = footnote; where a passage has more than one footnote, footnote number is added after *n*; *h* = headnotes.

Alphabetization is by key words mainly in noun or verb form.

A

Action, when advantageous, 11.6
  before enemy is ready, 11.7
  expecting to win with, 4.5
  following winning position, 4.5
  quick, 11.7
  reason for, on our side, 12.10
Action/Inaction, as stratagem, 1.12
Adept at War
  avoid when enemy's morale high, 7.9
  does not blame men, 5.9
  builds momentum, 5.6, 5.9
  cannot be sure of win over enemy, 4.1
  can direct an army as if one man, 11.16
  at defense, 6.4
  dislodged the enemy, 11.5
  not to draft men more than once, 2.3
  knows nine contingencies, 8.3
  made sure that no one could win over them, 4.1
  may be likened to *so-ran* snake, 11.14

made sure that no one could win over them, 4.1
  may be likened to *so-ran* snake, 11.14
  at offense, 6.4
  outmaneuvers enemy, 6.1
  produces orthodox and unorthodox formations, 5.2
  protective of support, 4.6
  responsible, for people's destiny, 2.7
  for state's security, 2.7
  not to seek provisions more than thrice, 2.3
  takes actions without hesitation, 10.19
  takes enemy without combat, 3.4
  takes position that cannot be defeated, 4.5
  is vigilant on Direction, 4.6
  won with ease, 4.5
Advance
  beyond defense, 6.5, 11.33
  in deep enemy territory, 11.18
  enemy disinclined to, 9.15

THE MIDWEST BOOK REVIEW

JAMES A. COX
Editor-in-Chief
mwbookrevw@aol.com
http://www.execpc.com/~mbr/bookwatch/

278 Orchard Drive
Oregon, WI 53575
(608) 835-7937
mbr@execpc.com

BUHLE'S BOOKSHELF

The Art Of Leadership By Sun Tzu
David H. Li, translator
Premier Publishing Company
PO Box 341267, Bethesda, MD 20827
0-9637852-9-X $25.00 1-301-469-7051 1-301-469-6544 (fax)

David H. Li draws upon his native fluency in Chinese and sixty-five years exposure to English to present an outstanding translation and annotation of Sun Tzu's (512 BCE) writings, integrating them with such diverse matters as war, the Year 2000 American presidential nomination process, war-stimulation games, and business. This informative and engaging work argues that the fundamental and unifying principle of leadership on or off the battlefield is professionalism, and that leadership in war management must be separated from leadership in state government. *The Art Of Leadership By Sun Tzu* is thoughtful, thought-provoking, and occasionally inspired and inspiring.

D

Dao *See* Direction

Deadly Land, Deadly Position, 11.1, 11.3
without exit as, 11.21
fear in, 11.10
fight way out, 8.1, 11.4
seek survival from, 11.29
show willingness not to live, 11.22

Death *See* also Life and Death
cannot be brought back to life, 12.10
over desertion, 11.10
fight in the face of, 11.10
when intelligence leaked, 13.10
from invading citadel, 3.3
and retreat, 11.12

Decree, Head of State's
not accepted, 8.2
and path to victory or defeat, 10.16

Defeat, defeatism and, 10.14
enemy feigning, 7.13
not knowing risks and distance and, 10.15
path to, and head of state decree, 10.16
predicting victory or, 1.12

Defeated, caring of, 12.8

Defeatism, Manifestation of, 10.9

Defend, Defense
compel enemy to redeploy as, 6.7
conceal when, 4.3
enemy's inability to, 6.4
      expected attack and, 6.3
exposed and, 6.9, 6.10
knowledge and, 6.8
scattered and, 6.7
sturdiness of, like mountain, 7.6
when inferior, 4.2
when unable to win, 4.2

Deploy, Deployment, Redeploy, Redeployment
disorderly, results in ruin, 10.12
dissention and, 9.21
enemy compelled to, 6.6
momentum and, 5.9
numerical superiority and, 3.5
provocation to deduce enemy's, 6.13
not responding to discipline and, 9.21
unsuspected route, 11.7
weighing alternatives before, 7.6

Desertion, and death, 11.10

Desperation,
indications of enemy's, 9.17

Destiny, enemy's, 6.4
people's, 2.7

Die, Willingness to
Direction and, 1.3
when soldier treated as son, 10.17

Diplomacy, and winning war, 3.2

Direction, 1.1, 13.17n4
administrative, as support, 1.7
attributes, 1.1n2
as common goal, 1.3
dao translated as, 1.1n2
estimating risk and proximity as commander-in-chief's, 10.15
as factor of war, 1.2, 1.8n13, 12.8n2
as inspiration to bravery, 11.16
as issue of victory or defeat, 1.9
and peace, 12.11
vigilant on, 4.6

Directive *See* Order

Discipline, and accord, 9.21
attribute of commandership, 1.6
chaos, organization, and, 5.7
disturbance and, 9.16
inconsistent, results in ruin, 10.12
as indication of enemy's incompetence, 9.18

D   INDEX ON WAR-RELATED CASES

This index covers war-related cases, written by this translator-annotator, for the specific purpose of illustrating text material included in this volume. For index covering Sun Wu's text and associated footnotes, see Appendix C, pp. 239ff; for index on cases related to the Year 2000 Presidential nomination process, see Appendix E, pp. 259ff.

Entries indexed are (1) people, (2) places, and (3) subjects. Authors of books referenced in the preparation of these cases are not indexed.

Alphabetization is by key words mainly in noun or verb form.

254

Cases Listed by Year of Campaign/Event

A

Abhisaras, Rajah of Jammu, W-G
Acheson,
  Secretary of State Dean, W-C
Alexander III (The Great), W-G
  as Asian monarch
  strength of army
Alexander, Tsar, W-A
  assumed commnadership
  decreed staff to submit plans
  relinquished commandership
Ambhi, King of Taxila, W-G
Ambush, W-E

Atlantic Wall, W-B
Attack vs destroy vs damage vs
  surround, W-E

B

Bao, the Prince of Wei, W-I
Battlefield vs Remote
  decision, W-E, W-H
  direction, W-E, W-H
  divergence, W-E, W-H
  planning, W-E, W-H
Bayeux , W-B

E   INDEX ON CASES RELATED TO
YEAR 2000 PRESIDENTIAL NOMINATION

This index covers events related to Year 2000's presidential nomination process, all written by this translator-annotator, for the specific purpose of illustrating text material included in this volume. For index covering Sun Wu's text and associated footnotes, see Appendix C, pp. 239ff; for index on war-related cases, see Appendix D, pp. 254ff.

     Entries indexed are (1) people, (2) places, and (3) subjects.

Cases Listed in Page Number Sequence

F TEXT PASSAGES REFERENCED IN CASES

Text passages referenced in cases included in this volume are summarized in this Appendix. References to war-related cases are given first (with prefix W), followed by those on the Year 2000 Presidential nomination process (prefix P), followed by war-simulation cases (WS) and by the lone business case.

There are, altogether, 26 cases, of which 5 war-related cases (W-B, World World II - Battle for Normandy; W-E, Gulf War - Desert Storm; W-H, American Civil War - Second Bull Run; W-J, World War I - The World's First Tank Battle; and W-K, The American Revolution - Washington and the Intelligence Community) are presented without passage references -- to allow our reader to do their own referencing.

Seventy-one passages, out of a total of 190 passages in this volume, or 37 percent, are referenced for a total of 115 times.

> **1.2,** P-1, P-2, P-8, WS-1, B-1
> **1.3,** W-C, P-8
> **1.8,** W-A, P-1, P-8
> **1.9,** W-A, W-D, P-10
> **1.12,** W-C, WS-2
> **1.13,** W-C, P-5, WS-2, WS-3
> **1.14,** W-C, W-I, WS-2
> **1.16,** W-A, P-4, P-7, P-8, WS-2, WS-3, B-1
>
> **2.1,** W-D
> **2.2,** W-A, W-D, P-2
> **2.3,** W-A, W-D
> **2.4,** W-A, W-D
> **2.7,** W-A, P-2
>
> **3.2,** W-A, W-I
> **3.7,** P-11
> **3.8,** W-C, P-3, WS-1
> **3.9,** W-C, P-11, WS-3

G   BIBLIOGRAPHY ON WAR-RELATED AND WAR-SIMULATION CASES

Page references:

W-A 33-37	**W-B** 45-51	**W-C** 59-64	**W-D** 72-76
W-E 85-91	**W-F** 113-115	**W-G** 126-133	**W-H** 146-153
W-I 168-175	**W-J** 183-188		**W-K** 197-200
WS-1 104-109	**WS-2** 134-140		**WS-3** 201-211

Ambrose, Stephen E., *The Victors - Eisenhower and His Boys: The Men of World War II* (New York: Simon & Schuster, 1998) **W-B**

Amiot, J. J. M., *Art Militaire des Chinois ou Recueil d'anciens sur la Guerre* (Paris: Didot l'ainé, 1772)   **W-A**

Anderson, Gerald F., *Are there any?* (Washington, 1945)   **WS-3**

Arrian, *The Anabasis of Alexander*, recorded in 2nd century (New York: Penguin)   **W-G**

Atkinson, Rick, *Crusade* (New York: Houghton Mifflin, 1993) **E**

AUSA Institute for Land Warfare, *The U.S. Army in Operation Desert Storm* (Arlington, AUSA, June 1991)   **W-E**

Bakeless, John, *Turncoats, Traitors, and Heroes* (Philadelphia: Lippincott, 1959)   **W-K**

Bender, David L., (ed), *The Vietnam War: Opposing Viewpoints* (St. Paul: Greenhaven Press, 1984)   **W-D**

Blair, Clay, *The Forgotten War: America in Korea, 1950-1953* (New York: Times Books, 1988)   **W-C**

Burg, David H., and Edward Purcell, *Almanac of World War I* (Louisville: University Press of Kentucky, 1998)
     "10 November 1917," p. 188   **W-J**

Burton, James G., "Pushing Them Out the Back Door," *Proceedings*, June 1993   **W-E**

Bruce, George (ed), *Harbottle's Dictionary of Battles* (London: Hart-Davis, 1971)

"Borodino - *Napoleonic Wars*," p. 46   **W-A**

"Cambrai - *World War I*," p. 55   **W-J**

"D-Day - *Operation Overlord - World War II*," p. 76 **W-B**

"Dien Bien Phu - *French-Vietnamese War*," p. 80   **W-D**

"Hydaspes -*Alexander's Asiatic Campaigns*," p.117 **W-G**

"Somme I - *World War I*," p. 238   **W-J**

"Thirty-Eighth Parallel - *Korean War*," pp. 251-252 **W-C**

"Vietnam War," pp.265-268   **W-D**

Chandler, Alfred D. (ed), *The Papers of Dwight David Eisenhower* (Baltimore 1970)   **W-B**

Cockburn, Alexander, *Idle Passion* - Chess and the Dance of Death (New York: Simon and Schuster, 1974)   **WS-2, WS-3**

Cohen, Eliot A., and John Gooch, *Military Misfortunes: The Anatomy of Failure in War* (New York: Free Press, 1990)

Chapter 7, "Aggregate Failure: The Defeat of the American Eighth Army in Korea, November - December 1950," at pp. 165-195   **W-C**

Cox, Jacob D., *The Second Battle of Bull Run* (Cincinnati: Thompson, 1882)   **W-H**

D'Este, Carlo, *Decision in Normandy* (New York: Dutton, 1983) **B**

Donnelly, Tom, "The Generals' War," *Army Times*, 2 March 1992
                W-E

Dupuy, R. Ernest (ed), *The Harper Encyclopedia of Military History* (New York: HarperCollins, 1993)

"The Korean War," pp. 1360-1363   **W-C**

"The Napoleonic Wars, 1800-1815," pp. 827-830   **W-A**

Eggenberger, David (ed), *An Encyclopedia of Battles* (New York: Dover, 1967, 1985)

"Alexander's Asiatic Campaigns," pp. 196-197   **W-G**

"Napoleonic Empire Wars," pp. 295-296   **W-A**

Eisenschiml, Otto, *The Celebrated Case of Fitz John Porter* (Boston: Houghton Mifflin, 1950)   **W-H**

Fischer, Bobby, *My 60 Memorable Games* (New York: Simon and Schuster, 1969)   **WS-2**

Gable, Henry, "The Fitz John Porter Case: Politics and Military Justice" (City University of New York Ph.D. Thesis, 1979) **W-H**

Gardner, Lloyd C., *The Korean War* (New York: Quadrangle Books, 1972)   **W-C**

George, Alexander, *The Chinese Communist Army in Action*: The Korean War and its Aftermath (New York: Columbia University Press, 1967)   **W-C**

Ginzburg, Ralph, "Bobby Fischer," *Harper's* (January 1962)
                                                        WS-2

Haythornwaite, Philip J., *The World War One Source Book* (London: Arms & Armour, 1992)
    "Haig, Sir Douglas, 1st Earl Haig of Bemersyde," pp. 328-330   **W-J**

Heller, Francis Howard, *The Truman White House* (Lawrence: Regents Press of Kansas, 1980) **C**

Kindsvatter, Peter S., "VII Corps in the Gulf War: Ground Offensive," *Military Review*, February 1992   **W-E**

Kriegspiel Connoisseur (Premier issue, August 1995)   **WS-3**

Lewis, Jon E. (ed), *The Mammoth Book of Battles* (New York: Carroll & Graf, 1995)
    Nigel Bagnall, "Omaha Beach (1944)," pp. 341-358 **W-B**
    Charles Mey, "Dien Bien Phu (1953)," pp. 433-443 **W-D**

Li, David H., *Chess Detective* - Kriegspiel Strategies, Endgames, and Problems (Bethesda: Premier, 1995)   **WS-3**

_____, *First Syllabus on Xiangqi* (Bethesda: Premier, 1996)
                                                  W-I, WS-1

_____, *The Genealogy of Chess* (Bethesda: Premier, 1998)
                                              W-I, WS-1, WS-2

_____, "Kriegspiel," *Chess* (UK), October, 1995   **WS-3**

_____, *Kriegspiel* - Chess Under Uncertainty (Bethesda: Premier, 1994)   **WS-3**

Lord, Theodore A., *A Summary of the Case of General Fitz-John Porter* (San Francisco, 1883) **W-H**

Macdonald, Lyn (ed), *1914-1918: Voices and Images of the Great War* (London: Michael Joseph, 1988) **W-J**

"Corporal A. E. Lee, A Battalion, of Tank Corps," pp. 167-168 **J**

Malik, Arjan Dass, *Alexander the Great: A Military Study* (New Dehli: Light & Life, 1976) **W-G**

Marshall, S. L. A., *Sinai Victory* (New York: Morrow, 1958) **W-C**

Montgomery, Bernard, *Memoirs* (London, 1958) **W-B**

National Training Center Handbook No. 100-91, *The Iraqi Army - Organization and Tactics* (National Training Center: S2, 177th Armored Brigade, January 1991) **W-E**

Neilson, Robert E., (ed), *Sun Tzu and Information Warfare* (Washington: National Defense University Press, 1997)
Carlson, Adolph, "Information Management and the Challenge of Battle Command" **W-E, W-H**

New York Times, November 22, 1917 **W-J**

O'Toole, G. J. A., *The Encyclopedia of American Intelligence & Espionage* (New York: Facts on File, 1988) **W-K**

Prior, Robin, and Trevor Wilson, *Passchendaele: the Untold Story* (New Haven: Yale University Press, 1996) **W-J**

Public Papers of the Presidents of the United States: Harry S. Truman (Washington: General Services Administration) **W-C**

Riehn, Richard K., *1812: Napoleon's Russian Campaign* (New York: McGraw-Hill, 1990) **W-A**

Rufus, Quintus Curtius, *The History of Alexander the Great* (circa 2nd century) **W-G**

Schiller, Eric, *World Champion Openings*; The Definitive Guide to the Concepts and Secrets of Chess Openings as Played by the World Champions (New York: Cardoza, 199) **WS-2**

H. Norman Schwarzkopf, *It Doesn't Take a Hero* (New York: Bantam Books, October 1992) **W-E**

Siculus, Diodorus, *The Histories*, recorded in the 1st century BCE
                                                            W-G

Sima Qian, *Shi Ji* (Historical Records) 1st century BCE
                                        In Chinese **W-F, W-I**

Sqain, Richard M., *Lucky Way* (Ft. Leavenworth KS: U.S.Army
    Command and General Staff College Press, 1994)   **W-E**

Thompson, W. Scott, and Donald D. E. Frizzell (ed), *The Lessons
    of Vietnam* (New York: Crane, Russak, 1977)   **W-D**

Trainor, Bernard E., "Schwarzkopf and His Generals," *Proceedings,*
    June 1994   **W-E**

United States Department of Defense, *Final Report to Congress*
    [Title V Report], April 1992   **W-E**

Venzon, Anne Cipriano (ed), *The United States in the First World
    War: an Encyclopedia* (New York: Garland, 1995)
        "Tanks," pp. 590-592   **W-J**

von Senger, Harro, *The Book of Stratagems: Tactics for Triumph
    and Survival* (New York: Viking, 1991)   **W-I**

The War of the Rebellion, A Compilation of the Official Records
    of *the Union and Confederate Armies* (Washington: Government
    Printing Office, 1885)   **W-H**

Warry, John, *Warfare in the Classical World* (Norman: University
    of Oklahoma Press, 1995)   **W-G**

Wood, Michael, *In the Footsteps of Alexander the Great* (Berkeley:
    University of California Press, 1997)   **W-G**

Yuan Wei (ed), *Encyclopedia of Chinese Military Campaigns -
    Volume 1: 3000 BC - 1919* (Beijing: Museum of Chinese Military
    Affairs, 1994) *In Chinese*   **W-I**

H   ABOUT THE TRANSLATOR-CUM-ANNOTATOR

David H. Li was born on October 7, 1928 (= 24th day of the 8th moon according to the lunar calendar) in Ningbo, Zhejiang Province. Moving to Shanghai shortly thereafter, he earned a BA (St. John's University, Shanghai) in 1949; an MBA (Wharton School, University of Pennylvania) in 1950; and a PhD (University of Illinois) in 1953.

Joining the academia in 1955, he was promoted to Professor at California State University at Fullerton in 1963, where he also served as the Chairman of Faculty Council in 1964-65. He later became Professor at the University of Washington, Seattle, 1965-74; and at the University of Texas at Dallas, 1980-83. He held two Ford Foundation Visiting Professorships, to the Chinese University of Hong Kong in 1967-69 and to the Indian Institute of Management, Calcutta, in 1970.

His 17 single-author English-language books include those written while in academia, as Director of Research of the EDP Auditing Foundation, and as a staff member of the World Bank Group. After retirement, he devotes full time to writing, mainly on Chinese culture. *The Happy Game of Mah-Jong* (1994) introduces the classical game as played in China; *First Syllabus on Xiangqi - Chinese Chess 1* (1996) and *Xiangqi Syllabus on Cannon - Chinese Chess 2* (1998) begin a series on the world's most played board game. *The Genealogy of Chess* (1998), the result of 18-month research at the Library of Congress that establishes China as the birthplace of chess, earned it a Book of the Year honor. This volume, following the critically accalimed *The Analects of Confucius - A New-Millennium Translation* (1999), represents the translator's second effort at book-length rendition of Chinese classics.